'My Dear Ones'

One Family and the Final Solution

Jonathan Wittenberg

**WILLIAM
COLLINS**

William Collins
An imprint of HarperCollins*Publishers*
1 London Bridge Street, London, SE1 9GF

WilliamCollinsBooks.com
This William Collins paperback edition published in 2017

22 21 20 19 18 17
10 9 8 7 6 5 4 3 2 1

First published in the United Kingdom by William Collins in 2016
Text © Jonathan Wittenberg, 2016

Jonathan Wittenberg asserts the moral right to be identified as the author
of this work.

A catalogue record for this book is available from the British Library.

ISBN 978-0-00-815806-4

Typeset by Palimpsest Book Production Ltd, Falkirk, Stirlingshire

Printed and bound in Great Britain by Clays Ltd, St Ives plc

MIX
Paper from
responsible sources
FSC **FSC® C007454**
www.fsc.org

FSC™ is a non-profit international organisation established to promote
the responsible management of the world's forests. Products carrying the
FSC label are independently certified to assure consumers that they come
from forests that are managed to meet the social, economic and
ecological needs of present and future generations,
and other controlled sources.

Find out more about HarperCollins and the environment at
www.harpercollins.co.uk/green

This book is dedicated to my father Adi Wittenberg
and to the memory of all the members of his family who perished;

To Daniella Nechama Moffson,
daughter of Sheera and Michael,
great-great-granddaughter of the quiet heroine of this book;

To my friend David Cesarani
without whose encouragement the work would never have
been written;

To my wife Nicky
and our children Mossy, Libbi and Kadya;

And to the future of all children,
especially those who have experienced the fate of the refugee.

ACKNOWLEDGEMENTS

I was looking forward to expressing my affectionate and respectful appreciation to my friend since university days, the acclaimed historian Professor David Cesarani, whom I simply think of as David. Without him I would not have had the confidence even to begin writing this book. During frequent conversations he would say 'You must read this!' and often the relevant work would arrive in the post or appear with him when he and his family joined us for a Sabbath meal. I'm still struggling to absorb the sad reality of his tragically early death; he is deeply missed.

I am grateful to my relatives, especially to my cousin Michal Hofmekler with whom I discovered the letters which form the basis of this book, to my father's cousins Jenny Michael in New York, Rachel and Professor Mark Steiner in Jerusalem, and Ruthie and Eliyahu Salpeter and Daniel Freimann in Tel Aviv, who advised me, told me more about our family's history and allowed me to search in cupboards, old cases and files for more letters, documents and photographs. Without their patience in answering questions, correcting errors and responding to repeated requests I would not have been able to recount the stories of our lost relatives.

I received invaluable assistance from many friends, old and new. Goetz Aly was kind enough to share his immense experience and skill as a researcher, historian and writer, and was kind enough to meet me in Berlin and offer essential advice. Jan Machala and Martin Strehlik of Holešov were both extremely helpful, Jan in inviting me to teach in Holešov and in sharing his own unique research into the history of the community during the Nazi occupation, and Martin in taking endless care and trouble to assist with every detail, from route planning to kosher food, in a visit to the town by a large group from my community in London. It may have been the first time services were held in the beautiful Shach Synagogue for over seventy years. From the mayor and his wife to the caretaker of the synagogue, the town offered us a warm welcome. Dr Katarzyna Person of the Jewish Historical Institute in Warsaw spent time and care searching for papers relating to my father's childhood in Rawitsch and Breslau, and helped to plan my visit with David and my son Mossy to Lublin, Lubartów and Ostrów Lubelski in 2015. Many researchers and archivists from Yad Vashem in Jerusalem, the Yivo Institute in New York, the Institute for Contemporary History in Munich, the Jewish Museum in Prague, as well as from other libraries and archives around the world, were extremely helpful. Their aid and advice in accessing records and finding local documents was constant and generous. Professor Dan Stone of Royal Holloway university stepped in at the last minute to allay my panic about possible mistakes in the more historical sections of the book; I am very grateful for his prompt kindness and perceptive advice. Needless to say, any errors are my own.

I am most grateful to Andy Lyon of William Collins for believing in this book from the start and for encouraging me at every stage of the work. But for his consistent support, I might well have abandoned the project. I am thankful to my agent Jonny Geller for his invaluable assistance in making the arrangements happen, and to Kathy Dyke and the entire team at William Collins who from the first greeted the project with great enthusiasm. I am, as ever, grateful to David Elliot.

This book is intended as a tribute to my family and to the many families who suffered similar and worse fortunes in the terrible years of Nazi persecution. It is written in recognition of the challenges faced by those who survived, and in tribute to the humanity and spiritual courage of those who were killed.

There have been too many terrible wars and acts of genocide since. The book is also offered as testament to what it means to have to flee for one's life from violent tyranny and as a plea for compassion, understanding and peaceful co-existence between all faiths and nations.

Studying the letters and documents which describe the fate of my father's family has taken me on a profound and at times perhaps over-absorbing journey into the past. This does not make me forget that the preciousness of existence is attested to most of all through appreciation of the gifts of the present, the beauty of the world, the wonder of life, the opportunity to try to do good, and the blessings of the family I am lucky enough to have around me. This book, and all my work as a community rabbi, is made possible by the love and understanding of my wife Nicky and our children Mossy, Libbi and Kadya, as well as by the support of my mother Isca and my brother Raphael and his family.

CONTENTS

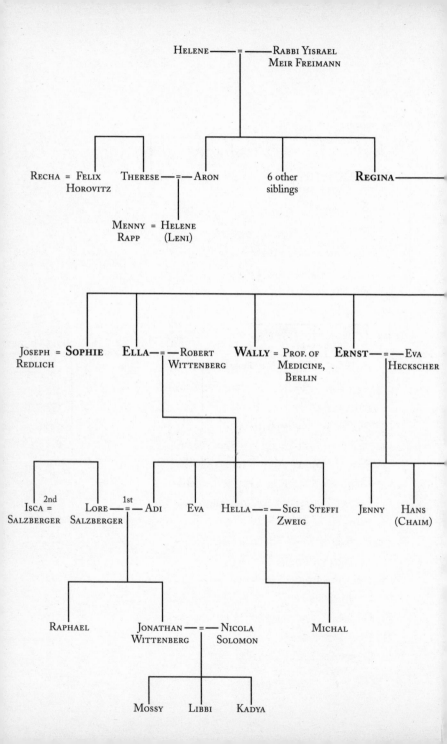

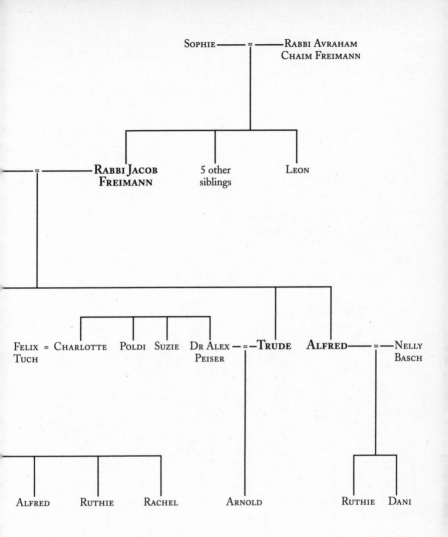

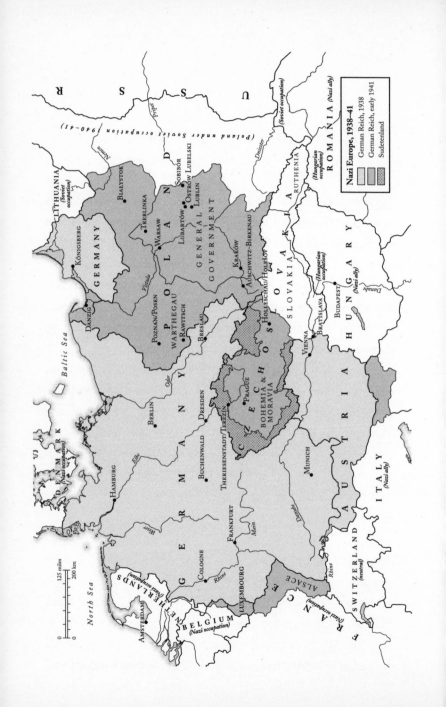

Nazi Europe, 1938–41

German Reich, 1938
German Reich, early 1941
Sudetenland

R U S S

(Soviet occupation)

(Poland under Soviet occupation 1940–41)

Niemen
Pripet
Dniester

LITHUANIA
(Soviet occupation)

ROMANIA *(Nazi ally)*

RUTHENIA

(Hungarian occupation)

KÖNIGSBERG

BIAŁYSTOK

P O L A N D

SOBIBÓR
OSTRÓW LUBELSKI
TREBLINKA
LUBARTÓW
LUBLIN
WARSAW

GERMANY

DANZIG

POZNAN/POSEN
WARTHEGAU
RAWITSCH
BRESLAU

KRAKÓW
AUSCHWITZ-BIRKENAU

G E N E R A L
G O V E R N M E N T

HOLLESCHAU/HOLEŠOV

Vistula
Oder

C Z E C H O S L O V A K I A

(Hungarian occupation)

Danube
BRATISLAVA

BUDAPEST

H U N G A R Y *(Nazi ally)*

VIENNA

Baltic Sea

BERLIN

DRESDEN
BUCHENWALD
THERIESENSTADT/TEREZÍN

PRAGUE
BOHEMIA &
MORAVIA

A U S T R I A

I T A L Y *(Nazi ally)*

D E N M A R K
(Nazi occupation)

G E R M A N Y

HAMBURG

Elbe

MUNICH

FRANKFURT
Main
Danube

SWITZERLAND
(neutral)

Rhine

COLOGNE
Rhine

LUXEMBOURG
ALSACE

N E T H E R L A N D S
(Nazi occupation)

AMSTERDAM

B E L G I U M
(Nazi occupation)

F R A N C E
(Nazi occupation)

North Sea

125 miles
200 km

0
0

My father's family had felt at home in Germany. They were leaders in the highly cultured world of German Jewry. They fought on the German side in the First World War; my grandfather's brother was welcomed home to great acclaim as a hero twice-wounded. They spoke German, wrote in German and baked kosher cakes according to German recipes. 'You have good family connections,' my father told me. His mother's father was a world-famous authority on Jewish law, from a dynasty of rabbis.

In 1945 all that was left of my father's family in Europe were scattered ashes, one grave, their former homes, of which the surviving members were never able to regain possession, and memories. 'So that you will know where to look for us afterwards,' his aunt Sophie had written in a final letter informing her brother of her impending deportation. But in her case, and that of her sister Trude and their families, there was no one left for their relatives to find.

'At first they did it all within the sanction of legality,' my father used to say. Step by step, in small measures which initially sometimes showed little of outright violence, the Nazis and their supporters removed the Jewish populations in their midst from their positions, hemmed them in with restrictions, laid claim to their belongings, stripped them of their savings, dispossessed them of their homes, isolated them from those they loved, starved and tortured them, robbed them of their lives and turned them into ashes.

Of course I knew as I was growing up that my father's family had come from Germany and that they had fled when he was in his teens. But I didn't understand about his part of the family in the same way as I knew the story on my mother's side. Her parents, also refugees from Germany, lived around the corner and I saw them several times each week. My father's relatives resided in faraway Jerusalem; his father had died even before my older brother was born, and I had met his mother only two or three times, on her occasional trips to London. She had struck me as generous, gentle and kind, but quiet and self-contained. It never occurred to me, a teenager absorbed in my own life, that it could be important to traverse her quietness and listen to who she was. She used to send us big wooden cases of oranges or grapefruits, an exciting treat from an Israel which I had never yet visited.

I knew, but I didn't really know; perhaps it would be more honest to say that I didn't pay sufficient attention or care. There are many things of which one is aware, but only at the periphery of the mind. They never properly penetrate the consciousness, but hover like a distant landscape beyond the parameters of one's immediate concerns. It doesn't occur to one to ask the important questions; nothing provokes one to enquire. Only after it is too late is one overcome by a compelling urgency, and in retrospect the failure to have shown sufficient curiosity while there was still time seems as inexplicable as it feels inexcusable: why did I never trouble to ask, before those who could have answered were all dead?

But my brother and I grew up safe in England, a long way

away from the past, too far to be minded to put the difficult questions while those who could have responded to them were still alive.

I remember one occasion when my father was in the scullery; I was in the kitchen rehearsing the script for the school assembly which was to be led the next day by the A level German set to which I belonged. It included a mocking comment about the Nazis. 'Don't forget that Hitler murdered millions of people,' my father, who wasn't in the habit of intervening, quietly observed. 'He turned thousands of them into bars of soap, including several of your relatives. Don't ever have anything to do with anyone who makes light of it, even in a joke.' I felt instantly ashamed.

A few years before he died, my father instructed me to make a record of all the family members who had perished in the Holocaust and Israel's wars. He carefully dictated their names in the vernacular and Hebrew, including the patronymic by which a person is referred to in formal Jewish documents. Slowly I typed them out, creating a testament which, following his wishes, I placed on the table every year on the bleak fast of the Ninth of Av, the date on which the Jewish people remembers its martyrs, and on the atonement fast of Yom Kippur. Then I would light a memorial candle and often, after coming home from the synagogue, sit and watch it flicker in the darkness, briefly illuminating the names, the walls and the small Ark containing the Torah scroll rescued by his family from the devastation. It was when he gave me that list that I understood for the first time the relationships between him and those people whom I had heard mentioned, though only infrequently and in passing, but never properly located on my internal family tree, his aunts Sophie and Trude and their families, his uncle Alfred, his grandmother Regina. It was then too that I began to realise quite how many of his family had perished and to ask myself what this must have meant to him and where in his heart he stored the sorrows of so much loss.

By then I understood his family better. I had stayed many times with his sisters Hella and Steffi in Jerusalem. There had been a third sister too, Eva, who had died very young, during the war. 'She had leukaemia. The doctor said, "She needs red wine and chicken." We can afford them now, but at that time in Palestine we had no money for such things. Who did?' I'm not sure my father ever showed me her picture. But she was more important to him than the paucity of his references suggested and in his final illness he would often call out, 'Eva, Eva, help me,' raising his arms and stretching out his bent hands as if his long-dead sister would reach down and raise him from his sickbed. It struck me as I listened to his semi-conscious pleading that the two of them must have been closer companions in those impoverished years in Palestine than he had previously allowed anyone to perceive.

I learnt equally little from my father about his grandmother Regina. From time to time he would refer to the famous rabbinic lineage to which the Freimann side of the family belonged. Regina had been married to the distinguished rabbi Jacob Freimann, of whom I had sometimes heard my father speak with deep respect and quiet pride. But that was virtually all I knew.

My father's reticence may also have been due to the complex geography of his life. From Breslau, then part of German Silesia, he had fled with his parents and sisters to Palestine when he was only sixteen; from there he had gone in 1955 to Glasgow with my mother, Lore, three years after their marriage and, after her death at the age of only forty-four, had moved with my brother and me to London in 1963, where he married Isca, Lore's younger sister, who now became my second mother. It took me a long time to realise how many losses had ruptured his life.

I find it hard, too, to understand my own ill-timed curiosity. Why had I asked him so little about his relatives, and why was I so full of questions now, when he was no longer there? Or maybe my need to explore the destiny of my father's family was part of my own mourning, both a tribute to him and an attempt at the impossible task of forming some kind of tally of what was lost. Or maybe there are questions that cannot be framed, not, at least, until long afterwards. 'Many people come to see me with their enquiries,' the German holocaust historian Goetz Aly told me. 'They almost all have one thing in common; they're over fifty, mostly over sixty, and those from whom they could once have enquired are dead.'

I was there in Jerusalem when Steffi died. The youngest of the four siblings, she'd been just ten when the family fled in 1937. She'd fallen in love at once with the new life in the developing Jewish homeland with its vital spirit, enthusiastic youthfulness and warm outdoors culture. She'd trained as a nurse and worked in Cyprus with the thousands of refugees held there by the British. Hoping to put the horrors of Nazi Europe behind them, they set sail from ports on the Black Sea or the Mediterranean, illegal immigrants on overcrowded boats, desperate to reach the shores of Palestine and begin fresh lives in the incipient Jewish state. Some made it safely to the new homeland; some drowned in sight of ports which offered them no anchorage; some were intercepted by the Royal Navy and interned. 'Whenever she was home for the weekend they'd come for her passport and use it to smuggle in new immigrants,' my father recalled; 'she'd have it back the following day.' Later she served for years in a small clinic in the Old City of Jerusalem. 'The first nurse in the Jewish Quarter', read the simple inscription Michal, my one and only cousin, later chose for her tombstone.

It was a burning June day when we buried her in the ancient Jewish cemetery high on the Mount of Olives overlooking the city she had loved. Few friends joined the small cortège of cabs which followed the hearse; this was East Jerusalem and the steep, narrow lanes bounded by high stone walls could not be considered completely safe. It would have been more convenient to have arranged the funeral elsewhere, but it felt appropriate to lay Steffi to rest in the same cemetery where Eva had been buried back in the Mandate days, before the State of Israel had been declared in 1948 and the city riven in two by the War of Independence. Remarkably, a space had been found where the two women could lie not quite next to each other but at least head to foot, and resume after sixty long and battle-ridden years their sisterly companionship in their final resting places.

After the grave had been filled with dust-dry soil and the memorial rites completed, I went for the first time to visit Eva about whose early death my father had so rarely spoken. I read the words on her gravestone:

Our precious daughter and sister
Chava Elka Wittenberg
daughter of Raphael z'l,
born on the 18th of the month of Menachem Av, 5682 (1922)
and taken in the midst of her days
on the 22nd of the month of Tammuz 5704 (1944)

This was puzzling. The letters 'z'l' stood for *zichrono liverachah* ('may his memory be for a blessing'). Eva's father Raphael, my grandfather, must therefore have been dead when these lines were composed. Yet he only passed away in 1954, ten years after Eva, a time in which those extra letters could scarcely have been added since the Mount of Olives was under Jordanian rule from 1948 until 1967 and Jews were allowed no access, even to the cemeteries. The inscription continued:

Granddaughter of the great Rabbi Jacob,
son of Rabbi Avraham Chaim Freimann,
who was born on the 21st of the month of Tishrei 5627 (1866)
and died on the 19th of the month of Tevet 5698 (1937)
and of Rebbetzin Rachel, daughter of Rabbi Yisrael Meir,
who was born on the 1st of the month of Shevat 5629 (1869)
and killed in the Holocaust for the sanctification of God's name,
in the month of Shevat 5704 (1944),
may God avenge her blood.
May their souls be bound up in the bond of life.

'For the sanctification of God's name' was the traditional phrase with which those killed for their faith were honoured. The objection that the Nazis persecuted the Jews not on account of their beliefs but simply due to their Jewish blood could not be raised here: my great-grandmother had perished not just because of, but deeply immersed in, her faith. As for the words 'May God avenge her blood', they had been found scrawled in blood itself on the insides of cells and on the stony surfaces of fortresses where Jews had been shot, kicked or bludgeoned to death.

I walked slowly through the rows of graves to the wall at the edge of the ancient terrace, looking out over the Temple Mount and the city beyond. When did the family first learn of my great-grandmother's fate? I remembered how my father had shown me a copy of the postcard she sent from Theresienstadt late in 1943, at the Nazis' behest of course, explaining to her family that all was well and that conditions in the town were perfectly satisfactory. But when did they know for certain that she had been murdered? It could not yet have been in that summer of 1944 when her granddaughter was laid to rest. The brutal facts of the Final Solution were not then understood in their entirety and the family wouldn't have relinquished prematurely the hope, however improbable, that they might yet hear when the war was over from *der lieben Mama*, their beloved mother, and that somehow she might have managed to survive.

It struck me then that years later, sometime after 1967 when the Mount of Olives was once more a part of Israel and she could again visit her daughter's grave, my grandmother must have chosen to commemorate her parents and her husband here, where her precious child already lay, bringing together in death all her loved ones who were prevented by visas, quotas, and decisions the ill-fated nature of which would only be revealed with hindsight, from ever meeting again while they were still alive. Her thoughts would have taken her not only to the memory of her beloved daughter, but of her whole family as once it had been, her father, mother, sisters and an entire world destroyed.

My father's last remaining sibling, Hella, died nine months after Steffi, just before the carnival festival of Purim. She too was buried on the Mount of Olives, close to her sisters. I went to Jerusalem for the funeral, then hurried home to be with my father during the *shivah*, the seven days of prescribed mourning. He was suffering from an unspecified illness associated with an autoimmune condition and had been growing progressively weaker for several years. But, as all the family agreed, it was the news of Hella's death which destroyed his will to live.

Before I left Israel, my cousin Michal and I met at the flat in Jerusalem where the family had lived since the end of the 1930s to go through their remaining possessions. It was the close of an era, especially for my cousin, to whom that apartment, on the first floor of 29 Rechov Ramban, the main route through the centre of the Rechavia district where so many German Jews had settled, had been home from her earliest childhood.

I too had strong associations with that apartment, where I had stayed many times on visits to Israel. There was the bookshelf with the old prayer books from Germany, most of which are now in my own home in London; here in the dining room hung the portrait of Rabbi Yacob Ettlinger, known after his chief work as the *Aruch LaNer;* outside on the balcony was a pile of old suitcases. As I remember, the case we opened that afternoon was one of those large wood-ribbed travelling trunks that used to be fashionable in the days when railway stations still had porters. Inside was a smaller suitcase in which we found an inauspicious-looking off-white linen bag. In it was a bundle of old papers, letters, bills and documents. In another package were notebooks written in a small, tidy hand. A quick examination showed that they were commentaries to verses from the Bible and jottings for lectures, presumably by my great-grandfather Rabbi Jacob Freimann.

But it was the letters that captured my curiosity. I picked up random envelopes and began to unfold the delicate sheets they contained. A brief glance showed that they were mostly written in German; the paper was thin and time had turned the ink of the addresses on the envelopes from blue to fading turquoise. It was the dates which caught my attention: June 1938; November 1938; March 1939. I began to read. Much of the handwriting eluded my first, hasty efforts to decipher it, but some of the letters were readily legible and a few were typed. I sat for several minutes absorbed and oblivious.

17 June 1938

Dear Mama,

Hopefully the parcel arrived safely. This Saturday is going to be sad for you . . . What's happening about your coming to visit us, dear Mama? Have you still not received any information?

The sender was Sophie, my father's aunt. Scarcely a month later she wrote again:

11 July 1938

Dearest Mama,

The weather has become so nice and cool that I'm going to send off a small box tomorrow. It'll hopefully be a duck and a chicken, and I'll pack the gaps with Omega and flour.

What, I wondered, was Omega, and why was her eldest daughter sending poultry to her mother through the post?

There was a list several pages long in pale black ink; the letters were slightly blurred around the edges indicating that this was probably a second or third copy, made by inserting a sheet of carbon paper between the pages. Every conceivable household object was itemised: one clock, twelve knives, twelve shirts, two belts. No doubt the top version had been sent elsewhere, or handed in at some office to satisfy its tedious bureaucratic requirements.

So far all the letters were from 1938. But then I drew an equally thin but larger sheet of writing paper out of its envelope; it was dated 10 January 1947:

Dear Frau Ella,

I received your letter of the 14 September at the end of November. I beg you not to be angry that I'm only answering it today . . . Your dear mother wrote the following words: in spite of everything my faith in God remains unshakeable. These words accompanied me through the long years of persecution and bombing, when more than once our life hung by a silken thread, and gave me the strength to bear it all and come through.

Ella was my grandmother; this letter had been posted in Berlin to her Jerusalem address. But who was the sender, Charlotte Tuch? This was not a name I had ever heard mentioned before. And what relationship did she bear to my great-grandmother that she should be aware of her innermost thoughts before she died?

'If it's all right with you, I'd like to keep these,' I half asked, half told my cousin as I returned the bundle to its off-white bag. I did not realise then the depth of the journey on which they would lead me.

I took the bag back with me to London, where we were all absorbed in caring for my father during his final days. I remember asking him about his aunt Sophie shortly before he entered that domain in which it was no longer possible to elicit the kind of information which is dependent on a practical and sequential awareness of the affairs of this world. 'She came to visit us in Palestine in 1937,' he said. 'We told her not to go back to Europe but she wouldn't listen. Her husband was a Czech nationalist; he believed they would be able to fight the Germans off. They were very wealthy in Czechoslovakia. "It isn't safe there; stay here with us," we told her. She wouldn't hear of it.'

That was the last time I was able to ask my father about such matters, or about anything else.

It was the following year, on the night of the fast of Tishah Be'Av, next to the light of the memorial candle and in the presence of the list of names of the martyred members of the family, which my father had enjoined me to place there, that I began to organise and file the papers I had found in that trunk. Now at last I could begin to study them.

2: AN UNWELCOME LETTER

9 November 1938

With reference to our telephone conversation we politely wish to inform you that, due to the small number of certificates made available by the Mandate Government, it will not be possible for the foreseeable future – at least according to current schedules – for you to obtain a Pensioner's Certificate to emigrate to Palestine.

We ask you to take due note of this information and remain, respectfully, yours

I've tried to imagine to myself the morning when my great-grandmother, Regina Freimann, received that letter. She would probably have been alone when the post was delivered. Glancing through it, she would at once have noticed the sender's address on the envelope and realised with a quiver of anxiety that this was the notification for which she had so urgently been waiting. All the family, but most especially her son Alfred, who had done so much to encourage her to submit the application, would be concerned to know the outcome.

The letter would have reached her at her relatively new address on the Güntzelstrasse in the Berlin district of Wilmersdorf; it was not long before then that she'd had to leave her previous home in the beautiful Oranienburgerstrasse, a few houses down from the magnificent synagogue which, with its gold cupola, dominated

PALÄSTINA TREUHAND-STELLE
DER JUDEN IN DEUTSCHLAND G.m.b.H.
BERLIN W 35, POTSDAMER STR. 72 2. HOF

Fernsprecher: Sammelnummer 22 89 36 · Telegramm-Adresse: PALTREU Berlin · Postscheckkonto: Berlin Nr. 37588
Bankkonten: M.M. Warburg & Co., Hamburg 1, Ferdinandstraße 75 · A.E. Wassermann, Berlin W 8, Wilhelmplatz 7
Sprechzeit 10-1 Uhr (außer Sonnabend)

Frau

R e g i n a F r e i m a n n

Berlin-Wilmersdorf,
Güntzelstr. 15.

Unser Zeichen	Ihr Zeichen	Ihr Schreiben vom	Tag
Dr.Fr/SW			9.11.38

Unter Bezugnahme auf das mit Ihnen geführte fernmündliche Gespräch teilen wir Ihnen höflichst mit, daß infolge der nur geringfügigen Anzahl von Zertifikaten, welche die Mandatsregierung zur Verfügung gestellt hat, es Ihnen auf absehbare Zeit - jedenfalls für die laufende Schedule - nicht möglich sein wird, auf Rentenzertifikat nach Palästina einzuwandern.

Wir bitten Sie, hiervon Kenntnis nehmen zu wollen und zeichnen

hochachtungsvoll
Palästina Treuhand-Stelle
der Juden in Deutschland G.m.b.H.

Letter to Regina Freimann from the Palästina Treuhand-Stelle.

the street. Probably that gracious flat had come with the position; as *Rav* and *Av Bet Din*, rabbi and head of the rabbinical court, her husband Jacob Freimann would have been looked after well by the community. But some months after his death his widow would have had to vacate the home they had shared together for close to ten productive but challenging years since they had come here from Poznań in 1928. To be selected to lead the rabbinical court in Berlin, a city with a large and influential Jewish community of over a hundred thousand souls, was a crowning mark of honour for a man whose Jewish legal and religious decisions were respected throughout Europe and beyond. No one could then have predicted how swiftly and insidiously National Socialism was gaining strength or how soon the fragile Weimar Republic would collapse.

The letter was sent from the offices of the *Palästina Treuhand-Stelle der Juden in Deutschland, G.m.b.H* (The Palestine Trust Company on behalf of the Jews of Germany Ltd). All applications for visas to Palestine had to be directed through its offices and were handled by its staff. They were expert not only in the intricacies of trying to leave Germany, but in the demands and conditions of the British Government which had effectively been ruling Palestine since 1918 under a United Nations mandate, due to expire in 1948. Beneath the stamp of the *Palästina Treuhand-Stelle* was an indecipherable signature, which only added to the bureaucratic impersonality of the message.

It was not an auspicious date on which to receive such news; the letter must have arrived in the immediate aftermath of Kristallnacht (9–10 November 1938). Now referred to in Germany as the *Reichspogromnacht* so as to avoid using the National Socialist expression, to most Jews this vicious and violent explosion will always be known as Kristallnacht (the Night of the Broken Glass), the date on which the true intent of the Nazi regime and its grip over the German and Austrian populations was revealed with a naked and grasping brutality which shattered irreparably the notion that life for the Jews could ever return to normal. Among the synagogues burnt down, Jewish premises destroyed and shops smashed and looted were the offices of the *Palästina Treuhand-Stelle* itself on the Meineckerstrasse. 'In Berlin, 5, then 15 synagogues burn down. Now popular anger rages . . . It should be given free reign,' Joseph Goebbels, the Nazi Minister for Propaganda who was largely responsible for instigating the violence, recorded in his diary.[1] The outburst, he explained, was simply the outpouring of the *kochende Volksseele,* a spontaneous expression of boiling popular feeling. He himself had given personal orders that the main Berlin synagogue on the Fasanenstrasse was to be destroyed. That night and over the following days tens of thousands of Jewish men were arrested and many murdered. It must have been a terrifying moment in which to learn that the key document on the obtaining of which one's chief hopes of leaving Germany rested was not to be forthcoming.

I have held that letter in my hand and stared at it many times. For my great-grandmother, it amounted to a death warrant. This was not, of course, literally the case. But the rejection of her application by the Mandate authorities at that critical time led her to make practical decisions which, while perfectly rational and probably the best choices she could have made in the circumstances known to her at the time, would prove with hindsight to have sealed her fate. Three days later, at a meeting chaired by Hermann Göring, Reinhard Heydrich, then head of the Security Police and subsequently directly responsible for the policies which led to Regina's murder, suggested that an agency be created under Nazi leadership to put into effect a nationwide policy to remove the Jews from the Reich. The chain of offices he created, with branches in Vienna and later in Prague with Adolf Eichmann at their head, would in fact lock the door against any chance of escape and rob hundreds of thousands of their possessions, hopes and lives. On the same day a fine of a billion marks was imposed on the Jewish community as punishment for the damage they had 'caused' on Kristallnacht.

In the event though, Regina was not at home in Berlin on the morning of 10 November. She was in fact in Frankfurt, helping her son Ernst and his wife Eva, who was in her ninth month of pregnancy with their fifth child.

When eventually Regina did open the letter she must have felt profoundly alone with the bad news. To whom could she turn? Whom could she phone to share the contents of that brief note and discuss what to do next? Among the papers in the bag I found in the old trunk were a number of telephone bills, but they carried no itemised list of calls or of the dates on which they were put through, so they were sadly of no use in discovering whether she still had a network of relatives and friends in the city. She may also have been aware that the phones were probably tapped and would have been cautious of sharing news over the telephone on such a delicate subject as emigration. The text of a telegram testified to her deep anxiety: '*Palästina-Amt total versagt. Hilfe dringend gebraucht*' ('the Palestine Office has let us down completely. Help urgently needed'). But the message wasn't dated and was probably not her first, immediate response; it was sent by her and Sophie, her eldest daughter, together, and Sophie didn't travel from Czechoslovakia to join her mother in Berlin until a few weeks later.

Of her six children, three had already fled Germany. Alfred, the youngest, was the first to leave, in 1933; Wally had followed him to Palestine in 1937. Ella, my grandmother, went later that same year. My grandfather, Robert, owned a timber mill in Rawitsch, a small town near Breslau. The city was the centre of one of the most swiftly Nazified regions in Germany and had a particularly vicious local leader. Tipped off by a German official that he was high on the Gestapo's list, Robert took his family and fled the city that same night. 'We laid the table as if we were planning to return very soon and packed just one small bag each so that nobody would be suspicious. Then we left for ever,' my father recalled. He put the place so far behind him emotionally as well, at least at a conscious level, that he never, to the best of my memory, even mentioned to his children the address at which he had lived.

Regina's other three children were still in Europe. Sophie had married and stayed in Holleschau, the small Moravian town where her father had served as rabbi for twenty years. After the collapse of the Austro-Hungarian Empire in the First World War it became part of Czechoslovakia and was renamed Holešov. Trude lived in Poznań, the second of Jacob Freimann's major rabbinical positions. Ernst, the only other son, a doctor in Frankfurt-am-Main, was closest in distance to Berlin. But, thanks to the Gestapo, he was in no position to help his mother. In fact, Regina, a pious and selfless woman whose first thoughts were always for her family, was almost certainly much more worried for Ernst and his wife and children than she was about herself.

More than anyone, though, Frau Dr Regina Freimann, as she was formally addressed on the envelopes of the letters, must have missed the presence of her husband. It was less than twelve months since he had died, suddenly, on 23 December of the previous year, while they were travelling to celebrate Sophie's twenty-fifth wedding anniversary in Czechoslovakia. He had been suffering from high blood pressure for a number of years and had already experienced several strokes. He was taken ill while on the train and died in the early hours of the following day in a hotel in the mountain resort of Spindlermühle.

A separate bundle inside the bag in the trunk contained letters and receipts pertaining to his funeral. Throughout 1938 Regina naturally remained preoccupied not only with the emotional but also with the practical aftermath of her husband's death. She had carefully kept all the relevant papers. A bill for two night-time visits showed that the local physician, Dr Franz Kindler, had twice been in attendance. There had evidently been nothing he could do to save the ailing rabbi's life. It may indeed have been a mercy that death came swiftly. A quote from Gustav Fischer's funeral services, based in Hohenelbe in the mountains of northern Czechoslovakia, itemised the expenses involved in the collection and transportation of the body, including the price of the coffin, the cost of procuring essential documentation, and smaller amounts for sundry telephone calls and telegrams. There were bills and receipts from the Burial Society and the Jewish Community of Holleschau, who provided the plot in the cemetery and supervised the actual funeral. A separate invoice from Leo Klein of the same town showed that there had been five *Sterbe-Wäscher* (washers of the dead), members of the Sacred Society privileged with the task of conducting the ritual preparation of the body and dressing it in the plain white linen vestments in which Jews are traditionally buried. A further list gave the costs of these garments, as well as of the sheets in which the body was cleaned and dried.

On a more mundane level, there were bills from the hotel in Spindlermühle, as well as from the establishment where they later stayed in Holleschau itself. The former listed every item separately: cups of coffee and tea, even a glass of cognac, no doubt badly needed, as well as linens, and four candles, probably for placing by the head of the dead man as Jewish tradition required. A receipt from the *Prager Tagblatt* (the Prague Daily) dated 30 December indicated that the family must have listed their loss in the then equivalent of its 'hatched, matched and dispatched' column. Strikingly, the bill for 400 thank-you cards and envelopes was dated earlier, 28 December. Overwhelmed by the numerous letters of condolence with which they would have been inundated, the family must have turned their attention quickly to how they would manage to acknowledge them all. Each major expense was carefully recorded by Josef Redlich in a letter he later sent to his wife Sophie, who had followed her mother back to Berlin after the period of ritual mourning was over. It was on account of their twenty-fifth wedding anniversary that everyone had gathered in Moravia. But instead of celebrating, they, as the wealthiest members, seem to have marked the occasion by defraying the costs of this family tragedy. 'My dear Sopherl,' he wrote, before proceeding to detail the various amounts including both those for which he had receipts and those for which no acknowledgement could normally be expected. One of the more substantial items was the distribution of 400 kroner to the local poor, prior to the commencement of the funeral service.

It had been Rabbi Freimann's wish that he be buried according to traditional rites and without undue fuss in the Jewish cemetery closest to the place where he died. In the event, he was interred in Holleschau, which probably wasn't the nearest orthodox burial ground but lay close enough to Spindlermühle and recommended itself both because it had been the seat of his longest rabbinical incumbency and because his daughter and son-in-law still lived there and could take care of the practical arrangements and later look after the grave. At any event, his body was not taken back to Berlin; had he died there he would surely have been laid to rest in the Sonderfeld, the special section of the vast Weissensee cemetery. It was there, amid the elaborate memorial chambers, that some hundreds of Jews, the starving and spectre-like living dead, managed to conceal themselves from the Nazis among the tombs and mausoleaums of the blessed dead in their eternal peace.

Rabbi Freimann was laid to rest in Holleschau's Jewish cemetery on 26 December 1937, on a freezing winter's day, next but one to the grave of Rabbi Shabbetai Hacohen, known after his initials as the Shach, the illustrious commentator to the key sixteenth-century code of Jewish law, the *Shulchan Aruch,* and also a former leader of the local community, who had been buried there in 1663. One of Rabbi Freimann's most important rabbinical tasks had been to deliver a learned lecture each year on the anniversary of the Shach's death, in which he shared the latter's teachings with the many scholars who came to visit his tomb. The field, with its tall gravestones and old funeral hall decorated with murals, remains undisturbed to this day.

Many people from all around the world attended the funeral of Rabbi Freimann, that is, those who were able to get to Holleschau. The ceremony reflected the great love and high esteem in which this towering figure was held . . . The practice of all the traditional rites by the Chevra Kaddisha of Berlin, as well as the active participation of many rabbinical figures from our city, ensured that the parting from our teacher was conducted with due simplicity and ceremony.[2]

'Those who were able to get to Holleschau' included neither Rabbi Freimann's older son Ernst, to whom the Nazis refused permission to leave Germany, nor his younger son Alfred, who observed the traditional mourning rites in Palestine together with the two of his sisters who by now also lived there. Regina would have been comforted by her other daughters, Trude and Sophie. Photographs shown to me by my father portrayed a long procession of men and women dressed in thick black coats and hats following the coffin on foot through the deep snow.

Ernst and his wife Eva wrote from Frankfurt:

It's terribly hard that we're not able to be with you. I had always believed that whatever happened we would be able to be together at once, but now there are mountains in between. Last time I parted from you, dear Mama, your heart was so heavy.

Did that final line indicate that Regina was well aware of the risk of a further stroke and afraid that something just like this might suddenly happen to her husband? Or was her mood occasioned by the terrible times?

Rabbi Jacob Freimann's funeral procession outside the synagogue in Holleschau.

A few days later Ella, my grandmother, wrote from Jerusalem; she had been waiting to hear more about the funeral:

Dear Mama,

We still can't comprehend the great misfortune which has overtaken us . . . We are constantly with you all in our thoughts. It's a relief to know that Trude was with you, dear Mama. All through these days we've been longing for news from you. Of course you won't be wanting to make any decisions right now, but it would be good if you would join us here in Jerusalem. Annchen wrote to us about how loving and attentive Sophie and Josef have been. This is a great comfort to us who are so far away.

A host of documents indicated that Regina spent much of the following months settling bills and dealing with the numerous administrative demands which follow any death, a painful task made all the more difficult by the hostile attitude which will have permeated most of the bureaucratic circles with which she had to deal. A copy of the will indicated that the couple had agreed that they would inherit each other's possessions and that, upon the death of the second partner, their fortunes would be divided equally among their six children. On 14 February 1938 Regina had to declare for the purposes of any potential tax liabilities that they had six adult sons and daughters of their own and no further step- or adopted children. She was required to provide addresses for all of them, a circumstance which was to prove invaluable to me in attempting to uncover the traces of their lives seventy-five years later.

At the same time as she was coping with the paperwork resulting from her husband's death, she also had to prepare a thorough inventory of her household possessions in readiness for shipping them to Tel Aviv, where, despite various hesitations, she hoped to go to escape Nazi Germany and rejoin the three of her children already in Palestine. Such lists were demanded by the Nazi authorities from anyone seeking to emigrate.

Amid all these pressing practical concerns Regina also had to make urgent decisions about her future. A letter to Alfred in Jerusalem from a family friend who was also a member of staff of the Palestine Office indicated that she was struggling to make up her mind what to do. That her preferred option was to go to Palestine was not in doubt. Her husband had firmly believed that God would redeem the divine promise and bring about the long-delayed return of the Jewish people to its ancestral land. But he was now dead and Regina had to face the future alone.

The Jewish community agreed to forward her widow's pension to Palestine if her application to emigrate were to prove successful, and the proposed sum of 350 Reichsmarks each month was generous. But what if the international situation should deteriorate still further and the transfer of monies became impossible? Would she then find herself penniless in a strange country, dependent on her family for support? Alfred's correspondent observed that most people were happy just to get out of Germany alive and to leave worrying about what would happen afterwards until they knew that they were safe. But Regina was clearly concerned lest she prove a burden to her children who were all now struggling to establish a new life in challenging circumstances in a land full of conflicts of its own. The last thing she wanted was to become a source of trouble to her nearest and dearest.

It would be impossible to judge whether these prepossessing concerns served to distract her from her grief, or to accentuate it. Her letters, both from this period and later, showed a selfless capacity to pass over or make light of her own sufferings. But her husband must have been in her thoughts all the time.

After all, they had been married for forty-six years. They were first cousins and had met in her parents' home in Ostrowo, when the young Jacob, still a teenager but already an orphan, had travelled there to study Torah with her father, Yisrael Meir Freimann, the town rabbi. Regina was probably just thirteen when the man with whom she was to share her life came to live in her parent's house. She no doubt looked up to him for his learning and diligence with proud admiration.

Back home in Holleschau, Sophie was well aware of where her

mother's thoughts lay. In a letter dated 11 July 1938 she included something special for her 'Dearest Mama':

The blue flowers in the envelope in the parcel grow near our dear departed Papa.

Regina Freimann, centre, surrounded by her family.

The first time I explored the old Jewish Quarter in Kraków was at night, walking along Szeroka Street past the Remu Synagogue, losing my way in small alleyways to find myself at the back of the ancient cemetery, staring through the railings at the worn gravestones of generations of scholars of Torah. I searched for the marks in the entranceways to courtyards and houses where the *mezuzot*, cases containing the tiny roll of parchment inscribed with the injunction to write on the doorposts of every home the command to love the Lord your God, had once been affixed. In my mind was the picture taken in secret by Roman Vishniac in the late 1930s of an old Jew studying Kabbalah by candlelight. Not long afterwards he, his world and virtually all its inhabitants were destroyed. Yet I imagined I might somehow encounter his spirit, together with the souls of those who had for generations devoted themselves to the love of Torah, among these places of prayer and learning, now empty of the Jews who had imbued them with their yearning and devotion.

I had also noticed the sign above an unobtrusive entrance in Jozefa Street: *Kove'a Ittim LaTorah* ('establish fixed times for Torah'), a name taken from the Talmudic dictum that every Jew must fix regular hours of the day and night for learning Torah. The building had once been a *Yeshivah*, a school for the intensive study of the classic Jewish texts and teachings. But I had no idea that there was any family connection. Here, however,

was where my great-great-great-grandfather, head of the
Rabbinical Court of Kraków, had taught his students Torah
every day.

Among his children were Avraham Chaim Freimann, who
would become the father of my great-grandfather, and Yisrael
Meir Freimann, who was to be the father of my great-grandmother.
Avraham Chaim remained as a rabbi and teacher of Torah in
Kraków. After learning intensively among the greatest Torah
scholars in Hungary, Yisrael Meir studied philosophy and oriental
languages, receiving his doctorate from the University of Jena in
1860. He was called to the rabbinate of the beautiful old town of
Filehne in the district of Posen in the same year. Also in that year
he married Helene, the third daughter of the famed teacher Rabbi
Yacob Ettlinger of Altona. When Steffi died and before it emerged
that there was a plot available close to her sister on the Mount
of Olives, I had been advised to tell the Burial Society that she
was his great-great-granddaughter; such ancestry, even after four
generations, would encourage them to accord her a place of honour
in the ancient cemetery.

A single surviving photograph of Helene shows her to have
been a beautiful and dignified lady; she was popular and much
loved in the family. My great-grandmother Regina was born in
Filehne on 12 January 1869. She was still a small child when the
family moved to the nearby town of Ostrowo where, after a unani-
mous election, Yisrael Meir was appointed rabbi, serving there
until his death. He was held in such esteem not only by the Jews
but by the entire local population that in 1900, over fifteen years
after he died, a street was named Freimannstrasse in his honour.

My great-grandfather Jacob was born in Kraków to Avraham

Rabbi Yisrael Meir Freimann and his wife Helene.

Chaim and his second wife Sophie on 1 October 1866, *Shemini Atzeret*, the conclusion of the harvest festival. Jacob grew up in the heart of the culture of intense and assiduous devotion to traditional Talmudic study which characterised much of the Jewish world of Eastern and Central Europe in the mid-nineteenth century. Among his teachers were the greatest analysts of Talmud and Jewish law of their generation. 'The boy received from his father the foundations of his Jewish education, that *girsa deyankuta,* that ineradicable childhood understanding of the Rabbinic-Talmudic way of life and thought,' wrote the editor of the Festschrift, the collection of scholarly essays presented to him as a tribute on his seventieth birthday.[1]

Jacob lost his parents at a young age; his mother Sophie died of typhoid fever in 1875 when he was only nine, and his father Avraham Chaim of cholera in 1882. I had visited the old cemetery, stopping by the burial places of the famous sixteenth-century scholar and legalist Rabbi Moses Isserles, before wandering off the trodden pathways into the grass to try to decipher the Hebrew inscriptions on the worn-down sandstone of the graves of the less illustrious dead. But in fact my great-grandfather's parents, Rabbi Avraham Chaim Freimann and his wife Sophie were not here. They were buried in the so-called 'new' cemetery, which was destroyed by the Nazis who used the gravestones to pave the nearby concentration camp of Plashov. After the war, when an attempt was made to restore them to their proper location, the family tried to find the headstones, but to no avail.

Jacob's brothers and sisters went to live with their uncle in America, a decision which would later help save the lives of part of the family trapped in Europe. A different existence beckoned to them in the new world. But Jacob preferred to remain within the trusted ambience of an intensely Jewish culture rooted in love and boundless dedication to Torah. He therefore chose to travel to his uncle Rabbi Israel Meir in Ostrowo, under whose direction he would be able to continue his studies.

Before leaving Kraków, Jacob, who was only sixteen when he was orphaned, noted down the inscriptions on his parents' graves in his beautiful cursive Hebrew script:

> My mother:
> in the midst of her days died a most honoured lady,
> young children seven she left behind;
> all who knew and cared for her wept and mourned . . .
> My father:
> here lies a most precious man
> who walked in the path of the perfect-hearted.

In this manner he carried his parents' characters and culture with him for the rest of his life.

Jacob had already earned a reputation as a *matmid*, a scholar devoted day and night to Torah. He took to Ostrowo a letter from some of the most famous teachers of the generation, testifying that he had 'an understanding heart to attend to and comprehend his studies'.

In his uncle's house Jacob completed his schooling and pursued his Talmudic education. Here, too, he met his future wife, his first cousin Regina. He would have been drawn to her not only on account of her personality, but because of the rich ambience of Jewish living and learning in which they had both been raised. Reflecting on God's promise to Adam that he would make him a fitting helpmeet, Jacob noted that 'whoever considers the upbringing of the woman he wants to marry, the education she received from her parents and the merits of the previous generations of her family, chooses well.'[2]

By the time he enrolled in the University of Berlin at the age of twenty, he was already in possession of a *Hatarat Hora'ah*, a diploma recognising him as an authoritative teacher of rabbinic Judaism. Since the middle of the nineteenth century traditional Jewry in the German lands had been influenced decisively by the philosophy of Samson Raphael Hirsch with its slogan of 'Torah together with the way of the world', combining unwavering adherence to Jewish law and ritual with full participation in the life and concerns of the culture and society in which one lived. For almost the first time in the long Jewish experience of exile it was possible to be a *Yisroelmensch*, a faithful Jew and a full citizen of one's country, equal among others. This outlook became a cornerstone of German-Jewish Orthodoxy. It was partly also a response to the attrition suffered by the traditional community when, with the attainment of increasing civil rights through the late eighteenth and nineteenth centuries, German cultured society and its professions became accessible to Jews, many of whom aspired to its ways and were assimilated within its ranks. Hirsch's philosophy was embodied in the educational principles of Ezriel Hildesheimer, in whose name a seminary was established in Berlin for the training of orthodox rabbis. It was here that Jacob Freimann came to study. He also took courses at the university; the German authorities required religious leaders in official positions and thus salaried by the state to possess a university education to doctoral level. Freimann followed courses in literature, oriental studies and philosophy before writing his thesis at the University of Tübingen on a Syriac translation of the Book of Daniel.

On 5 February 1891, equipped with his doctorate and his *Semichah*, his rabbinic ordination, he married his cousin Regina Freimann in her home town of Ostrowo. Her father had meanwhile died, but her mother, Helene, would live to be a much-loved grandparent. The marriage was close, respectful and happy. In a comment on the verse from Genesis, 'It is not good for a man to be alone', Rabbi Jacob noted the Talmud's observation: 'If your wife is low and gentle, bend down and seek her counsel in domestic matters.' Photographs show that Regina was indeed considerably shorter than her husband, and she was certainly gentle in spirit. By 'domestic matters' a patronising confinement of the woman's role to the kitchen was not meant, but rather the spirit and values of the home and what it represented, the heart and kernel of the

Freimann couple's life. One sensed that they were rarely, if ever, geographically, intellectually or spiritually apart.

After a brief period in Kanitz they settled in Holleschau with their two small daughters, Sophie, their eldest child, and Ella, who would become my grandmother. Soon after their arrival, on 3 September 1893 a new synagogue was dedicated. I was proudly shown the list of dignitaries in attendance; Rabbi Freimann's signature appeared in the middle and it was he who conducted the opening ceremony. Sadly, the building was not destined to reach its half-century; it was burnt down by the Germans in 1941.

Not long after the dedication, a new house was constructed for the rabbi and his family. A graceful building, it stood opposite the synagogue, separated only by a vegetable garden. Ernst remembered it warmly:

It had eight rooms. In one of them the roof could be lifted up by springs and was used as our *Sukka* [the booth roofed with branches in which the harvest festival is celebrated]. Between this house and the synagogue was a garden with flowers and a part with vegetables. In the back was a shed for wood and coal, and for chickens, turkeys and ducks, a coop for the geese, and a laundry room. There were also trees: one plum tree, one pear tree, and one 'Reine Claude', a kind of plum. There were two toilets, a cellar and an attic.[3]

Water was drawn daily by the maid from a well near the entrance to the house and stored in a large covered barrel. The surrounding lands were fertile; local farmers came to the market to sell poultry, vegetables and fruit. In a letter to her mother in the summer of

1938 Sophie referred to the cherries, blueberries, blackberries, raspberries and damsons that she had bottled or turned into jam.

But life in Moravia was by no means always easy for Jews, as Jacob Freimann recorded in his history of the town. The community was probably first formed after it was driven out of nearby Olmütz in 1454. By the seventeenth century it was thriving, but the congregation had constantly to renew its privileges, as the local rulers kept changing. A document from 1631 listed the conditions under which it was tolerated: Jews were permitted to maintain a school, synagogue, hospital, ritual baths, cemetery and houses. They were allowed to practise their ceremonies and pursue their trade in cloth, wool, leather and linens. In return they had to provide the duke and a large number of lesser dignitaries with numerous gifts, anything from geese for Christmas to sugar, pepper, saffron and spices. In 1899 a blood libel led to pogroms across the Czech lands; in Holleschau hundreds of people went on the rampage, invading the Jewish quarter and robbing the houses, creating a challenging crisis for the still young and relatively inexperienced rabbi. It wasn't until the birth of Czechoslovakia in 1919 as an independent nation that the autonomous Jewish community, effectively a twin settlement existing in parallel to the Christian town, merged with it into one civic entity.

These were good years for Rabbi Jacob and his wife. It was here that their third daughter Wally was born in 1894. Ernst, the first boy, followed in 1897, Trude in 1898, and their youngest child, Alfred, in 1899. The rabbi was able to find time to follow both his professional duties and his academic pursuits. He had a deep interest in history and became an important contributor to the work of *Mekitsei Nirdamim,* an international society devoted to the publication of scholarly editions of classic Jewish texts. He was appointed inspector of religion for the Jewish schools of northern Moravia and became chairman of the union of rabbis of Moravia and Silesia. It was in this capacity that he received a telegram from the Austro-Hungarian Emperor Franz Josef in 1906 thanking him for the 'patriotic tribute' he had offered on behalf of his colleagues, though it was not clear what the occasion was on which he had contributed these congenial greetings.

Rabbi Jacob Freimann teaching in the synagogue.

In 1914 Jacob Freimann was called to the rabbinic seat of Posen, made famous by his illustrious predecessor Rabbi Akiva Eger.

Twenty years later, in an accolade on his seventieth birthday, an admirer described his life there:

. . . his outstanding diplomatic skills, and above all the exemplary and deeply Jewish rabbinical home, run with tact and dedication by his life's partner, created the atmosphere of his rabbinic incumbency. Then came the war years; it was necessary to look after wounded soldiers, prisoners of war and brothers in occupied lands. More than ever before, the troubles which afflicted the surrounding communities with their rich Jewish life poured into Posen. All important legal and political issues came before the Posen rabbinate for resolution.

When Posen became part of Poland as a result of the Treaty of Versailles following Germany's defeat in the First World War, most of the city's Jews, who spoke German, identified with German culture, and who felt threatened by the rising anti-Semitic tones of Polish nationalism backed by major elements of the Catholic Church, left to live in the Reich. However, Jacob and Regina remained until 1928, when they eventually moved to Berlin after he was offered the position of rabbi of the city's oldest synagogue in the Heidereuterstrasse. 'The Nazis destroyed it; there's nothing left of it,' my father told me. Nevertheless I went to visit the site where it had once stood. My father was correct; all that remained was a plaque noting that this had been the first of Berlin's many synagogues: 'Consecrated in 1714, the last service was held here in 1942, before the building was destroyed in 1945.'

Though he was sixty-two when he came to Berlin, Rabbi Freimann's energies were in no way depleted. He taught history, literature, and practical rabbinics at the Hildesheimer Seminary where he himself had studied forty years earlier. He was appointed *Av Bet Din*, head of the rabbinical court. His reputation and authority extended well beyond the city, and beyond Germany itself; questions of Jewish law and scholarship were sent to him for his opinion from all over the world.

The early years in Berlin should have been a period of profound satisfaction for Jacob and Regina. Their six children were well settled in their lives; they were all married and their sons and sons-in-law were successful at their occupations. Their eldest daughter, Sophie, had remained in Holleschau where she had married Josef Redlich, grandson of the town's former rabbi, whose family had been manufacturers of spirits for two generations. According to one account they possessed a rum distillery. But it seems more likely that they produced a variety of liquors. They were wealthy, but, after almost two decades of marriage, not blessed with children. They felt deeply at home in Czechoslovakia and had a wide circle of clients and friends across the neighbouring towns and villages. Trude had stayed in Poznań where she married Alex Peiser, a doctor at the city's Jewish hospital; they had one child, Arnold, born in 1928. Jacob and Regina's older son Ernst had studied medicine and, after serving in the Austro-Hungarian Army for the duration of the First World War, settled in Frankfurt, the city with Germany's second largest, but oldest and most famous, Jewish community. Despite his professional obligations he was an ardent student of Judaism; in his memoirs he carefully recorded the names of all the major scholars and teachers with whom he had learnt Torah in every city in which he had lived. He had married Eva Heckscher, the daughter of a banker from Hamburg, and they soon had a thriving young family. The youngest of Jacob and Regina's six children, Alfred, had completed his studies and was shortly to be appointed to the judiciary in Königsberg. Although it had been the city of Kant, it wasn't renowned for its Jewish community, but the government had posted him there and events were soon to prove that the move to East Prussia was *beschert* (ordained in heaven) – as the Yiddish term succinctly put it. For it was here that he would meet his future wife. Wally too was married, to an eminent doctor; he had a passion for song-birds which, to the horror of other members of the family, he allowed to flap freely around their home. Wally was the only one of the six siblings later to be divorced. Sadly, she had no children. I remember visiting her when she was an old lady, a wizened figure who made a living by administering injections, existing in rather Spartan style in a flat on King George Street in the centre of Jerusalem. In fact, she had really wanted to become a doctor but because at the time women were apparently not allowed to study medicine, she had to settle for being a nurse instead. She was a brilliant cook. I stayed with her on my first ever visit to Israel when the somewhat grim asceticism of her manner rather frightened me. I never met her at her best or had the opportunity to appreciate the person she really was.

Ella and Robert Wittenberg, my grandparents, had initially settled in the small town of Rawitsch, where my grandfather owned a timber mill. My father once showed me a picture taken after the war, possibly as late as the early 1960s. The name Wittenberg was still displayed in large letters on a board by the entrance; nobody had thought it necessary to take it down. Evidently the possibility that any members of the family might one day return was too remote to merit consideration. After he died I searched every folder of my father's papers but was not able to recover that photograph. My father was born in Rawitsch in 1921; two years later the family moved to nearby Breslau. My father would have been too young to understand but the move was probably occasioned by the election of a nationalist mayor, Kazimierz Czyszewski, in 1922. The Polish Nationalist Party was notoriously anti-Semitic. The Jews of Rawitsch suffered discrimination and persecution, including the refusal to hand them the keys to the synagogue. In October 1923 the Jewish community of Rawitsch was formally dissolved and its properties made over to the State Treasury.

Ella and Robert Wittenberg, my grandparents.

Breslau, a beautiful city on the Oder, had a substantial Jewish population and a famous rabbinical seminary named after the nineteenth-century founder of Conservative Judaism, Zecharias

Frankel. I visited the town in 2010 for the rededication of its best-known synagogue, *Zum Weissen Storch* (At the White Stork). I wasn't even able to look for ghosts; my father had never told me where they lived or what synagogue they had attended. I only knew that he had been a pupil at the Jewish school; a small photograph showed a rather bare and miserable playground. It was there that he and his classmates used to play football whenever their Jewish studies teacher was called to the phone in the middle of the lesson, according to my father a rather frequent occurrence. He vividly remembered how those boys too slow to return to their seats on time would be lifted back through the window by their ears. 'Yes,' he said, 'It did hurt.' The family had been prosperous. 'At midnight we would break for a large meal, with goose fat,' my father said, remembering how they had honoured the custom of studying Torah all night on the festival of the Giving of the Law. 'My mother's recipes would say "Take twenty eggs," he recalled, listening to my brother or me as we read out the more modest list of ingredients for a cake from some new-fangled, cholesterol-conscious work. 'Who would dream of doing that today?'

It appeared too that the Wittenberg parents rather spoiled their children, as the disapproving tone of a letter from Sophie to Alfred in September 1937 indicated:

The Wittenbergs are finally on their way to join you [in Palestine]. Hopefully they'll all soon find occupations. It's particularly important for the children so that they can finally understand the seriousness of their situation. For the money they spent on their stay in Basel they could have lived for half a year. Sadly, Robert and Ella don't seem to be very firm with the children and indulge them in things which don't suit with their situation, like excursions, bike riding and so forth, instead of mending clothes, ironing and such like.

I remember my father telling me that after fleeing Breslau they had indeed gone to stay with relatives in Switzerland while waiting for their visas to come through, no doubt so as to be out of the way of the Gestapo. But nothing about my father suggested a spoilt childhood.

In 1936 Jacob Freimann marked his seventieth birthday; Alfred was already in Palestine, but no doubt the rest of the family gathered in Berlin for the occasion. It was the end of the summer during which the city had hosted the Olympic Games. Hitler had been at pains to show the world only the positive face of Germany; there had even been a brief reprieve in the more public measures against Jews. For the Freimann family, this would prove to be the last ever major celebration. The rabbi's colleagues prepared a Jubilee volume in his honour; a family friend, Harry Levy, wrote the foreword:

Alongside an inherited rabbinical bearing, he possessed an even temperament, a psychological gift for empathy and relating to people, and most of all a flexibility of spirit which had its roots in the natural piety of a secure personality, as well as a powerful measure of common sense and understanding which matured increasingly over the years into wisdom. Added to that, he was equally well rooted in two almost diametrically opposed worlds, the eastern world of the Talmud, where he rejoiced in the minutiae of its argumentation, and the scholarly culture of Western Europe. Only such an inner harmony could render the sheer quantity of his achievements comprehensible.

In that suitcase in Jerusalem had been letters of tribute from colleagues and institutions of learning all around the world. One was even written on parchment. The event was to prove the crowning acknowledgement of his life's work.

A little over a year later Jacob Freimann was dead. The *Israelitisches Familienblatt* carried a gracious obituary:

Others are noted and respected for their knowledge and learning, but he was loved by all who were privileged to draw close to him for his human qualities first and foremost, for his simplicity, his nobility of character, his inability to do anything unjust, his love of fairness and truth. It wasn't at the pulpit, nor in his writings, nor at meetings that Jacob Freimann was most completely himself; he was truly himself in his own home which was as simple as he was, when he guided a small circle of people through the teachings of Judaism.

Though she was not mentioned directly, the words were clearly also an acknowledgement of his indebtedness to his wife. But no tribute is ever as honest, or as meaningful, as that of a person's own children. Fifty years later, when he himself was in his eighties, Ernst made no distinction between his parents when he wrote about their values and their way of life:

It is hard for me to describe the unique characters of my parents. They were both meticulous in preserving the Jewish way of life in all its fine details. At the same time they showed tolerance towards all people, even those far from keeping the commandments. They were full of love for their children. They were very generous to the poor who came to their door; most of whom were given food to eat. They succeeded in helping to resolve the problems faced by many people in all their different aspects.

In a sermon dated 1929 on the opening chapter of Genesis, Rabbi Freimann noted:

Scripture tells us that 'God saw that [creation] was good' with the sole exception of man . . . All other creatures have just the one sole option – to remain at the level on which they were created and behave according to their inborn nature. To man alone is given the capacity for choice, the possibility of determining the course of his life according to his own free will. To man alone the task is granted of aspiring to perfection, of diligently devoting all the days of his life to its attainment.

A few lines further on he considered God's famous question to Adam after he had eaten from the tree of knowledge:

'God called out and said to the man, "Where are you?"' This is no mere enquiry about his physical location but an expression of surprise and admonition: 'See to where you have come by forsaking the path along which I commanded you to walk!'

He died before the depths to which that abandonment could lead were revealed in the destinies of his widow and their children.

On 16 July 1938 a friend working for the Palestine Office in Berlin replied to Alfred's urgent enquiries on behalf of his mother, about whose situation he was deeply worried:

Dear Alfred,

Many thanks for your lines. They led me to make a long-intended visit to your mother to discuss her situation with her. Sadly, the matter is in several respects more difficult than it looked back in May because circumstances have become significantly worse in a number of ways.

The letter explained in great detail the various options which might still remain open; its author was closely conversant with the advantages and disadvantages of each of the categories under which it was possible to apply to the British Mandate authorities for a visa to Palestine.

Of all the six children it was Alfred who was most aware of the urgency of getting his mother out of Germany and who was most able to act. By now two of his sisters had joined him in Palestine, but he was the longest settled in the country and his legal background equipped him best to understand the numerous difficulties which had to be overcome.

The youngest of the Freimann children, born in 1899, Alfred had thrived in the atmosphere of intense Jewish study in his parents' house. 'As he was always at home he learnt much more from my father than I,' his older brother Ernst recalled. 'He was always reading or learning.' Whereas Ernst had been obliged to serve during the First World War, Alfred didn't turn eighteen until close to the end of hostilities and the Jewish farmer to whom he was sent for war work allowed him to stay at home with his books. This enabled him to write, at the age of just eighteen, a highly commended biography of the famous thirteenth-fourteenth century legal authority, Rabbi Asher ben Yechiel. Throughout his life his great love was Jewish scholarship. In the autumn of 1922 he wrote to the committee of the nascent Hebrew University, then based in London; he had heard that the department of philosophy was looking for teaching staff. 'I trust you won't think me, most respected sirs, over-bold in turning to you in this regard,' he began. He described his studies with his father, 'where I drank my fill of the Babylonian and Jerusalem Talmuds and numerous legal works. My longing for Torah grew ever stronger; I laboured in it and found reward.' He wrote of his fascination with the history of Hebrew literature; he mentioned his book and noted that it had been favourably received by the leading scholars of the generation. But his real passion was Hebrew jurisprudence; it was to this subject that he wished to dedicate his life. Alfred was not quite twenty-three when he wrote the letter. Almost two decades would pass, bringing with them events unimaginable at the beginning of the Weimar Republic, before he was eventually invited to join the Faculty of Humanities of the Hebrew University in Jerusalem.

In the meantime he opted for the law as a way of earning a living. He was made Gerichtsassessor in 1926, a two-year probationary placement, and was scarcely thirty when he was appointed to the Prussian judiciary. The constitution of the Weimar Republic made discrimination in access to the professions illegal, affirming that 'admission to public office was to be independent of religious affiliation'. His certificate of appointment, dated 25 June 1928 and written in magnificent Gothic script, declared that 'Probationary judge Dr Alfred Freimann in Tilsit is herewith appointed to the position of regional, and at the same time that of district, judge.'

He was sent by the Prussian Ministry of Justice to Königsberg in East Prussia, where he met and fell in love with a friend of the daughter of the lady who managed the establishment in which he took lodgings. Nelly Basch, originally from Luxembourg, had lost her parents at an early age and was brought up in an orphanage. The couple were married in the summer of 1928 in Posen. The civil certificate was stamped with the seal of Alfred's father; officiating at the wedding of his son must have been one of Jacob Freimann's last, and happiest, duties before leaving for Berlin.

I remember Nelly well; she was a kind, homely, down-to-earth and practical woman, devoted to her family, and served wonderful cakes. She possessed great strength of character, no doubt forged in her challenging childhood and toughened by the subsequent tragedies which continued to punctuate her life.

In 1933, when the Nazi party came to power, there were more than three thousand Jewish lawyers in Prussia, over a quarter of the total number of practitioners in the region. This 'over-representation' was resented; on 31 March the Prussian Minister of Justice, Hanns Kerrl, announced measures dismissing most Jews working in the civil service and the law, ordering that 'only certain Jewish attorneys shall practise, generally corresponding to the proportion of Jews in the rest of the population.' This figure would have stood at less than one per cent. It seems that Kerrl took these steps on his own initiative, prior even to the promulgation one week later by the Nazi government of the Law for the Restoration of the Civil Service that mandated the dismissal of all non-Aryans. The latter category was defined as excluding 'anyone descended from non-Aryan, particularly Jewish, parents or grandparents'. To lose one's job, just one 'wrong' grandparent sufficed.

Alfred had been practising his profession for scarcely three years when he was removed from his post. A subsequent letter from the Prussian Ministry of Justice, dated 3 July 1933, by which time he was already in Berlin, informed him of the supposedly 'initial' duration of his 'retirement':

By means of this letter, you are discharged from your duties as of 7 April 1933 until 1 November 1933, on the basis of section 3 of the Law for the Restoration of the Civil Service. Your retirement will continue until this date.

Referring to a series of bye-laws, the letter made it clear that 'no severance payments are due'. The signature was illegible. The envelope was marked *persönlich*, followed by an exclamation mark. One might wonder why; Alfred's colleagues would surely have known exactly what the receipt of such a missive meant. Perhaps the sender didn't want other eyes to see the cold details of how the ministry dismissed its faithful servants. It would be hard to imagine a letter which showed less personal concern.

The act in question, the Law for the Restoration of the Civil

Der Preußische Justizminister

II a 2022.

Berlin W 8, den 3.Juli 193 3.
Wilhelmstraße 65
Fernsprecher: A 1 Jäger Nr. 0044.

Anlage: Abschied.

       Durch den beifolgenden Abschied sind Sie auf Grund des § 3 des Gesetzes zur Wiederherstellung des Berufsbeamtentums vom 7.April 1933 (RGBl.I S.175) zum 1.November 1933 in den Ruhestand versetzt. Ihre Beurlaubung dauert bis zu diesem Zeitpunkt fort.

       Ein Ruhegehalt steht Ihnen auf Grund des § 8 aaO. in Verbindung mit Ziff. 2,3 zu § 8 der Dritten Verordnung zur Durchführung des Gesetzes zur Wiederherstellung des Berufs= beamtentums vom 6.Mai 1933 (RGBl.I S.245) nicht zu (vgl. auch Ziff 24 und 25 der 3.Preußischen Ausführungsvorschrift vom 15.Juni 1933 -Ges.S.202-).

An

Herrn Land= und Amtsgerichtsrat
Dr.Alfred F r e i m a n n - Persönlich! "

       in

       B e r l i n N.24.

Letter to Alfred Freimann discharging him from his post in the Prussian judiciary.

Service, was to affect many thousands of people, often costing them the positions to which they had given decades of diligent service. In Frankfurt, Alfred's uncle Aron, a notable scholar who had devoted his life to developing the Judaica collection in the municipal library into one of the finest and most extensive in the world, was summarily 'retired' and shortly afterwards required to hand in his keys to the building.

Soon after receiving notification of his dismissal, Alfred was tipped off by a non-Jewish colleague who had seen his name on a Gestapo list. He advised him to leave Königsberg at once. Alfred departed for his parents' home in Berlin with little more than the coat on his back. Nelly followed two days later with their three-year-old daughter Ruthie. They, too, took no luggage; nobody could be trusted, not even the nanny. Safer in the comparative anonymity of the capital, and close to the offices of the *Treuhand-Stelle,* they applied, successfully, for certificates for Palestine. Parting from his parents must have been hard; Alfred was perhaps the closest to his father of the six children in temperament and interests and even in 1933 it must have been far from certain that they would ever see one another again.

A year after arriving in Palestine Alfred left the country, albeit temporarily, drawn by the opportunity of teaching at the University of Rome. But it was not to prove an attractive option. 'We went to Italy,' Nelly told me. 'Mussolini was already in power. I said to Alfred: "We're not staying here. We've seen it all before. There's only one place we're going to live."' They returned to Palestine where, with no opportunities available in the academic sphere, Alfred took a position as legal advisor to an insurance company. At night he followed his passion for scholarship. Paper was in short supply; he used the backs of insurance forms, covering them with notes for the book he was preparing on Jewish marriage law, to this day considered a classic study on the subject. Further jottings showed that he was already at work on the sequel, a history of the Jewish law of divorce. All through his life he had a passion for Jewish books, which he collected avidly despite the limited means at his disposal.

In 1935, Nelly gave birth to their son Dani, the first member of the family to be born outside Europe. Alfred's parents travelled from Berlin to join them for the celebration of the circumcision. It was a journey Regina would longingly recall:

This week brings Passover . . . In the year of '35 we arrived in Palestine during these very days; the joy of our dear departed Papa when he saw the land from the ship was indescribable. What has happened since that time!

Had it not been for his sense of duty towards his beleaguered congregants back in Berlin, Rabbi Freimann would have remained in Palestine, Alfred's daughter Ruthie told me as we sat in her home in Tel Aviv seventy-five years later. She must have been just five when they came to visit; it was the last time she would ever see either of her grandparents.

By the summer of 1938 Alfred and his family were well settled in Jerusalem. Reports from more recent arrivals from Germany, who included two of his sisters, made the extreme urgency of his mother's position all too clear. The situation had deteriorated greatly since he himself had fled; there were no ways out of Germany that did not present major difficulties. Restrictive quotas made the waiting period for visas to the United States extremely lengthy. Exactly how long depended on one's nationality; separate immigration quotas were fixed for each country. Who could foresee what might happen by the date their number came up, maybe sometime as far distant as 1941 or 1942? After Kristallnacht, when it was no longer possible to cling to the illusion that things would get better, it was clear that an indefinite wait might well amount to a delayed death sentence. The British authorities had meanwhile also had placed far tighter restrictions on entry into Palestine. It was sometimes easier to obtain visas for a number of South American countries or for the Far East, but how was one to know what life was really like in those faraway places, or if one could make a living and put food in the mouths of one's family?

While it grew ever harder to leave, it also became increasingly difficult to remain in Germany. Jews were progressively stripped of their status, their right to access amenities, their opportunities to work and their economic assets. On 15 September 1935 at the party rally in Nuremberg the promulgation of two new laws was announced to the Reichstag. The first, the Law for the Protection of German Blood and Honour, prohibited marriages and sexual relations between Jews and Germans. It also forbade Jews to employ German women under the age of forty-five in their households, 'in case of *Rassenschande*' (racial pollution). The second, the Reich Citizenship Law, defined those not of German blood as merely subjects of the state, in contrast to Aryans who were full *Reichsbürger* (citizens of the Reich). This effectively stripped Jews of all their rights as citizens and placed them outside the protection of the law. It is not surprising that numerous Jews, many of whom had lost their sons, or had themselves fought with honour for their beloved *Vaterland* in the First World War, found it hard to fathom such a deep and utter betrayal. Henceforth Germany's Jews, as well as Roma and other non-Aryans, were legally relegated to the rank of a lesser species. Among the few documents I found relating to my father and his parents were those indicating that they had ceased to be citizens of Germany: 'German citizenship declared void following the announcement of 7 November 1940', the cards stated, though why they were issued on this date, by which time the family had already been out of the country for over three years, remained unclear to me.

Less than a year later, in 1936, the *Sicherheitsdienst* (security police), led by Reinhard Heydrich, created a special department, *Amt II*, for internal intelligence and surveillance. Subsection 112 was tasked with preparing a card index of all Jews living inside the Reich. My father never forgot the impact of this sinister gathering of data. Over fifty years later, when, during the course of returning a questionnaire for teachers about their background and experience,

I was on the point of filling in a box about ethnic origins he demanded with uncharacteristic anger that I leave it blank. When I demurred, he insisted: 'That's how they found all the Jews.'

Growing self-confidence and increasing disregard for foreign reactions led the leading Nazis to be ever more outspoken in their anti-Jewish pronouncements. In his address on National Peasants Day in November 1935, Heinrich Himmler, head of the *Schutzstaffel* (SS), ostensibly a bodyguard for Hitler and other leading Nazi personalities, but in effect a racial and military elite carefully nurtured to promulgate and enforce all aspects of Nazi ideology, described the Jews as:

this people composed of the waste products of all the people and nations of this planet on which it has imprinted the features of its Jewish blood, the people whose goal is the domination of the world, whose breath is destruction, whose will is extermination, whose religion is atheism, whose idea is Bolshevism . . .[1]

Two years later, Propaganda Minister Joseph Goebbels used similar language at the Party Congress of Labour on 11 September 1937, describing the Jew as:

the enemy of the world, the destroyer of cultures, the parasite among the nations, the son of chaos, the incarnation of evil, the ferment of decomposition, the visible demon of the decay of humanity.[2]

While there was nothing new in the sentiments themselves, their public expression by the top Nazi leadership at major gatherings served as a clear indicator of the rising tenor of anti-Jewish incitement.

For Jews it was a time of ever-increasing hopelessness and terror. Many people committed suicide; 'In the flat downstairs the couple took their lives together,' my mother's mother recalled.

The only lull in the rising level of racist activity had come in the summer of 1936, for the Olympic Games, when Hitler wanted his country to present to the world a benign and industrious image. 'I went to see them,' my father told me. 'Hitler walked past me not this far away,' I think I recall him saying, indicating a distance of two or three yards. I never asked him why he had gone or how the experience had felt; even the memory of the conversation feels like a chimera.

It was during 1938 that it became unambiguously clear how tight the noose around the Reich's Jews had already been drawn. At the beginning of the year all Jews were required to hand in their passports; new documents would be issued only to those about to emigrate. My mother, who did not leave Germany until 9 April 1939 and vividly remembered Kristallnacht, following which her father was interned in Dachau, told me how frightening she had found a particular experience during a visit to Germany fifty years later. On being informed that she had to leave her passport at the concierge's desk, she spent the hours of darkness caught between anxious sleeplessness and nightmares.

Jews were excluded from virtually every part of the economy. While they had already been subject for years to public humiliation and mockery, discriminatory legislation, financial abuse, constant threats and periodic violence, 1938 marked a change of pace in the rise of naked hatred and blatant exploitation. By this time the German national debt, caused not only by the reparations required by the Treaty of Versailles, but especially by Hitler's huge rearmament programme, was out of control. From where better could the money be taken to plug the hole in the accounts than the plunder of Jewish possessions?

In April 1938 a decree was promulgated requiring Jews to register all remaining assets over the value of 5,000 Reichsmarks. The information had to be provided by the end of June, though in the event the date was put back because it proved impossible to distribute the forms sufficiently quickly. On 23 June Regina received a letter from the Council of the Jewish Community of Berlin alerting her to the fact that:

In our estimation the pension which you draw from us is subject to declaration under the order of 16 April 1938 (RGBi I. S. 414) concerning the disclosure of assets belonging to Jews. In case you have not already done so, we recommend that you obtain a declaration form as soon as possible from the police station nearest to your home and fill in the details of your pension on side 3.

The reminder further advised her that any other sources of income, such as from national insurance or similar pension plans, had also to be disclosed.

The combined wealth of Germany and Austria's Jews was estimated by the Ministry of Economics at 8 billion Reichsmarks; that could now be channelled systematically into the coffers of the Reich.

All this information, together with numerous reports on the terrors of life in Germany and the difficulty of obtaining visas would have been well known to Alfred not only from his own family members but from refugees newly arrived in Palestine and from conversations in every quarter. It was abundantly clear to him that his mother had to leave the country as soon as possible. But by what route would she be able to get out of Germany and how was he to persuade her to take action? His friend's letter would have brought him little comfort, both because of its frank appraisal of the chances of success and because it showed how hard his mother was finding it to come to any kind of decision:

Your mother believes that she could still get 1,000 Palestinian pounds from the Berlin community as a settlement. As the 1,000 LP costs at least 25,700 Reichsmarks, with taxes on top, that would be a sum of at least 30,000 Reichsmarks. That your mother would still be able to transfer the 1,000 LP is out of the question. Firstly, we can't provide her with the so-called 'age certificate' because she's over sixty, and secondly, even with the certificate she would only get a higher Reichs-bank number and it would still be three years before she would be able to make the transfer. At the moment we can't take anyone out of the queue at the normal price of 25,700. Preferential treatment costs 35,000 and is almost always only agreed to for families.

There followed a no less detailed paragraph in which he weighed the possibilities should Regina decide to make her settlement over to her son Ernst. He had recently been to stay with his mother in Berlin over *Shavuot*, the celebration of the Giving of the Torah, which fell that year in early June. ('It's nice that Ernst and little Jenny spent the festival with you,' Nelly, who was always interested in family matters, had written from Jerusalem in reply to news from her mother-in-law.) Regina was well aware of the many difficulties with which the family of four young children, with a fifth on the way, were confronted.

Alfred's correspondent then put forward a different option:

If we leave Ernst entirely out of the picture, it still remains to be considered whether your mother shouldn't apply for a pensioner's certificate. At the moment there are no more pensioner's certificates to be had, but from 1 October a new quota will become available. Pensioner's certificates are distributed solely by the government in Jerusalem. The Palestine Office can only offer advice and the consulate here can only accept applications for the purpose of forwarding them on. You therefore need to link up with the government department for immigration over there; in many cases this has proved very useful. It would be a prerequisite that the *Ha'avara* arrange the transfer of the pension. At the moment it is being more generous than seems to me likely to be judged warranted, in that it's ready to transfer not just 8 Palestinian pounds per person per month but the entire pension up to the amount of 550 Reichsmarks. Your mother understandably raises the objection that the transfer of pensions is liable to be stopped at any moment and that she will then find herself over there without any means. Here too it's a question of making the decision as to whether one is prepared to accept the risk or not. Most of the people with whom I speak would be happy if they could only get into the country on a pensioner's certificate.

The writer was using a terminology that was closely familiar to him as an advisor in the *Treuhand-Stelle* organisation, but it is probably right to assume that the details would have been depressingly familiar to the mass of Jews desperate to leave Nazi Germany. But what in fact was this organisation which played such a decisive role in the lives of tens of thousands, and how was Regina, subject to different pressures from the various members of her family, to reach her decision?

All applications from Germany for immigration to Palestine had to be made through the offices of the *Palästina Treuhand-Stelle* (the Palestine Trust). The organisation had a remarkable history and was substantially different from the Nazi-run emigration offices later set up in Vienna and Prague by Adolf Eichmann, and which Reinhard Heydrich, as head of the SS under Himmler, was resolved after Kristallnacht to replicate in Berlin.

The *Treuhand-Stelle*'s partner, the Trust and Transfer Office Ha'avara Ltd in Tel Aviv, known simply as the *Ha'avara*, or 'Transfer', was established in the summer of 1933 as a result of a strange confluence of interests between the agricultural needs of the growing Jewish settlement in Palestine and the more rationally motivated departments of the Nazi government. A less likely coincidence of concerns would be hard to imagine. Yet ultimately the agreement, which was supported not only by the German Foreign office and the Treasury but even for a time by parts of the SS because it appeared to offer a practical resolution to the 'Jewish problem', allowed many thousands of Jews to escape Germany and avoid total destitution while enabling the Nazi state to rob them of most of their assets within the sanction of an ostensibly legal framework. It wasn't until the second year of war, when the policy of removing the Jews beyond the borders of the Reich proved impracticable and no longer appealing to Nazi ideology that the words 'solution' and 'Jewish problem' combined irrevocably to form a rather different meaning. While filled with murderous rhetoric and contemptuous violence from the first, it was not initially obvious that Nazi policy would necessarily lead to systematically organised, comprehensive mass extermination, or how it would do so.

The agreement also had to conform to the policies of the British administration under which Palestine had been ruled since the League of Nations formally appointed his Britannic Majesty as the Mandatory for the territories in July 1922. This act incorporated almost verbatim the wording of the Balfour Declaration in which, in a letter dated 2 November 1917, Lord James Balfour announced to Lionel Rothschild, then chairman of the Zionist Federation, that His Majesty's Government:

viewed with favour the establishment in Palestine of a national home for the Jewish people, [it being] clearly understood that nothing might be done which would prejudice the existing civil and religious rights of existing non-Jewish communities.

The meaning of 'favour' and the implications of the concurrent 'understanding' were to vary in the minds of the territory's British rulers as the relationship between Jews and Arabs in Palestine deteriorated over the following years, with disastrous implications for the Jews of Europe.

Negotiations with the German authorities began in 1932, the last year of the Weimar Republic, after the German government under Chancellor Brüning imposed a ban on the removal of capital from Germany in response to the global economic crisis following the great depression. A certain Sam Cohen ran a citrus growing company in Palestine, Hanotaiah Ltd of Tel Aviv, and was keenly aware of the need for heavy equipment to develop the land. In March 1933 he signed an agreement with the German

Foreign Ministry to enable the transfer, in the form of agricultural machinery, of up to a million Reichsmarks belonging to German Jews. Through this device Jews already anxious to leave Germany could take with them a small portion of their assets, just enough to avoid immediate penury on their arrival in a country where, as the popular saying went, the only commodities available in plenty were sun, sand and stone. They were required to deposit a significant sum in a special account in Germany as payment for the equipment bought by Hanotaiah Ltd and other interested companies, and were subsequently reimbursed upon their arrival in Palestine by the importers, who paid in this manner for their purchases.

Obtaining the necessary papers to enter Palestine was far less difficult in the early 1930s than it would later become, because British policy was still relatively relaxed with regard to Jewish immigration. However, a White Paper issued by Colonial Secretary Passfield in October 1930 had expressed the view that the Balfour Declaration imposed on Britain an equal obligation to both Jews and Arabs, and that immigration should not be allowed to rise to a rate which would put the local Arab population out of work. But, due to the influence of Chaim Weizmann, who had the diplomatic skills and personal charisma of a world-class statesman without at that point representing a state, and to whom Britain felt indebted for his invention at a critical stage in the First World War of a way of manufacturing acetone out of maize, any change in policy was swiftly rejected. As a result, Palestine received between 40,000 and 60,000 Jewish immigrants each year, with an even greater total in 1936. How immigrants were chosen was left largely to the discretion of the Jewish Agency, recognised by Britain in 1930 as the authoritative body in this regard and named in Article

4 of the Palestine Mandate of the League of Nations. It was during this comparatively relaxed period that Alfred and his family were able to procure certificates with relative ease.

Although Hitler's rhetoric had long threatened them with a far more sinister fate, and violence was rife, Nazi policy throughout the 1930s was chiefly aimed at forcing the Jews out of Germany. With few countries willing to accept immigrants, let alone impoverished refugees, Palestine provided an essential destination. It wasn't until towards the end of the decade that the Nazi leadership began to feel concern lest the establishment of a national homeland would allow the forces of international Jewry an increased opportunity to exercise their demonic influence over world affairs. Before then, the possibility that the Jews would actually succeed in forming a country of their own had seemed to them too remote to merit serious consideration. The Nazi government and the Zionist infrastructure thus found in one another improbable partners in promoting, for entirely different reasons, a common agenda of encouraging Jews to remove themselves from the Reich and resettle in Palestine.

But solving its Jewish problem wasn't the only concern behind the readiness of the Nazi leadership to listen with interest to the overtures from Palestine. Germany badly needed foreign income and the Middle East offered a potential new market for its exports. Hjalmar Schacht, director of the Reichsbank, was a realist. He was well aware that too rapid an exclusion of Jews from Germany's business infrastructure would be disastrous for the economy. From after the initial boycott of Jewish shops and businesses across Germany on 1 April 1933 until his eventual dismissal by Hitler in 1937, he sought to exercise a restraining influence on the Führer and his more militant ministers. He favoured the gradual and orderly takeover of Jewish assets, not out of concern for Germany's Jews, but because he considered this to be in the country's best economic interests. Hitler, too, came to understand that it was unwise to act drastically until the economy was sufficiently robust to finance the forthcoming war, which he had always regarded as inevitable, that is to say, desirable. The transfer of funds in such a way as allowed the greater part to be confiscated in the process with the apparent consent of their owners, and the sale of German goods abroad with the benefits it brought to the country's balance of payments, both served these ends well.

There was yet another reason for the Nazi interest in establishing a trade relationship with the Jewish settlement in Palestine. Such an agreement would be a particularly eloquent way of breaking the boycott of German goods, which was perceived as being led by international Jewry abroad. In actual terms the boycott probably did relatively little damage to Germany, but it was taken very seriously in Berlin, precisely because of the exaggerated importance attributed to the influence of international Jewry. The myth that Jews were immensely wealthy and manipulated world affairs through their control of international finance and the media was not only carefully exploited, as evidenced by Joseph Goebbels' propaganda films, but widely credited, and not only by the Nazis.

The question of the boycott was hotly debated in Jewish circles as well. It came to a head at the eighteenth World Zionist Congress, held in the late summer of 1933 in Prague. In the end, it was judged that a pragmatic approach to helping Jews to get out of an ever more threatening Germany was more important than the boycott and would in the long term have a more constructive effect on the Jewish future.

As a result of this unlikely combination of interests, an agreement was signed on 25 August in which the Warburg Bank of Hamburg and the Wassermann Bank of Berlin, along with the Anglo-Palestine Bank, established the *Palästina Treuhand-Stelle der Juden in Deutschland, G.m.b.H.* (The Palestine Trust Company on behalf of the Jews of Germany Ltd), subsequently known simply as *Paltreu*, in Berlin. Its offices were located on the Meinekestrasse. There can be no stranger measure of its support for this endeavour to expedite the departure of Jews from Germany than that, when the premises were sacked on Kristallnacht, the SS apparently helped them to reopen as quickly as possible, and even ordered the release from prisons in Berlin and Vienna of Jews connected with the *Palästina-Amt*.[3]

In simple terms, the *Ha'avara* – or transfer – system worked as follows: Jews planning to emigrate to Palestine could, whether or not they already had the necessary travel documents, deposit sums in the relevant account in Germany, known simply as *Konto 1*. If they were successful in reaching Palestine, a percentage of the money would be returned to them by the Anglo-Palestine Bank after their arrival, either in currency, movables or real estate. In this way they were able to take a fraction of their capital with them out of Germany. At the same time agriculturalists in Palestine could purchase from German manufacturers the essential equipment they needed. Meanwhile, by far the greatest proportion of the assets of all German Jews was simply stripped from them in the form of special levies and stolen by the state.

It was from the offices of *Paltreu* that Regina had received her fateful letter after Kristallnacht in 1938. Matters had changed drastically since Alfred had obtained his papers five years earlier.

Two separate elements had contributed to the worsening of the situation. In the first instance, Nazi policy towards the Jews had become increasingly more savage, contemptuous and brutal. Yet for many the second factor constituted, at least until the outbreak of war, no less of a barrier to escaping from Germany. The attitude of the British government towards Palestine had altered sharply. In 1936 what became known as the Arab Revolt began with violent protests against what was seen as excessive Jewish immigration. It continued with varying levels of intensity for several years. At the same time, the probability of war became ever more imminent. With major bases in Egypt and North Africa as well as in Palestine itself, Britain was anxious not to jeopardise its position in the Middle East by antagonising local populations and their leadership. This concern culminated in the White Paper of May 1939 that limited Jewish immigration to 75,000 over the following five years, a figure calculated to ensure that Jews would not exceed a third of Palestine's total population. To David Ben-Gurion, then head of the Jewish Agency, and to the leadership of the embryonic Jewish state, this constituted a betrayal of the commitments promised in the Balfour Declaration. For many Jews stuck in Europe and desperate to get out, it would prove fatal.

In the meantime, applicants faced further dilemmas. The already severely limited number of places on the British quota was further divided into categories. For which kind of certificate should they apply? Category A, itself split into five sections, was for immigrants with their own means of support. Visas issued in this class were known as 'capitalist certificates'. Category A1 was for those with at least 1,000 Palestinian pounds available to them in the country. To qualify for category A2 one had to be a practitioner of one of the 'free professions' and to possess at least 500 Palestinian pounds. The category recommended by Alfred's friend on the *Paltreu* team was A4; it applied to those in receipt of a regular pension of not less than 4 Palestinian pounds per month. But it had also become virtually impossible to move money out of Germany. As Alfred was to write later in the year concerning the desperate situation of his brother, one needed relatives or friends abroad to guarantee the funds. But at least at this point in time, the Jewish community was still able and willing to forward her full pension, should Regina succeed in emigrating to Palestine.

Regina, however, was troubled. What if the political situation should degenerate to the point where it was no longer possible to send any monies out of Germany at all? She didn't want to become a burden to her children who were struggling to make ends meet in a new and impoverished country. Yet matters were only going to get worse and soon there might be no opportunities left for leaving Germany at all, with or without funds. As Alfred's friend had written:

I would urgently advise you to get the process of obtaining a pensioner's certificate underway before it is too late. As the transfer of funds to Palestine is congested and is no longer available at all for other countries, one hears every day of people who emigrate leaving their entire fortune behind. Also, it's always better to take the risk that one can still count on the transfer of enough to live on for another 6 or 12 or 18 months, than to wait until this opportunity too has passed.

Regina made the application, and was refused.

Buchenwald, the concentration camp in which Ernst Freimann was interned after Kristallnacht. (Yad Vashem Photo Archive)

While Regina was opening her letter, Ernst was in the concentration camp of Buchenwald. The Gestapo had found him at home in his flat above the synagogue in Frankfurt on the morning after Kristallnacht, and took him away.

Ernst loved Frankfurt: *'Wie kann ein Mensch nicht aus Frankfurt sein'* ('How can anyone not hale from Frankfurt'), he wrote fondly in his memoirs, quoting the local poet Friedrich Stoltze, though no doubt the reputation of the Jewish community and its many illustrious rabbis interested him more than the renown of the great city itself. He'd lived there since his early twenties, when he obtained a much sought-after internship at the university hospital. 'I found a furnished room next door to the apartment building where my uncle lived,' he recalled; wholesome kosher meals were provided every day. The uncle referred to was his mother's younger brother Aron, curator of the Judaica section at the municipal library.

Ernst had been halfway through his medical studies in Breslau when he was drafted into the Austro-Hungarian Army as a health inspector; he was awarded the Iron Cross for his services. Following demobilisation he completed his degree in Würzburg with a dissertation on Arabic medicine. He began his career by serving there as assistant doctor at the pharmacological institute, before settling in Frankfurt in 1924, where 'family connections opened me to even the houses of the richest and most choosy families.' He faithfully recorded the names of the rabbis and relatives he met in the city, with whom he regularly studied Torah, and how his medical practice had functioned. As it began to thrive, he moved to a two-room apartment heated by a coal-fired stove and equipped with a gas burner which 'I used for cooking and urine examinations.' He was one of the first people in Frankfurt to acquire a direct-dial telephone. Initially most of his patients were poor East European Jews whom he treated for free, but he gradually acquired more affluent clients and was able to earn a respectable income. This was of particular importance because 'it was the custom in Germany that one married only if one was able to make a living'. The best families were not slow in coming forward with suggestions as to whom such an eligible young man, son of a famous rabbi and an up-and-coming doctor, should meet.

'Many attempts to get me married failed,' he noted wryly. But then a lady patient whom he was treating for pulmonary tuberculosis suggested he be introduced to a niece of her friend, a young woman called Eva from the well-known and well-to-do Heckscher family. He took his aunt Therese, Uncle Aron's wife, with him on his second visit to the lady in question because he 'trusted her judgment in such important matters'. His confidence was to prove well-founded; Ernst and Eva would enjoy a marriage of over sixty years. I remember them well from their annual visits to London. He was a quietly spoken gentleman; she a spritely and down-to-earth lady concerned for the welfare of each and every member of the family. Ernst lived to be 97, Eva 102. 'Every year I make a point of reading a different commentary to the Torah,' Ernst told me, the sacred books he was currently studying lying close by on the table. It was a small glimpse into the world of Torah-learning coupled with excellence in the professions and a deep interest in culture which formed the hallmark of German Jewish orthodoxy at its best.

Ernst and Eva were married in Hamburg in November 1928, on the New Moon of the month of Kislev; it was no doubt a Jewish high society occasion. Eva grew close to her parents-in-law, who in turn welcomed her into the family and took her to their heart. Life was good to the young couple. 'We often went to plays and concerts,' Ernst recalled. He became deeply involved in the charitable life of the city. He sat on the board of the community, on the committee of a day centre for unemployed Jewish youth and as trustee of a fund to help the destitute Jewish elderly. More unusually, he also served as medical coach to the Jewish football club and as chair of the Jewish gymnastics association.

He became the medical director of the Jewish Hospital. His private practice prospered; to make house calls easier he even learnt to drive 'and nearly bought a car, but was prevented by the change in the political conditions'. It was just as well; the Nazis presently disallowed Jews from holding a driver's licence and enriched themselves by taking possession of Jewish-owned automobiles. In 1930 Eva gave birth to their first child, a son, who died three days later of internal bleeding. Ernst was to recall the night when he had to turn the guests away and inform them that no, there was to be no *shalom zachar*, no customary celebration with words of Torah and a glass of Schnapps on the first Shabbat after the newborn boy's arrival, as the most painful of his entire life.

Jacob and Regina with Ernst and Eva on their wedding day.

In April of the following year Jenny was born; Jenny in whose beautiful New York flat I sat so many times and, plugging in my computer, plied her with questions about the family; at whose table I went through so many folders of letters and uncovered the record of so much suffering, courage and hope.

Soon after the Nazi accession to power, the Ministry of Employment removed Ernst from the list of doctors allowed to offer treatment under the national insurance scheme. On 1 September 1933 he was further banned from practising under private health insurance arrangements. He protested: as a recipient of the Iron Cross for his services to the German cause in the First World War he should surely have been exempted from such bans. He succeeded in having them lifted until the beginning of 1938, when not even having risked life and limb for the Fatherland could serve any longer as protection against the ferocity of the Nazis' decrees.

Life grew ever more threatening. In 1937 the Nazis held a vast rally in Frankfurt. Hitler visited the city on 31 March 1938, shortly after the *Anschluss* with Austria, and addressed cheering crowds from the balcony of the Römer building in the old city. Everywhere were posters declaring '*Die Juden sind unser Unglück*' ('The Jews are our misfortune'), the slogan penned by Heinrich von Treitschke in 1879 and popularised by Julius Streicher's anti-Semitic hate paper *Der Stürmer*. 'One couldn't react,' my mother's father, who was a rabbi in the same city, recalled. 'Everywhere there were Nazis, watching.'

As well as having plentiful concerns of their own, Ernst and Eva were worried about Regina. With the summer holidays approaching, Eva wrote to her mother-in-law:

Frankfurt

19 June 1938

Dear Mama,

Your letter arrived today. I hope you're also looking after yourself and taking lots of walks. One needs to keep one's nerves in good order, and you know that our beloved Papa, may his memory be for a blessing, set great store by this. One lives for others, as long as one lives, and one has no right to neglect oneself. Jenny very much wants to visit you in the holidays. I'm very concerned though that it'll be too much for you. I want to hear from you often about how you are. I also haven't heard if there are any travelling companions. I want to hear from you first. Perhaps you could send me an answer soon, as I might enrol her for the holiday games and that needs to be done soon. We had a long letter from Trude. Here one could never invite thirty-eight people over for coffee. Ernst will write you out a new calendar, or I will. It may go on Sunday. Gertrud Rosenbaum is with us today. She is on the way back from a Kindertransport. Otherwise I know of nothing new. The children are all, thank God, in good health and happy and looking good. Jenny can read a lot better now and I hope she'll manage until the summer holidays. She's not so defensive any more. What are you going to have for Shabbat? I've got a stuffed pike, just like you make it, even though it's become a real treat. Many greetings and good Shabbes. Are you on your own or will you have visitors? Your Eva.

Eva's concern was touching. I had always thought of Regina as a strong woman, but Eva was clearly worried about her state of mind, reminding her that her late husband would have wanted her to look after herself and keep up her spirits by remembering that one has to go on living for the sake of other people. The domestic details suggested that the two women were very close and kept in frequent contact. In a small note, which had probably been tucked into the same envelope, Eva added: 'Dear Mama! I just spoke about the thermos. If the flask isn't completely full it doesn't stay hot. Give it a try. Otherwise it needs to be exchanged. Greetings, Eva.' Such gadgets were apparently new to her mother-in-law and her first attempt at using them to keep the water hot over the Sabbath, when it is forbidden to boil it back up, hadn't been a success.

Stuffed pike was obviously a special family tradition. My father used to tell me how his mother would prepare it for Shabbat; now I knew where the custom had come from. I once saw whole pike for sale at the local fishmongers, their sharp teeth distinguishing them from the other fish on the counter. I thought of buying one for my father, but he was already too ill to have been able to tell me the proper way of cooking it and finding a random recipe in a book wouldn't have been the same, even if I had succeeded in producing something edible.

The reference to the Kindertransport was especially interesting; evidently the term was current and children were being sent abroad in groups several months before the operation known as The Kindertransport *par excellence*, commenced, in which approximately ten thousand children were sent without their parents from Germany, Austria and Czechoslovakia to find refuge in Britain.

The reasons no Jew in Germany would have thirty-eight people for a celebration were sinister; who could trust, with that great a number of guests, even were a gathering of that size permitted, that no one would betray them? My mother's father told of an anti-Nazi friend, a non-Jew, who held a modest birthday party. He was arrested immediately afterwards. Fortunate to return from the Gestapo, he promptly invited the same group of people and asked them bluntly who had given him away. They all denied having done so. The man's son then emerged from the bathroom and declared that it had been he who had told on his father. In the Nazi Youth, he explained, we were ordered to inform on anything our parents said.

By the autumn of 1938 Ernst and Eva had four children; Jenny was the eldest, followed by two boys, Hans and Alfred, and a little sister, Ruthie. When, on 10 November, the morning after Kristallnacht, the Gestapo came to arrest Ernst, a fifth child was expected at any time. It was to be a baby girl, stillborn while her father was in detention in Buchenwald. She was a breech presentation and specialist help was urgently needed. But, driven to despair by the hopelessness of his situation in Nazi Germany, the family obstetrician had committed suicide a few days earlier and, in Ernst's forbearing words, 'the young resident did not have much experience'.

Ernst and Eva explored all avenues of escape.

The *Anschluss,* the Nazi annexation of Austria on 12 March 1938, brought a further 185,000 Jews under German rule. Very few countries were willing to offer shelter to the many tens of thousands desperate to flee the Reich. A conference was convened on the initiative of the President of the United States to consider how to respond to the refugee crisis. Representatives of thirty-two countries gathered in the French resort of Évian-les-Bains between 9 and 16 July. The event proved worse than a mere failure, the chief outcome being a propaganda victory for the Nazis. The British delegation argued that unemployment prevented the country from accepting further refugees; its sole concession was that British territories in East Africa agreed to admit a small number. France declared that it had reached the point of extreme saturation. The United States offered to fill those places which had not yet been taken up in its pre-existing quotas for Germany and Austria. Only the Dominican Republic was prepared to provide asylum for additional numbers, in return for significant sums of money. The unwillingness of the participating countries to offer shelter to those frantically seeking safety allowed Hitler and Goebbels to declare with superior irony how astounding it was that Germany was criticised for its treatment of the Jews when no one else wanted them either.

Eva's brother, Alex Heckscher, who had moved to London with his family some years earlier, made a special trip to Chicago to persuade Leon Freeman, a wealthy uncle with no children of his own, to stand guarantor for his sister and her family. On the strength of his affidavit the American Consulate in Stuttgart allocated Ernst, who was born in Czechoslovakia, a place on the Czech list. He was fortunate; many others, including my mother's parents, who had travelled to Stuttgart on the day before Kristallnacht, returned home to ponder the futility of their endeavours. Many committed suicide. On 18 August Ernst was allocated sixty-first place in the Czech quota. Even though this was a relatively high position, the wait was estimated at up to two years. Who could know if the family would be able to survive in Germany for that length of time? Ernst could not afford to abandon other plans and maintained close contact with Alfred in Palestine. But by then, he noted in his memoirs, the cost of a 'capitalist' certificate had risen to 60,000 marks. The figure was extraordinarily high given the sums cited just a few months earlier by Alfred's friend after visiting Regina, but it presumably included the costs for the whole family of six. Places were hard to obtain at any price and Ernst had seemingly left the matter rather late.

They arrested him early on 10 November. 'I don't remember them coming for my father,' Jenny, who was just seven at the time, reflected. 'Later in the morning our relative Recha arrived with a big car to pick us up. There was a door from our flat which led directly into the robing room of the synagogue. From there, a second door opened onto the ladies' gallery. That morning those doors were gone and I could see straight through into the ruins of the synagogue. The black sky and charred remains of the metal supports of the huge dome haunted me in nightmares for years.' That was all which remained of the great and beautiful house of prayer on Frankfurt's Boerneplatz. Strangely, my mother's father, for thirty years a rabbi to Frankfurt's liberal community, was at that very moment observing the same view from the other side of the ruins. Alleging that he possessed the keys, a claim they must have known to be false as it was a strictly orthodox synagogue, the Gestapo had ordered him to come immediately to the burning building. There were firemen present, he recalled, but no one did anything to extinguish the flames. As he walked through the crowds watching the spectacle he heard people say: '*Das wird sich rächen*' ('this will be avenged').

Disregarding Regina's remonstrations that, with his wife so heavily pregnant, Ernst was badly needed at home, the Gestapo took him away. They brought him first to the local police station and from there to the *Festhalle*, the concert hall, which my mother's father also remembered all too well from his own arrest. There Ernst found his uncle Aron whom the Nazis had rewarded for his outstanding services to the city by dismissing him from his post just weeks after they came to power. When, at 1.20 a.m. on the morning of 10 November, Reinhard Heydrich, head of the Reich Security Service, issued orders that 'as many Jews, especially rich ones, are to be arrested as can be accommodated in the existing jails',[1] he stipulated that only males in good health were to be taken and specifically excluded the elderly. But age did not protect Uncle Aron; they picked him up anyway. He was one of the very few later to be released from that hall, where hundreds of Jewish men were gathered, humiliated, intimidated and beaten, prior to their deportation to concentration camps. Soon afterwards he managed to escape to the United States with his wife and daughter.

Ernst himself was not so fortunate. Of the three camps to which thousands of Jews were deported in the following days, Dachau, Sachsenhausen and Buchenwald, the last was widely considered the worst. Construction had begun in 1937, but in the autumn of 1938 the site was still in a primitive state. What huts there were often had no floors, only wet earth. The water supply was almost non-existent and there was no proper provision for sewage; open latrines made even elemental hygiene virtually impossible. Ernst was part of the first group of men to be sent there from Frankfurt and was therefore able to find some kind of shelter. Prisoners who arrived later were simply left out in the open for hours or even days:

MY DEAR ONES | 82

We came to a large barracks where there were bunks in three tiers. I at once went to the highest and found some people there. One of them felt bad because he had some money on him, which was forbidden. I borrowed 120 marks, which was useful for me as I decided to do as I did in the army – not to eat any of their *treifa* [unkosher] food. The next morning I found someone who had taken along his *Tefillin* [phylacteries, small leather boxes containing verses from the Torah worn during weekday morning prayers] which I could use at any time. They cut all our hair off our heads and gave us black striped prison uniforms. I managed to put my watch and money in my pockets.

These brief sentences convey little of what Ernst was made to undergo. The journey itself must have been appalling. He and three hundred other Jews from Frankfurt, all men, had been taken to a goods siding and loaded into fourth-class carriages. When they arrived at the station in Weimar, from where they had to walk the remaining distance to the camp, the platforms had, out of sheer sadism, been smeared with soap. On entering the camp many of the prisoners were severely beaten. 'Of atrocities I saw only public flagellation,' Ernst recalled. 'The guards used vulgar words at any opportunity they saw a Jew. I tried to calm my neighbours down by telling them that they wouldn't be offended if a dog barked at them in the street.' Ernst was given the prisoner number 10205 and labelled an *Aktionsjude*, a Jew arrested during the 'actions', or round-ups, following Kristallnacht.

Keeping kosher, in so far as there was anything available at all which could be called food, no doubt took great courage. Reciting prayers also brought the risk of violence if caught. One political prisoner, Karl Wack, reported having to record the name of a dying man who had been hit over the head repeatedly by an SS officer for praying aloud.[2] Yet Ernst faithfully maintained his strict standards of Jewish observance, as he had done throughout his army service in the First World War. His conduct must have served as an inspiring example to his comrades; it also saved him from an illness which plagued many others:

They put bicarbonate of soda into the food claiming that this calms people down, but it only caused diarrhoea. They made us stand for hours without permitting the use of a toilet.

Meanwhile the family were doing everything possible to obtain his release. Despite being nine months pregnant, Eva, like tens of thousands of other women across Germany whose husbands had been sent to concentration camps, did her utmost to gain the essential papers, which, with the promise of a visa, might procure her husband's freedom. The British Consulate on the Guiollettstrasse in Frankfurt's West End became a focal point for thousands of desperate people; queues often stretched across the pavement and round the block. The staff struggled to bring comfort and hope to the throngs of people waiting anxiously in every corner of the building and in the streets outside. 'They offered us tea and sandwiches; they spoke to us like human beings and gave us back our dignity,' one lady remembered. The Deputy Consul, Arthur Dowden, even drove round the streets seeking out terrified people, to whom he gave food and drink.

From Jerusalem, Alfred wrote to relatives in Amsterdam requesting their urgent intervention. By now he was all too familiar with every detail of the immigration process for Palestine. But how were matters to be arranged, with Ernst in a concentration camp and his heavily pregnant wife living in a hospital with their four young children because their home and the adjacent synagogue had been burnt down? In particular, how could the necessary funds be made available in Tel Aviv for a certificate to Palestine, when the Nazis had made it illegal to transfer money out of Germany?

Jerusalem

18 November 1938

My dear ones,

We have received news from Frankfurt that Ernst too has been arrested. Eva, who's expecting a child any day, is in hospital in the Gagernstrasse, where the other children also are. They were living until now in the Boerneplatz, in what used to be the rabbi's home, which is, as we suppose, no longer habitable. The only way to get Ernst and his family out of Germany is to obtain permission to immigrate into Palestine.

But because of the huge demand all the certificates have been taken, with the exception of the capitalist category. The only possibility still remaining open is to obtain one for Ernst by indirect means. This indirect route is necessary because he is not allowed by the German authorities to own any money abroad, and the British administration and its consulates require him to have a sum of at least 1,000 Palestinian pounds at his sole and free disposal.

After much breaking of our heads and after consultation with experts we've hit upon a plan that should work quickly and inexpensively and be difficult to object to. However, it requires the cooperation of friends abroad: Ernst needs to be given at least 1,030 LP (1,030 English or Palestinian pounds), from a source from whom such a gift is credible on personal grounds . . .

This operation can't be undertaken in Palestine itself, because the immigration certificate is only granted where the above-mentioned minimum amount of fresh capital is brought into the country from abroad. My brothers and sisters in Posen and in Czechoslovakia are themselves subject to the local foreign exchange controls, so nothing can be done from that end. I must therefore turn to you for help in this extraordinary emergency. My big request is that you formally make available to Ernst this sum of 1,030 pounds. This amount must be transferred to the account of Dr Ernst Freimann at the Anglo-Palestine Bank Limited in Jerusalem. I have made all the arrangements here to ensure that the money returns to you as soon as Ernst has emigrated and his papers are in order. Should Ernst for any reason not be able to emigrate, I will be in a position to undertake the repayment.

Should you not at present have the requisite sum at your disposal, please ask Herr Sigmund Seligmann for his assistance. In these circumstances, where it's a matter of saving lives, he will surely do everything within his power. I will gladly take responsibility for any costs incurred. With heartfelt greetings . . .

Alfred may or may not have known that even as he was writing his letter, the Nazis were sending the ashes of their victims back home to their families in urns wrapped up as parcels. 'One dreaded the approach of the postman,' my mother remembered; her father had been sent to Dachau on 14 November. They cremated the bodies, noted Ernst, so that it would be impossible to prove how their victims had perished. The families were then informed that their loved ones had 'regrettably' been taken ill and that it had 'sadly' proved impossible to save their lives. The truth, of course, was that they had been murdered.

Three weeks later Alfred had still received no news. Having heard that his older sister Sophie had travelled from Holleschau to help Eva and the children, he wrote to her husband Josef in the hope that he might know more. His anxiety was apparent:

9 December 1938

We suppose dear Sophie is already in Frankfurt and that you, dear Josef, are better informed. We know neither what's been happening in Frankfurt nor what's going on now. On the one hand we've had letters that Ernst has not yet come home, which means that he's still interned; on the other hand we're told that Ernst and Eva have already got their tickets for the ship and are leaving on 19 December. We've no idea for where. According to the earlier reports we have to suppose that the flat in the Dominikanerplatz no longer exists, that it was either burnt down together with the synagogue or destroyed in some other way. Dear Josef, if you have any further information, we beg you to tell us fully and in detail.

With enormous difficulty we've managed to meet all the requirements to obtain certificates to Palestine for Ernst and his family. It would of course be a terrible shame if all this should have been done in vain because in the meantime entirely different travel plans for Ernst have been put in place. For example, we don't know whether in the meanwhile on the basis of the affidavit a visa for America has been issued. We don't dare send a telegraph directly to Frankfurt because we don't know if such a telegram mightn't cause harm. I've also been to much trouble here personally to obtain Ernst's release, and there are grounds for hoping that these efforts will prove successful.

Eva's brother in London wrote to us that he's trying to obtain immigration documents for Ernst and Eva. He asked us about living expenses for the family. But this question can't be relevant because Ernst and his family will of course come here as soon as they receive the certificates . . .

Alfred assumed that his brother would rather go to Palestine than to Britain or the States; hadn't they been brought up to see the Land of Israel as the ancestral home of the Jewish people and had their father not fallen in love with it on first sight as he watched the Carmel mountains grow nearer from the ship which brought him to Haifa in 1935?

In the event, it was the London option that came through first. Ernst very likely owed his life to the British Consul-General, Robert Smallbones, and his staff. Smallbones himself had been in London on the night of Kristallnacht, where his wife had telegraphed him to tell him that the consulate building was filled to overflowing with desperate people, in all the rooms, on the staircase and outside. They could not possibly turn them away and were doing their best to provide them with food and offer what comfort and consolation they could. He, Robert, 'simply had to do something!' He succeeded in persuading the British Home Office that it would not require a change in the law for the authorities to issue temporary visas allowing their holders to remain in Britain for up to six months, on condition that they intended to travel on elsewhere and that they promised not to seek employment. This was subsequently known as the Smallbones Scheme; it is estimated that up to 48,000 Jewish and other desperate people may have managed to escape Nazi Germany as a result of its provisions. Returning to Frankfurt, Smallbones met the local

Gestapo leader to arrange for Jews already interned in concentration camps to be released if their families could produce a letter stating that they would presently be issued with such a visa for Britain. A fierce argument followed: 'I started shouting in the proper German manner,' Smallbones recalled. 'When I jumped up and said that my proposal to help Germany be rid of some of its Jews was off . . . the Gestapo bully collapsed and we made an agreement.'

'I usually worked about eighteen hours a day,' Smallbones later wrote. 'The longest stretch I remember was from early in the morning until midnight when I fell asleep for a few minutes on my desk . . . I went to bed . . . After two hours' sleep my conscience pricked me. The feeling was horrible that there were people in concentration camps whom I could get out and that I was comfortable in bed . . . I returned to my desk and stayed there until the next midnight.' Some months later he had a nervous breakdown. 'The last straw that broke my back was the case of a person who died in a concentration camp because one of my staff had failed to get my signature and to dispatch the promise of a visa which was in order.'[3]

It was such a promise which obtained Ernst's release from Buchenwald.

British Consulate General,
62, Guiollettstrasse,
Frankfurt a. Main
5 December 1938
For the purposes of representation to the relevant German authorities, I hereby confirm that I am willing to provide you with a visa for entry into England as soon as you are in possession of a valid passport.

This authorisation is provided for prisoners in two copies. One copy should be handed in to the Secret Police together with the application for the release of prisoners. The other copy should be handed in to the office responsible for the issue of passports together with the passport application form.

This letter of authorisation is valid for:

Dr Ernst Freimann and his wife,

resident at Dominkanerplatz 16, Frankfurt / Main,

currently living at Gagernstrasse 36

Underneath was the personal signature of Robert Smallbones himself.

Ernst was released. The discharge note he was issued with in Buchenwald bore the date of 1 December. However, this was contradicted by the timing of Smallbones' letter, written four days later, on the fifth of the month, clearly on the understanding that Ernst was still in detention. Two documents from the *Comité Internationale* of the Red Cross gave different dates again, 12 or 18 December, either of which was plausible. But it is hard to avoid the conclusion that the date on the papers provided by the Nazi authorities was a fabrication, intended to make the period of his imprisonment appear shorter that it actually was. Before being allowed to leave the camp Ernst was made to sign a form declaring that he had received back all the articles which he had been obliged to hand over on his internment. The list included shoes, coat, jacket, trousers, shirt, underwear and a hat. He was no doubt also forced to declare, as was my mother's father prior to his release from Dachau, that he had not in any way been mistreated during his time in detention. He would have been warned that if he dared

British Consulate General,
62, Guiollettstrasse
Frankfurt a. Main

Ref No. 26/5/2797

den, 5 Dezember 1938.

Zum Zwecke der Vorlage bei den zuständigen
deutschen Behörden bestätige ich hiermit, dass ich
bereit bin Ihnen ein Sichtvermerk zur Einreise nach
England zu erteilen, sobald Sie im Besitze eines
gültigen Reisepasses sind.

Diese Bescheinigung wird für Häftlinge in
doppelter Ausführung ausgestellt. Ein Exemplar
ist mit dem Haftentlassungsantrag der Geheimen
Staatspolizei einzureichen. Das andere Exemplar
ist mit dem Passantrag an die zuständige Stelle
einzureichen, welche Reisepässe ausstellt.

Diese Bescheinigung ist gültig für:

Herrn Dr. Ernst Freimann und dessen Ehefrau
Dominikanerplatz 16,
Frankfurt/Main.

z.Zt. Gagernstrasse 36.

[signature]

Kgl.Grossbrit. Generalkonsul

Letter from Robert Smallbones granting Ernst and Eva a temporary visa for Britain.

to speak of his experiences to anyone anywhere he would be liable to re-arrest 'for his own safety'. Nevertheless, in response to accusations of British brutality by the Nazi leadership, in late 1939

His Majesty's Government published a short but grim Command Paper which included excerpts from numerous accounts received in consulates throughout Germany, all quoted anonymously, detailing the kinds of abuse to which detainees in concentration camps were constantly subject. 'The conditions in Germany and the treatment accorded to Germans . . . are reminiscent of the darkest ages in the history of man,' observed the author. Over sixty Jews from Frankfurt, imprisoned alongside Ernst, died in those bitter months in Buchenwald.

Ernst's description of his return home was characteristically matter-of-fact: 'Uncle Alex got from the British Government permission for us to stay in England until we had a chance to go either to Palestine or the United States. So one day they discharged me from the concentration camp.' It was a grim home-coming: 'I went straight to the house where we lived, but found only the remnant of the now completely destroyed synagogue and nobody in the apartment, which was partly looted.' His aunt Therese, Uncle Aron's wife, had managed to procure rooms for the family in the Jewish hospital; it was there that Eva had meanwhile given birth to their stillborn daughter. Reunited with his family, Ernst was greeted by his son with the words, 'They said you are in prison.'

The weeks before they were able to leave Germany must have been terrifying. Ernst was required to report daily to the police. He and Eva had to obtain passports, settle all their affairs and pay the so-called emigration tax. On 29 November Eva had handed in their applications for a passport. A careful examination of a copy of the document showed that, following the words 'valid for travel abroad' something, possibly a destination, had been written in by hand. The word was hard to decipher but may have read 'Bolivia'. On 7 December she obtained from the tax office of the local finance department the critical *Unbedenklichkeitsbescheinigung* certifying that the family owed no money and was therefore at liberty to emigrate. The document was renewed on 16 January. The later copy contained an additional sentence affirming that they had duly paid the *Reichsfluchtsteuer*, a penalty tax for 'fleeing the Reich', a further device by which the Nazi authorities stripped their victims of their assets. On the same date they paid the remittance of three marks each to obtain identity cards. The middle name 'Israel' was inserted between 'Ernst' and 'Freimann' as required by the Nazi authorities lest Jews with German-sounding surnames should manage to escape their attentions by submerging themselves in the Aryan crowd. 'The emigration tax alone brought in around one billion marks between 1933 and 1945 – the highest annual total being 342,521,000 marks in the fiscal year 1938–39, the year in which state-sponsored pogroms led the greatest number of German Jews to flee the country,' noted the historian Goetz Aly.[4] That was aside from the pillage of the property and possessions refugees from Nazism were obliged to leave behind. Faced with widespread looting by profiteering officials, and later in Eastern Europe by local fascists, Nazi documents emphasised time and again that vacated homes and their abandoned contents were the property of the state. No less a figure than Göring himself stressed in a speech to Gauleiters on 6 December that money raised from the sale of Jewish possessions was to go solely to the central government of the Reich and was not to line the pockets of local leaders. The funds were urgently needed for the Nazi war chest.

Scrutiny of their papers suggests that what happened to Ernst and Eva was precisely what so many Jews trying to leave Germany so greatly feared. While they were waiting to obtain one set of documents, the dates on another lapsed. They would then have to go through the whole nerve-racking and uncertain process of renewing them in the hope that this time they would have all the necessary papers in their possession and in good order at one and the same time. The sentence indicating that the holders of the *Unbedenklichkeitsbescheinigung* had access to such money as they were permitted to take out of the Reich was crossed out on the second set of forms issued to Ernst and Eva on 16 January 1939. Like so many others, they must have left Germany virtually penniless. They were however more fortunate than most in having relatives with means abroad.

Through arrangements which must have brought them as much heartache as relief, Ernst and Eva succeeded in sending their children out of Germany to the safety of Switzerland, where they would be able to remain until such time as the family could hopefully be reunited. 'Aunt Therese arranged it,' Jenny remembered:

We left on 1 January from the Hauptbahnhof in Frankfurt. We joined a group of one hundred children. That was all agreed with the Gestapo. But we were four extras. When they came round to check everyone's papers we were quietly moved from compartment to compartment. Years later when we asked our parents what had been the worst day of their lives, Mama said it was then, parting from us at the station when we boarded that train.

At least Eva and Ernst's own plans were well advanced and, painful as the separation from their children must have been, there was a high likelihood that they would be reunited with them in the coming months. Many parents whose children left with the Kindertransport must have returned home to empty apartments with utter despair in their hearts.

The girls went to Zurich. The boys were taken to a home for Jewish children in the mountain resort of Celerina. Over a year was to pass before the family was together once again, in a Britain by then at war.

On 11 January Ernst received notification from the Government of Palestine, Department of Migration and Statistics, Jerusalem Immigration Office:

Sir,

I refer to your application for the admission to Palestine of Dr Ernst Freimann and family as immigrants in Category A(1) and have to inform you with regret that your application cannot be considered during the present quota period.

Renewed application may be made after 1 April, 1939, or such other date as may be notified by announcement, and that application will be considered in the light of policy prevailing at the time.

I am, Sir,

Your obedient servant,

This was no doubt as a result of Alfred's efforts on his behalf. In the event it was just as well that the possibility of leaving for London came through first; papers for Palestine were subject to unpredictable delays.

The following day Ernst visited Regina in Berlin to mark her seventieth birthday. It was the last time mother and son would ever see one another. The deep faith they both shared would have taught them to avoid negative thoughts and bolster each other's hopes, but in their heart of hearts they must surely have known that this might be their final meeting.

Ernst and Eva finally left Germany for England in late January 1939. They broke their journey to meet relatives in Amsterdam and Den Haag, then sailed for England on the Hoek to Harwich ferry. 'The weather was bad and we all got very seasick,' noted Ernst, making no mention of any other feelings. On 25 January he wrote to his mother from Sneath Avenue in Golders Green, round the corner from where I grew up and a world away from Nazi Germany:

We were all seasick during the night. It's an illness most people long for the opportunity to have. What's going to happen in the future we don't as yet know. First we have to get used to our new circumstances. I know very little English. Your faithful Ernst sends you his greetings. Hopefully we'll soon get good news about your departure.

As ever, Eva added a note of her own:

Dear Mama! I'm very curious to know how far you've managed to get. We're very happy to have made it to the first stage. Now we're considering what comes next. The journey was very interesting. Everything went very well. The boat, the sleeper, it was all new for us. Lots of greetings and wishes for a good Shabbes, from your Eva.

Well aware that the visas on which they had been allowed to enter Britain were only temporary, they lost no time in pursuing further options. Just one day after arriving in the city, Ernst wrote to the American Consulate in London, informing the relevant department that he was registered with the American Consulate in Stuttgart for a visa 'under quota No. 61 of the CSR Quota' and asking to know when he might expect it to be granted, as the matter was 'of great importance to me to emigrate to the United States as soon as ever possible'.

Alfred, however, expected his older brother to join him in Palestine at the earliest opportunity. The deposit he had so urgently requested on his behalf was waiting safely in an account at the Anglo Palestine Bank. The amount of '1,000 Palestinian pounds is to be paid to that Gentleman (Herr Dr Ernst Freimann) after his immigration to Palestine. This credit is irrevocably valid until 31 December 1939', wrote a certain Jules Roos of Ellern's Bank in Tel Aviv, presumably addressing himself to Alfred.

Yet Alfred must have been deeply relieved that at least one more branch of his extensive family was safe. It only remained to get them to Palestine before their temporary visa for Britain expired, as he indicated when he wrote in late December to thank the relatives who had put up the money:

Dear Families Rapp and Darmstädter,

Yesterday we received the happy news that dear Ernst has come home in good health. The children are due to travel to Switzerland this week. Ernst and Eva have to leave Germany by the 19th of the month. They'll go in the first instance to Eva's brother in London.

On Sunday 11 December the monies sent by you arrived. On Monday I promptly handed in the request for a certificate. It was accepted, but only towards the next quota in April because meanwhile all the available certificates were already allocated. As the permit for London is of limited duration, Ernst will surely still need the immigration visa. Please accept once again my heartfelt gratitude for all the trouble you've taken. I ask you once more to let me know all the costs you've incurred so that I can arrange for their immediate repayment.

Hopefully all your loved ones have by now joined you. News from Germany is so sparse that one learns little even about the narrowest circle of one's relatives . . . A Good Chanukkah and heartfelt greetings.

Now the family could turn their full attention to their mother's situation. With Ernst, Eva and their children out of Germany, by the close of January 1939 Regina was the only member of the immediate family living under Nazi rule, though not the only one close to danger.

Sophie in her late teens.

Throughout the previous year Sophie had been in constant contact with her mother. Out of all the members of the family, it was easiest for her to travel, for three reasons: she had a Czech passport, she and her husband possessed the means, and she did not have the daily responsibility of looking after children. In January 1938 she had followed her mother back to Berlin. In the autumn she went to Frankfurt after Ernst's arrest to help her sister-in-law Eva. Soon afterwards she was back in Berlin, assisting her mother in packing up her affairs. In the intervals she kept in close touch by letter, while engaging in other travels of a more social nature. Thus she wrote from Holleschau in June, worrying about her mother being on her own for the Sabbath and suggesting she visit Trude in Poznań. She had been shaken by the sudden death of a family friend, Herr Levy, presumably the Harry Levy who had written the foreword to the Jubilee volume for her father, since she continued, 'it all reminds me of our own misfortune'. Josef added a quick line with an alternative proposal, 'Dearest Mama, when are you intending and when will you have the opportunity to come to us?' It seems that everyone in the family referred to Regina as 'Mama', not only because she was indeed the matriarch, but because she was deeply loved. The title was passed on to my grandmother; I remember how when my parents spoke of her she was always simply 'Mama'.

A month later Sophie had written in a more relaxed mood. Some weeks spent in her garden, safe from the Nazis in the brave Czech state, had done her good.

11 July 1938

Dearest Mama,

The weather has become so nice and cool that I'm going to send off a small box tomorrow. It'll hopefully be a duck and a chicken, and I'll pack the gaps with Omega and flour. We received a picture of Arnold from Posen, together with a detailed description of the celebrations. Aunty Frieda has surely told you all about it. The boy got magnificent presents. On Thursday I was in K. to pay a condolence visit to Irka

Fuchs and also went to see Erna Fall who had again come back from radiotherapy. She died today. She was sadly well aware of her situation and had said to the official that the next funeral would be hers.

I've got a great deal of washing this week. It'll have rained itself out by Wednesday, so we'll be able to dry it in the garden. It's a bad year here for preserving fruit; the cherries were all spoiled. On the other hand, I've put away ten kilos of blackcurrant compote and five of blueberries. I've still got so much jam from last year that I'm going to leave it until the raspberries before starting again. The damson jam from the dried fruits is wonderful. On Friday it's Josef's birthday; I've had silk nightshirts made for him in three different colours in a workshop in Prosnitz, because he so hates wearing pyjamas. I'm going to collect them tomorrow afternoon. Paula Beer always buys me everything I need in Prosnitz. Here, many people have gone on holiday, but they've all stayed in the country . . . One doesn't know what the next week will bring, so it's better to stay at home.

Your Sophie sends you, dear Mama, and dear Annchen her heartfelt greetings. The blue flowers in the envelope in the parcel grow near our dear departed Papa.

The Annchen to whom she was referring had married into the family but her husband had died young; kind and beautiful, she remained popular with everyone and proved a loyal support.

It's strange how touching I find the details about the fruit. A vivid memory draws me back to the kitchen in my parents' house where my father is showing me how to bottle gooseberries. He's taking the large Kilner jars out of the oven and ladling in the hot fruit. He carefully adds sufficient syrup so that the liquid rises to just below the rim, then covers each jar with a circle of greaseproof paper, allowing in no air so as to ensure a vacuum. He places each glass lid inside the metal screw-top ring and checks that the rubber band which creates the seal is not twisted or out of place. Then he sets each one carefully on top of its jar and turns it a couple of times. He reserves the final tightening until later, when the glass and its boiling contents have begun to cool and contract. I remember with sadness when we eventually disposed of those large jars; it was after my father had died and they'd been standing empty for years, the tops gritty with rust. Who would ever use them now, when it was so easy to pop things into plastic bags and stick them in the freezer? But the jars are back in fashion today and I've been thinking of buying a few for the currants and damsons my wife and I pick yearly in our North London garden. I shall imagine that Sophie is standing next to me as I anxiously heat up the fruit in the kitchen, on a gentle flame so that it doesn't boil too hard and disintegrate, before dispensing it into the oven-warmed jars.

I've always felt a special closeness to Sophie, ever since I first saw her photograph. I have just two pictures of her. The first shows a young girl, in her late teens, perhaps twenty at the most. She looks pensive, wistful, even somewhat sad. The second is taken in Holešov; Sophie and Josef are sitting together on a garden seat behind which three stone steps lead up to the entrance of an elegant house. Sophie has a fur stole around her shoulders; one hand is on her lap, with the other she holds the metal end of the bench. She is beautiful. I also have her *Ketubah*, her Jewish marriage contract, though how and why it ended up in that bag of letters I shall never understand. No Jewish couple is supposed to live together without having a valid *Ketubah* in their possession; it seems improbable that

Sophie would have forwarded the document to any of her relatives in Palestine. The notion that someone found it afterwards in their abandoned house and knew to whom to send it is scarcely credible.

Sophie and Josef sitting together on a garden seat in Holešov.

Sophie and Josef's wedding had been celebrated in Holleschau on the fifteenth of the Hebrew month of Tevet in the year 5763. It was a Wednesday. Tuesday is a traditional day for Jewish weddings because it is the third day of creation, of which the Torah says twice that God 'saw that it was good', once in approval of the emergence of dry land out of the sea and a second time in appreciation of the flourishing of the grasses, plants and trees.

Wednesdays are a more unusual choice. The explanation is that it was Christmas Day. The year was 1912 and it must have felt on that wonderful afternoon in which the rabbi of the town married off his eldest child, 'Sheva daughter of our rabbi and teacher of our teachers, Jacob, to Josef, son of our rabbi and teacher Abraham', that all was right with the world. A simple decorative pattern framed the words of the contract. On each of the top corners was a red Star of David; in the star on the right were the words of the wedding blessing 'the voice of gladness and the voice of joy', in the star on the left the words 'the voice of the bridegroom and the voice of the bride'.

The New Year of 1939 found Regina still in Berlin, where Sophie had gone to help her pack up her affairs and send them ahead to Palestine in the expectation that their dear Mama would soon be able to follow them. After all, the family could not leave their no-longer-youthful mother alone in Berlin. Matters were only getting worse. On 28 November 1938 Himmler had published an article in the SS bulletin *Das Schwarze Korps,* ('The Black Unit'), in which he spoke of 'the vital necessity to exterminate this Jewish subhumanity, as we exterminate all criminals in our ordered country: by the fire and the sword. The outcome will be the final catastrophe for Jewry in Germany, its total annihilation.'[1] It may have been this piece which prompted the American Consul General in Berlin, Raymond Geist, to note that the Nazi objective was ultimately annihilation. Hitler had both the national and the international audience in mind when he employed the term in his annual speech to the Reichstag on 30 January, the anniversary of his ascent to the chancellorship. Never before had his threats against the Jews been so explicit:

At the time of my struggle for power it was mostly the Jewish people who laughed at the prophecy that one day I would attain in Germany the leadership of the state and therewith of the entire nation, and that among other problems I would also solve the Jewish one. I think that the uproarious laughter of that time has in the meantime remained stuck in German Jewry's throat. Today I want to be a prophet again: if international Jewry inside and outside Europe again succeeds in precipitating the nations into a world war, the result will not be the Bolshevisation of the earth and with it the victory of Jewry, but the annihilation of the Jewish race in Europe.[2]

Over the following six years Hitler referred back repeatedly to this pronouncement. To his ministers, who saw their function as 'working towards the Führer', that is, turning his general expressions of intention into specific plans of action, these words came to be seen as establishing the final goal of the Nazi racial ideal and as legitimising whatever means might be necessary for its attainment. This did not mean that the death camps were already constructed in the Nazi thought-process at the beginning of 1939. But the notion of extermination was being prepared as an idea; a path was being carved through the imagination which would make subsequent implementation practicable and acceptable, no more than that to which the mind had years earlier given its assent.

Throughout 1939 it grew ever more difficult for Jews to get out of Germany. 'Early in the morning, Jews appear at travel agencies and stand in long lines waiting to ask what visas one can obtain that day,' wrote Georg Landauer, director of the Central Bureau for the Settlement of German Jews in Palestine, to his colleague Arthur Rupin in Jerusalem.[3] Orders had been issued by Göring, the founder of the Gestapo, to replace the *Palästina Treuhand-Stelle*, which, although operating within numerous constraints, had been largely in the hands of the Jewish community itself and from which Regina had received her letter the previous November, with an office under the direction of the Reich Central Bureau for Jewish Emigration, run entirely by the Nazis. Reinhard Heydrich appointed Heinrich Müller, head of the Gestapo, the secret state police, to take charge. A similar office had already been opened in Vienna, under the direction of Adolf Eichmann.

Nothing could have been easy for Regina. The first anniversary of her husband's death had just passed; the relief of knowing that her older son had been released from Buchenwald had been followed by yet another parting, and packing away a lifetime of personal effects with all their associated memories must have been a miserable undertaking, especially as it remained uncertain whether she would ever see them again. Extraordinarily, a family friend chose this moment to write offering his warmest congratulations and inviting Regina 'to look back on a lifetime of shared achievements' in which her role as Rebbetzin, rabbi's wife, had been of central importance in facilitating her husband's successes. True as this no doubt was, it is hard to see how she could have appreciated the expression of those sentiments at such a time. Perhaps the sender had been searching for some way in which to support her morale.

On 8 February 1939 Regina wrote to Jerusalem:

My dear children!

I wrote just yesterday and sent the letter to our dear Alfred and Nelly. But I know you will get to read it too, and that you will all pass on in the opposite direction the letters addressed to your dear siblings.

We're still here and it's impossible to see how everything's going to develop. I still have the flat until 30 March. If I had the certificate, or if I knew where I might be able to go, I would do things differently. I would also like to know for sure that the mortal remains of our dear blessed Papa will be brought to Palestine. Annchen has made the arrangements with the *Chevra Kaddisha* [burial society] in Breslau. It costs 2000 marks, which I could perhaps still obtain from here.

Dear Sophie can't stay here indefinitely and it's going to be too much for dear Josef too. You can imagine my mood; but how good it would be for me if our beloved Papa would have taken me along back then.

The letter was particularly hard to decipher; perhaps the terrible times and her state of mind had affected Regina's handwriting. What did Regina mean by 'taken me along back then'? Was she referring to their visit to Palestine in 1935, when Alfred and Nelly tried to persuade them to stay but were not successful, because her husband had said that at times like these he could not possibly abandon his community? Or was this a wish, formed in her mourning and strengthened by the terrors of those grim months that they could have shared the end of their lives just as they had shared its many happier years? The letter revealed what perhaps amounted to a very rare moment of inner despair. I often wondered whether her decision to travel with her daughter to Holleschau, sensible and practical as it must have seemed, was not most profoundly rooted in her desire to be near her beloved husband and to keep him company at the graveside in the town where they had spent, long since, their happiest years.

Whatever efforts Regina may have made to obtain her papers,

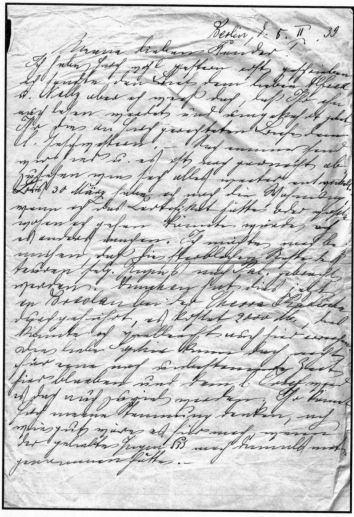

Regina's letter to Jerusalem, 8 February 1939.

there appears to have been no further response from the Palestine Trust Office until several months later. The undated draft of a telegram to Alfred summed up her and Sophie's mood:

Palestine Office entirely negative

Artur's intervention by telegraph urgently needed

Lift ready end of February

Then able to travel to Holleschau

Mama Sophie

The 'lift' referred to was the transportation of her belongings to Palestine. 'Artur' was probably Arthur Rupin, the former head of the Jewish Agency, who had personally helped to resettle large numbers of Jewish refugees from Germany. Whether or not he was approached to intervene on her behalf, no surviving letters indicate any progress with her application for a certificate to join her children in Palestine until May, well after she had made the decision to leave Berlin. By the time she could respond, her affairs had come at least partly under the jurisdiction of the office in Prague, where all matters pertaining to emigration were governed, at least from that summer onwards, by the policies determined by Heydrich and Eichmann.

Regina now had six weeks left to vacate her flat. Sophie was by all accounts a practical and down-to-earth, as well as a beautiful and elegant, woman. With her help, her mother made good progress in packing up her affairs. Two copies of a long list, running to six pages and 168 entries, itemised all her possessions, from kitchen forks and waste paper baskets to prayer books and candlesticks. It was this which had come to my attention when I first found the letters in Jerusalem. One copy was on the headed paper of the firm of Brokerhoff and Lipschütz of Berlin, international removers. The other declared that the list had been prepared for the purpose of transporting furniture from Berlin to Tel Aviv. There were special

Internationales Speditions-Büro
Brokerhoff & Lipschütz
G. m. b. H.
BERLIN C 2, Frommelstraße 1a
Fernsprecher: 42 06 21
Postscheck-Konto: 37987
Tel-Adr.: Welttransport

Umzugsgut des Auswanderers:

Name: Frau Regina Freimann, Berlin-Wilmersdorf
Güntzelstrasse 15
vor dem 1.1.1933 in meinem Besitz
Adresse:

Lfde. Nr.	Gegenstände — Stück	Gegenstände — Art	Zeitpunkt der Anschaffung	Wert der nach dem 1. 1. 1933 erworbenen Gegenstände	Bemerkungen
	3	Wanduhren	1900/32		
	1	kleine Stehuhr			
	18	Familienbilder			
	2	Teppiche			
	2	Brücken			
	5	Bettvorleger			
	10	Fenstergardienen			
	2	Couch			
	2	Tische			
	1	Nähtisch			
	1	Schreibtisch			
	17	Stühle			
	1	Liegestuhl			
	2	Rauchtische			
	1	Blumentisch			
	4	Schränke			
	4	Bettstellen m.Matrazen			
	1	Anrichtetisch			
	1	Grammophon mit Platten (einige)			
	1	Chaiselonguedecke			
	6	Sofakissen			
	1	Schreibtischlampe			
	1	Stehlampe			
	3	Hängelampen			
	2	Nachttischlampen			
	2	Nachttische			
	1	Nähmaschine	1903		
	1	Truhe			
	1	Waschgeschirr 3teilig	1900/32		
	1	Kommode			
	1	kleiner elektr. Wärmespender			
	1	elektr. Kochtopf			
	1	" Bügeleisen			
	1	" Kochplatte			
	1	" Staubsauger			
	1	" Uhr			
	1	Schreibmaschine Stoewer altes Model			
	1	alter Fussbodenbelag			
	3	Spiegel m.Tisch			
	2	Tischdecken			
	6	Tabletts			
	2	Papierkörbe			
	1	Handtuchhalter			
	5	Hutkoffer			
	1	Koffer			
	1	Schreibtischgarnitur			
	1	Rauchservice			
	1	Toilett-Eimer			
	1	kleiner Kasten m.Decken und ...ie			

Regina's list itemising her possessions to be transported to Tel Aviv.

columns requiring details of the date of purchase and value of any items acquired after the 1 January 1933. In a handwritten comment

Regina noted that virtually all the objects were wedding gifts that had been in her possession for forty years, adding that she was now seventy years old. The few exceptions included a hoover and a refrigerator, the latter made by Brown Boveri and bought in 1937 for the seemingly exorbitant price of 455 marks, presumably because the family had told her that if there was one single piece of equipment needed more than any other for her new life in Palestine it was a decent fridge.

Among all the kitchenware, 'Various kitchen and household objects, including pots, pans, sieves, bowls, boards, spoons, trays, cutlery made of non-precious metals etc.', were mentioned '150 prayer books and biblical writings, etc', 'three Torah scrolls with crowns, (old family heirlooms)' and 'a number of Torah breast-plates and pointers'. Whenever I stayed with my father's sisters in their flat in Jerusalem my eye was drawn to the small bookshelf with the old *machzorim*, prayerbooks for the cycle of the Jewish year. Bound in their complete sets, they possessed a certain beauty, a presence which evoked an awareness of their provenance else-where, as if they had become imbued with the history of the Jewish people as reflected in the words of the prayers and the very pages had absorbed the lives, journeys and destinies of the family. When the flat was cleared after my father and his sisters had died, I asked if I might have them. They now occupy a bookshelf in my home, from which I carefully withdraw the respective volumes for each festival, anxious lest the spines, which survived so many travails, should become broken. Whenever I open them, with reverence for their age and the experiences to which they bear witness, I feel as if I'm standing at the border between the living and the dead, whose spirits transform the heavy print of the old pages into the depths and melodies of prayer.

On 14 February Regina swore on oath before the chief of police of the 156th police district of Berlin that the objects enumerated on pages 1–6 of the attached list 'are my possessions, have been in my use here and are to be transported to Tel Aviv for my immigration where they will again serve for my personal use'. She duly signed as Regina Sara Freimann, the middle name Sara being added as demanded by the Nazis.

It was time to leave Germany. Apart from the pressures of the general situation, Sophie was by now much missed back at home. On 6 February Josef had written:

Dear Mama, my dear Sopherl,

I'd written to you yesterday afternoon, and the day before, but I just received your precious letter with the picture and that is cause enough to write again at once and thank you from the bottom of my heart for that photograph of you with which I'm truly delighted. You've brought me great happiness. But the happiness is marred by the fact that dear Mama does not look well. You must, dear Mama, allow yourself to recover. I'm glad that you've finally received the letter from the Italian Consulate; hopefully the matter will now move forwards swiftly to a good conclusion. I wasn't in Napajedla, first of all because I had work to do in the office and secondly because Frau Hermine Batscha has already been visiting there since Saturday morning and wants to stay until Monday morning. I'm going to do the Tlumačov-Otrokovice circuit during the week and then come back home via Napajedla. This morning I was in Bystritz. This time I didn't pick up Frau Fuchs; she came here with me last time and doesn't make the trip every fortnight. She's sold her house in Bystritz

and is moving to her daughter in Brno. I'll give Faniuka your letter and
I enclose one from her for you. I greet you and kiss you. My thanks
and warmest greetings to dear Mama. Your Josef.

Two days later he wrote again:

Dear Mama, dearest Sopherl,

I received your cards this morning and thank you and dear Mama
for your lines. I'm always really happy when I get news from you. The
parcel's going today, just as you asked. Sadly the only things to be
had are chickens and I'd so much wanted to send you a turkey again
but there are none to be had. It's very cold here again. Karel's been
gone with the van yesterday and today, and he'll be travelling with it
tomorrow as well . . . I'll write to you again on Friday. I greet you
and kiss you and remain your Josef. Warmest greetings to dear Mama
and Annchen.

Josef's repeated and affectionate concern for his mother-in-law
was touching. They must have known each other well; the
Freimanns had been living in Holleschau for almost twenty years
by the time Josef married their eldest daughter. Afterwards they
would have virtually been neighbours, until the Freimanns left
for Posen.

But Josef wasn't the only person missing Sophie; he duly
enclosed Faniuka's letter as promised. Her proper name was in
fact Frantiska; she had been employed in the household for several
years as cook and presumably lived in. The warm tone suggested
that, in spite of the social and religious distance between them,
the two women were close.

Dear Mistress,

I was reminded to write you a few lines, which I am very pleased to do although I do not know if it is now convenient for you. I hope I am not detaining you while you read my letter. You missed a great deal this year as you were unable to ski here. The weather suitable for skiing lasted about a month. The son of Volak had another skiing accident this year. For a long time he walked with a bump on his head and before that he had to be in bed. Jarka is ill with flu. You could have at least taken your warm slippers, which are now here for the second year keeping a box warm in the wardrobe and I am sure your feet are cold. My skis, which I have from Eva, I lent to my sister, as she was asking me for them. Then she wrote to me that she had learned to ski but she injured her forehead when she fell (on skis) and hit a tree. Then she went to a ball on Sunday. Her mother did not want to go with her as she was upset at how her nose and forehead looked – all the other girls looked pretty but she looked like she came back injured from the front. But at the end she was talked into going with her. She wrote to me afterwards to say how much she enjoyed the ball and how she danced – they all wanted to know what happened to her . . . But she just danced more and more. Excuse me mistress if what I write is not very interesting for you. If so I could write somehow differently next time. For Christmas I prepared a Christmas cake for dear Franc and for the ever-complaining Karel, which I got baked at the baker's. He baked them very beautifully, except for one that did not rise, which I took for myself. I received the money for Christmas. I have not yet decided how to spend it but maybe I'll buy myself something to wear. Franc's wife is expecting a baby. I can just see how Franc's going to celebrate. To conclude, I send my heartfelt greetings to you and to your mother and cousin and I hope that you'll return soon.

The letter was graciously poised between affection and deference; Frantiska knew that her mistress liked to have warm feet and that she enjoyed hearing the local news. But she also understood that she was in service. The tone suggested that its author was quite young, certainly well under 45 (and probably less than half of that), the age below which the Nuremberg laws forbade the employment of non-Jewish girls in Jewish homes, just in case. But Sophie somehow managed to maintain good relationships with those around her, Jewish and non-Jewish, as they did with her. She was fond of her home, her town and her neighbours.

By mid-February it was time for Sophie to go back to Czechoslovakia, taking her mother with her. They sent the lift, gave up the flat in Berlin, and took the train together for Holleschau.

Unlike their owner, Regina's possessions arrived safely in Palestine, two months ahead of the war which would soon close the Mediterranean to civilian traffic. On 14 July the Orient Shipping Agency wrote to Alfred (in German) asking him to pay the outstanding sum of 31 Palestinian pounds for invoice no. 1866, to include delivery, so that they could pass the goods as soon as possible to the firm of Kober and Jellinek for transportation to Jerusalem. The writer also asked Alfred to provide an address where the items could be deposited. Six weeks later they sent him a somewhat impatient reminder, complaining that in his absence an altogether unnecessary correspondence with his brother-in-law had delayed matters and that the sum, which had been clearly and unambiguously stated, had still not been paid. Presumably Alfred once again came up with the money. He would no doubt have had more important matters on his mind, such as if and when his mother could be rescued from Europe to rejoin her possessions in the comparative security of Mandate Palestine. But only her cutlery and clothes were destined ever to get there, together with the letters and papers in that suitcase, which remained shut for six decades on the balcony in Rechavia until my cousin and I eventually opened it.

It must have been with a considerable degree of relief that Sophie brought her mother with her to Czechoslovakia. There she could look after her in the comfort of her own home and with the support of her husband. But it must have been a strange journey for Regina. The last time she had set out south-east from Berlin, her husband had become fatally ill on the train. The shadow of that journey, and of his presence, must have accompanied her. When they changed onto the branch line, or perhaps were collected by motorcar, at nearby Hulin and approached Holleschau she must have been possessed by an overwhelming multiplicity of feelings: the happy associations of the vanished days when everything was future and family, now all refracted through the prism of loss, and her fears over a lonely and uncertain future. But she was a giving, not a self-centred, lady; she would have set her mind on the fact that she would be together with her daughter and would make every effort to assist her and her son-in-law in whatever ways she was able. Together they would write to every member of the family and preserve by means of letters the affectionate bonds which physical distance would not be allowed to unravel. She was also a woman of faith; the spirit of her husband would be with her and their children, together with whom she would see once again the beautiful coastline of Palestine.

Sophie arrived back in her home town with her mother less than a month before the Nazis marched in.

'We should go together to Holleschau,' my father would sometimes say. It had a position on my personal map of my father long before I knew the geographical location of the town. There was a reverence to his tone when he said the name 'Holleschau'; that was how people spoke about someone long dead for whom they still carried silent love in the depths of their heart. He conveyed a sense of fidelity and humility, as if the place still possessed the power of something sacred despite the decades since the family's devastation. To go there would not be a journey but a pilgrimage. Sadly, it was not one we ever undertook together. My father was eight years dead before my eighteen-year-old daughter Libbi and I travelled to Holleschau together, searched the streets for the houses where the family had lived, wandered along the grass path to my great-grandfather's grave, took photographs of the murals in the old synagogue and stared at the railway tracks along which Sophie, Josef and Regina had been taken away.

The town lay on the edge of the Hostyn Hills, the westernmost beginnings of the Carpathian Mountains which rose just out of view to the east. My father always referred to it as 'Holleschau'. That had been its name during the centuries of German influence, while the region formed part of the Austro-Hungarian Empire. After its defeat in the First World War and the creation of Czechoslovakia in 1918, the place took the Czech name of Holešov.

The Nazis, who bestowed upon the provinces of Bohemia and Moravia, in the latter of which the town lay, the unsought title of 'Protectorate', called the town Holleschau once again. That is how I too think of it; not, of course, because of the Nazis, but in honour of my father and his family, and because the traditional spelling of the name in Hebrew, הלעשויא, follows the German pronunciation.

In his short history of Jewish life there, my great-grandfather recorded that, of all the difficult events in the history of its Jewish quarter:

The worst disaster struck on 4 December 1918, when an armed mob of some two hundred men attacked the community, murdered two Jewish soldiers just back from the war, and robbed several Jewish families of all they had. Following this last pogrom, from which the community has to this day not recovered, only a few Jewish families remained in the town.

Among those who stayed were Sophie and Josef Redlich. No doubt it was chiefly Josef's business which kept him there, but the couple also loved and felt at home in the place. It was immediately after the 1918 pogrom, at the very time when the administration of the Jewish town on the site of the former ghetto was finally united with that of the larger Christian settlement into one civic entity, that Josef Redlich became a leader in local affairs.

In a register of the Jewish inhabitants of the region of the community of Holešov, compiled sometime after the Nazis occupied Bohemia and Moravia on 15 March, he was listed simply as 'Kaufmann', a businessman. In fact, he had inherited a thriving liquor business, established by his father in 1866. After the latter's death, the company's letterhead was altered to read 'Adolf Redlich's Sohn, Likörerzeugung'. In 1937 it employed a staff of four and had a turnover of 700,000 kroner; in 1938 this rose to 750,000. It was the only factory in the region producing spirits and liquors, a status which was to prove of the utmost importance when the town fell under Nazi occupation. The family were wealthy, owning two properties in the central Masarykstrasse. Josef had inherited the second home on the death of his father in 1927; it contained eleven apartments, as well as a small guest house frequented by people from the surrounding villages whose business compelled them to spend the occasional night in town. The manager was German and not Jewish, a detail which was to prove critical for its future.

In May 1938 Josef Redlich stood for the town council on the Jewish party's list; it received 131 votes and Josef was duly elected. It was not to be for long; on 26 June 1939 he resigned together with the two other Jews on official committees, presumably under duress. They were replaced by members of the Vlajka, the Czech fascist party; their names were crossed off the official list, with the date of this 'improvement', 6 May 1940, carefully inserted by hand. A month earlier it had been declared illegal for Jews to occupy official positions or work in a large range of professions throughout the Czech lands.

However patriotic Josef may have felt, he couldn't have been unaware of how perilous the international situation had become. Following the agreement finalised in Munich at a meeting between Hitler, Chamberlain and Daladier on 29 September 1938, Czechoslovakia, which was not even represented at the decisive session, was obliged to agree to the immediate German occupation of the Sudetenland. This entailed the abandonment of the Masaryk Line, the crucial military bulwark which the young democracy had been constructing since 1936. It must have been obvious to everyone that the situation for the remainder of the country was hopeless. A passionate lover of Czechoslovakia, Josef had no doubt founded his hopes on the inclusive policies of President Tomáš Masaryk and his successor Dr Edvard Beneš, whom the fascists branded as 'the hireling of the Jews'. Their enlightened leadership had turned Czechoslovakia into the staunchest liberal democracy in Central Europe. Czech fascists later demolished the statues of the two men and melted down the metal to make weapons. Thus by the autumn of 1938 even Josef had become extremely anxious about the situation. He, too, turned to Alfred, asking his brother-in-law to make enquiries on his behalf in Palestine. The procedures he outlined in his reply were familiar enough, as were the difficulties; though, since the country was not – yet – under German occupation, the transfer of money out of Czechoslovakia might still prove possible:

9 December 1938

Now to your affairs: Our previous letters must have crossed. As we already wrote to you, you can only apply for the certificates through the British Embassy in Prague. The application could only be made in Palestine if the advance sum of at least 1,000 Palestinian pounds was already deposited in a local bank and made over indisputably in your name and in the names of the two other applicants mentioned by you. So that you understand in full: for every applicant 1,000 Palestinian pounds, that is 3,000 Palestinian pounds in all, must already have been deposited here in Palestine. As the conditions where you live are very new, we've so far got no experience here as to whether it's possible to transfer the advance of 1,000 Palestinian pounds per family [*sic*] prior to emigration or whether, as is the case in Germany, this can only be done at the same time as you emigrate. On that point you need to get precise information from the Palestine office in Prague. Perhaps, dear Josef, you could write to us more clearly about the advice you've been given by the Palestine office. Should they advise you to try to obtain the certificates by means of a bank credit, this is not only very difficult but also very expensive, costing 70 to 80 Palestinian pounds per person. They'll also need here the exact details of every immigrant, as is the case with all applications for certificates (name, place and date of birth, status, names and ages of each member of the family, present occupation, passport number and place of issue, present address, religion and nationality). Because of the high pressure of demand from Germany and Austria the remaining number of capitalist certificates in the present quota (that is until 1 April 1939) is extremely limited; there were only 1950 such certificates for the entire current half year.

The numbers of people by now desperate to leave a Europe in which Germany's growing domination presented an ever more immediate danger must have been incomparably higher than the disturbingly low figure agreed by Great Britain. One can only guess at the numbers for whom this meagre quota must have meant that the most obvious, perhaps even the only, route to safety was now, cruelly, closed.

Alfred proceeded to address the question of Josef's prospects should he eventually be able to reach Palestine:

Concerning your question about the beverage industry, all we can say at present is that there are of course in Palestine enterprises for the production of every kind of alcoholic and non-alcoholic drink, as well as the major wine cellars which also produce cognac and liqueurs, and a large brewery and a factory making fruit juice. What we're trying to get clear information about is whether, dear Josef, an employment opportunity within the framework of these enterprises might be best for you. This information cannot be obtained in Jerusalem, only on location. We'll report back to you about that too, soon and in full.

Josef was unlikely to have felt encouraged by this news. But there is no evidence to suggest that he pursued the possibility of potential employment in Palestine. Nothing in any of the surviving correspondence, the vast majority of which was no doubt admittedly lost, gave any indication that Sophie and Josef felt an urgent need to leave Holešov or were making serious efforts to get out of the country. Yet they could not but have felt a degree of envy towards those who had taken the decision and succeeded in negotiating their escape from Europe, as the continuation of the letter Josef had written to Sophie in February 1939 indicated:

Think, my dear Sopherl, what luck some people have. Löbowitsch was here until ten o'clock last night, showing me letters from South Africa where he's already been accepted; the local community has procured permission for him to immigrate. All he now needs are various documents that I'm supposed to get for him, which of course I shall. On Monday he's already off to Prague, to the British Consulate, to hand in his papers. You'll be amazed how he's managed it. A few years ago a rich Jew from South Africa was on business in Bohemia. He asked

Löbowitsch to show him the Synagogue in his community. He left Löbowitsch his visiting card, which he kept. A couple of months ago he wrote to the gentleman in South Africa; thus came about this happy state of affairs. Otherwise there's nothing new to report.

For obvious reasons, no surviving letters described what Regina or Sophie felt when the Nazis marched into Czechoslovakia; when, on the following day, 16 March, Hitler displayed himself from the very windows of the Hradčany Castle in Prague where the Czech presidents had stood on state occasions to proclaim the liberty of their country; when he signed the decree incorporating the Czech lands into the Reich under the title of 'the Protectorate of Bohemia and Moravia'; or when the very laws which had deprived Regina of citizenship in Germany caught up with her on midsummer's day in her former home town and rendered her an outcast once again.

For Hitler the seizure of Czechoslovakia had been a triumph. As Karl Wolff, her father's adjutant, wrote to Himmler's daughter Gudrun, towards whom he clearly felt an attachment, 'The Führer went into a barely furnished room, turned to your father and embraced him [saying] isn't it wonderful that we are standing here, here we are and we shall never leave.'[1] Himmler had indeed played an essential role in the operation, allocating two SS *Einsatzgruppen* units to the occupying forces. They immediately began to seize documents and carry out arrests, unimpeded by any process of law.

Holleschau wouldn't have seemed a sufficiently important place to necessitate a large military presence. Nor was it on the main road to anywhere else significant. Yet photographs from the town

chronicles for 15 March showed a large number of armoured vehicles parked in the main square. The caption recorded how at
7.45 in the morning 'a German plane circled like a bird of prey
before flying away to the east'. At 11.30 the first wave of advanced
troops arrived on motorcycles, followed shortly afterwards by mech-
anised units. The mayor summoned the town council and briefly
welcomed the commanding officer, informing him that 'they were
at his disposal'. Noting the sombre mood, the *Wehrmacht* soldier
responded with the fatuous request: '*Meine Herren, nur keine saueren
Gesichter machen!*' ('*Gentleman, no sour faces!*')

*Military vehicles in Holešov's main square, 15 March 1939. (Municipal
Library, Holešov)*

'The Jewish population is terrified,' wrote the American
Ambassador Wilbur Carr to the US Secretary of State a few days
later; across the Protectorate there were widespread arrests conducted
'in the usual Nazi manner'.[2] The latter were conveniently able to

leave many of the initial assaults on Jews to the Czech fascists. On 18 March it was decreed that all Jewish-owned shops had to display a sign saying '*Jüdisches Geschäft*'. Three days later this ruling was revoked; instead, all 'Aryan' shops had to show that they belonged to Aryan proprietors. On 30 March the synagogue in nearby Ostrava was burnt down, a terrifying indication to a Jewish population which had felt deeply at home and safe under Czech rule. Following the edict issued by the Reichsprotektor on 21 June that all businesses had to be under Aryan management, Josef had foisted upon his liquor enterprise the appointment of an Aryan director. Jewish and Czech assets were systematically channelled into the coffers of the Reich to fund the very armies which were now occupying the country. In the summer of 1939 alone 800,000 ounces of gold were removed from the Czech National Bank to Berlin. The highly developed Škoda munitions works were harnessed for the German war machine; the weapons produced in Czechoslovakia may have given the Germans as much as a year's advantage over Britain in the race to re-arm.

These and virtually all subsequent decrees, which gradually but systematically reduced the scope of their life to an ever-narrowing and impoverished circle, passed almost unmentioned in Regina's and Sophie's letters. This was no doubt because they didn't want to fall foul of the censor and imperil the opportunity of being able to correspond with the rest of the family; but it is also likely that they wanted to avoid troubling their relatives in the free world with an even greater burden of anxiety than they must already have felt on their account. Thus the letters endeavoured to maintain a reassuring tone. For Regina especially, the one great solace was to be able to exchange news with her beloved children.

Sophie was generally rather practical in manner; a deep faith and stoical wisdom flowed quietly but constantly through Regina's lines. One has to be patient, she maintained; it must surely be God's will that these trials would eventually end; the family would be reunited in peacetime; she would see her dear children once again. She often concluded her letters with the greeting 'Eure treue Mutter'; the literal translation, 'your *faithful* mother', giving no adequate sense of the deep loyalty and steadfastness conveyed by her use of the word.

On 31 May Regina wrote to Palestine:

My dear children!

Your dear letter with the greetings from your lovely children for Yom Tov [the festival] brought us special pleasure. The letters from all our dear children for Yom Tov arrived in good time. We find out what's happening to you from the *Jüdisches Nachrichtenblatt* [Jewish newsletter] which Aunt Judith gives us every week. Hopefully tempers will calm down and such times will begin as are a blessing for all. Just now Mr Leopold Meisel came by, I usually lend him the paper, there's hardly any Jewish life here. Mr M. complains that his mother left with the last general transport and that they've now been in Athens, i.e. Piraeus, for two months.

Dear Josef, whom I told this afternoon about this conversation said that young people don't know what it means to endure suffering and need. He spent 20 months starving and full of lice in the war.

Sophie has gone as usual to the tailor in Olmütz and the milliner in Prosnitz and has taken Ms De Hayek and Ms Batscha along. Yesterday Sophie went to the corset-maker in Zlin and came back in the evening with dear Josef.

Each in their own way, Josef and Sophie were evidently preparing to last the German occupation out, Josef by reminding those around him that they'd endured worse in the past and Sophie by doing her best to carry on with life in the same way as before. For Regina, alongside keeping in touch with her children, the overriding concern remained the question of emigration. In her next letter to Alfred she copied out a series of notes from the *Palästina Treuhand-Stelle* in Berlin, all sent to her before the end of May. It appeared that with her move to Czechoslovakia a number of important documents had gone astray. Two letters addressed the question of whether or not her pension could still be transferred to Palestine should she be able to obtain a certificate, the issue which had so troubled her when Alfred's friend had come to see her in Berlin a year earlier:

For the information of the British Passport Office, we hereby certify that Ha'avara Ltd of Tel-Aviv is willing to transfer your pension of 363 Reichsmarks per month provided by the Synagogue Congregation of Berlin, up to the value of £4 each month, so long as the provisions regarding transfer transactions to Palestine set out in the circular from the government office for the regulation of foreign exchange pertain, and as long as the Foreign Exchange Office approves of payments into Special Account I of a sum of Reichsmarks sufficient to cover the transfer of a monthly amount of £4.

To this positive news was added a rider; with the outbreak of war ever more probable, any arrangement for the international transfer of money was bound to be fragile. Besides this obvious caution, the authors of the letter may have had a further, unstated, concern:

large numbers of impoverished Jews, deprived of any opportunity for gaining an income in Germany and German-occupied lands and excluded from all forms of governmental social support, had nowhere else to turn other than to the offices of the Jewish community, which had less and less funds available with which to provide for them. Would a pension agreement with someone who had by then hopefully managed to leave Europe rank among the organisation's top priorities? It had to be made clear to Frau Freimann that if the Ha'avara Office in Tel Aviv did not receive the money from Germany it couldn't be held liable for making any payments:

We are enclosing the documents for you to submit to the British Passport Office in order to obtain an A IV (Pensioner's) Certificate. We must apprise you of the fact that Ha'avara Ltd Tel-Aviv cannot guarantee to make the monthly payment of £4 to you in Palestine if the money transferred into the Special Account I according to current transfer rates is not sufficient to pay £4 on a monthly basis. Equally, the attached declaration from the Ha'avara does not indicate any obligation to make any payments to you should money cease to be paid into the Special Account I, or in case delays and difficulties make such a payout impossible. We also wish to state that this arrangement will only apply for as long as the transfer agreements with the Office for Foreign Exchange Controls remain valid.

What was Regina to do now? Once again she turned to Alfred for advice:

I hope to hear from you, dear Alfred, how I should answer those letters. In Prague they wanted you to give a guarantee. Obviously I would prefer it if the Berlin community could do this. I need immediate advice on how I should respond to the British Passport Office. Dear Sophie is travelling and I don't want this letter to wait here any longer. All my love, from your faithful mother.

Regina couldn't have known that, scarcely a fortnight earlier, the British government had issued its new White Paper limiting the total number of Jews permitted to enter the country over the following five years to 75,000. Thereafter there was to be no further immigration without the agreement of the Arabs of Palestine. The Jewish Agency had been quick to respond:

The Jewish people regards this breach of faith as a surrender to Arab terrorism. It delivers Great Britain's friends into the hands of those who are fighting against her. The new regime announced in the White Paper will be devoid of any moral basis and contrary to international law.[3]

The statement had expressed anger that the British had given in to the violence of the Arab Revolt and were effectively playing into the hands of Nazi sympathisers, whereas the Jewish population of Palestine was ready and eager to take up arms in Britain's cause.

Meanwhile ways had been found to escape from Europe without the benefit of the requisite documents. 'Illegal' ships were already departing from Athens and the Black Sea ports. It was presumably for such an opportunity that the family referred to by Regina were waiting in Piraeus. Such boats set sail in 1939, throughout the war years and afterwards, until the establishment of the State of Israel in May 1948. Some reached the shores of Palestine safely; others were intercepted by the Royal Navy and their passengers transferred to British camps or colonies. Some were prevented from landing anywhere. There were many tragedies. The *Salvador* sank in a storm in the Sea of Marmora in February 1940. In November of the same year the steamer *Patria* exploded in Haifa harbour and 251 lives were lost. In December 1941, 769 refugees set sail across the Black Sea from Rumania in the *Struma*; the Turkish authorities refused to let the passengers disembark unless they were first assured that the Mandate administration would allow them to enter Palestine. As the Jewish agency was unable to procure the necessary permissions the ship was forced to set sail once again and blew up in the open sea with the loss of all lives on board except two. Those who did make it safely to Palestine did not necessarily pass beneath the British radar; the latter simply deducted the number of such immigrants from the quota of certificates they were prepared to supply.

The perils entailed in following such an 'illegal' route were hardly likely to make it appealing to a lady in her seventies.

That summer Regina wrote again; the date is unclear, but Ernst's birthday was 1 July:

My beloved children!

It seems such a long time since I heard from you. Today is dear Ernst's birthday; we receive regular news from him. Unfortunately we have not yet heard what we wish for them from the bottom of our heart. The beloved little ones are now together in Celerina. For five months the parents have been separated from their children and although they are in good hands among friends, they long for them deeply. The dear children can sense this. Mrs Levy, Annchen's mother, wrote that Uncle Aron had a post in N. Rh. Do you, my dear, know anything about that? M.K.'s practice was not very lucrative, this doesn't happen very quickly anywhere . . . For everything you need a bit of *mazel* [good luck]; hopefully that will also come for dear Ernst and Eva, who are very impatient. Today I received the last meat. I am sending you, dear Alfred, the letter from the Palestine Trust Society. I am very disappointed that I get so little. When I left it was supposed to be double. I haven't received any of my pension payments since 1 April and nothing has been transferred to me over here. I haven't got anyone here who can advise me and in Berlin nobody is left who could speak on my behalf. On the eve of the New Moon we went to the grave of dear Papa; may he bless us all with his protection. Where are you going to send dear Ruth for the holidays? Even Trude, who celebrated her birthday so nicely – she had thirty-five guests and the best presents, and she was treated to the best things – doesn't know where to send her dear Arnold during the two months of holidays. I send my love and all the warmest wishes in my heart, your faithful mother.

It was fortunate for Regina that her affairs were still at least partially handled by the office of the *Palästina Treuhand-Stelle* in Berlin. In the very month that she was writing to Alfred, Reinhard Heydrich was instructing his Security Police to prevent an exodus of Jews from the Protectorate at the expense of the emigration quotas from the Altreich. He was concerned that, with a limited number of countries prepared to accept any refugees at all and most of those offering entry only to a very small number, places taken up by Jews from recently occupied lands might delay the attainment of the primary Nazi objective of making the Reich itself fully *Judenfrei* (free of Jews). Thus it wasn't until the summer that he gave his consent to the establishment in Prague of an office to deal with Jewish emigration on the lines of the *Zentralstelle für jüdische*

Auswanderung (the Central Office for Jewish Emigration) set up in Vienna. But this was no support organisation intended to help Jews leave Nazi-occupied Europe. In theory its aims may have been to assist potential emigrants in obtaining all the necessary documents and to work with travel agencies, shipping lines and Jewish organisations to facilitate the speediest possible departure of the Jews from the Protectorate. But in practice the Office had been instructed to extract money from the Czech Jews, who were forced to make payments into its accounts. The pretext, that the funds would help their by now largely pauperised coreligionists to get out of Germany, was simply a cover for stealing their assets. Adolf Eichmann, who had developed the Austrian branch with brutal efficiency, was brought to Prague to run the new agency. It opened on 15 July with an initial remit to serve the capital and the surrounding area only. It would have been to this office, had he chosen to pursue the possibility of emigration, that Josef would have turned.

In the event, it was almost certainly not the delays in obtaining her papers which prevented Regina's escape from Europe, but the start of the war in the early hours of 1 September. As Alfred later noted with bitter frustration, her papers were finally issued, but they came too late. On 26 September the Jerusalem Office of the Department for Migration wrote to Alfred's lawyer:

The Assistant Commissioner for Migration at Jerusalem presents his compliments to Dr F. S. Perles and has the honour to state that an immigration certificate has been issued in favour of Mrs Regina Freimann and transmitted to the British Passport Control Officer, Berlin, on 24 August 1939.

It was a pro forma letter; only the names and places were specially typed in, with the date entered by hand. The certificate was issued just eight days before Germany attacked Poland. But a month had already gone by before Alfred received his notification. By the time Regina would have learnt of the arrival of the certificate further vital days, if not weeks, would have been lost.

Dr Perles informed Alfred, who must immediately have written to the Immigration Department of the Jewish Agency for Palestine, located temporarily in Geneva. Following the start of the war he could no longer correspond directly with his mother. They replied on 23 October, saying that they had been in contact with the Palestine offices in Berlin and Prague and that they would 'in due course' do their utmost to help his mother make *Aliyah*, the traditional phrase for going to live in the land of Israel. Enclosed with the letter was an information sheet about travel options. The problem lay with the words 'in due course'; the war and the unrelenting pursuit by the Nazis of their Jewish policy had already made all but the most risky 'travel options' unfeasible.

The sheet explained that the Jewish Agency had a standing arrangement with the Adriatica Company, whose ships sailed from Trieste. The Italian authorities, no doubt short of foreign exchange, were insisting that tickets be purchased in dollars only. The schedule listed sailings by a veritable fleet of liners; the names must have rung with the sound of unattainable freedom: *Esperia, Egeo, Calitea, Marco Polo, Filippo Grimani, Palestina, Gerusalemme, Galilea*. Ports of call included Genoa, Naples, Syracuse, Piraeus, Rhodes, Alexandria, Haifa and Beirut, as well as Istanbul. The next ship was due to set sail on 17 October.

Company brochures from 1937, the year in which my grandparents travelled with my father and his sisters, described the facilities and activities on board ship, which included dancing, cinema, a wireless newssheet, libraries, reading rooms and a photographic service. A splendid menu ensured that passengers would not go hungry. Such luxuries would scarcely have been the primary concern of Jewish passengers, who, grateful to have escaped Nazi Europe, would have been preoccupied with worry about family and friends left behind and by anxiety over the challenges which now faced them in an unknown land. My father recalled how their ship docked in Haifa on the festival of Tabernacles in late September. Following the strictures of Jewish law they had to wait until the holiday had concluded at dusk before disembarking. Arriving in Palestine with virtually no possessions, they found strictly orthodox relatives busy throwing out all their pots and pans after the local Jewish butcher had been exposed for passing off unkosher camel meat as kosher veal. They rescued the discarded kitchenware from the dustbin, put it through the due process of ritual cleansing and settled down to a new life in the difficult conditions of the ancient homeland now ruled by a country soon to be at war.

But for Regina it was simply too late. The outbreak of hostilities put an end to virtually all emigration from the Protectorate; official routes by land and sea were effectively closed. This didn't prevent the *Zentralstelle* in Prague from insisting that wealthy Jews had to submit emigration plans, but this was solely with the aim of extorting large sums from them in the form of emigration taxes. A series of increasingly severe decrees required the Jews of the region to make over their money and possessions to the *Auswanderungsfond*, the so-called 'emigration fund' which was subsequently used by the Nazis to pay for the murder of those from whom they had extorted it.

Had Regina stayed in Berlin her papers might perhaps have arrived earlier. Perhaps, too, she might have managed to leave the country, even after the outbreak of war. Perhaps. Almost two years later, in a letter dated May 1941, she wrote to Ernst that 'the tickets can no longer be extended'. It must have been a torment to her to know that the documents which could have saved her life and reunited her with at least three of her beloved children had finally reached her hands only to be rendered useless by the disastrous turn of events.

Across the so-called Protectorate Nazi decrees followed each other at a quickening pace and with intensifying cruelty. As early as March 1939, a ban was imposed on the sale of Jewish properties and businesses, preventing Jews from liquidating their assets and taking something with them should they be able to emigrate. On 23 June Jews were forbidden to export personal effects and valuables. On 5 August restaurant owners were required to serve Jews in special rooms only; shortly afterwards certain restaurants were declared off limits to Jews altogether. On 1 September, no doubt as a show of force on the day they started the war, the Nazis arrested five of Holešov's leading Jews and sent them to concentration camps. Two in fact survived. On 21 November the town council decided to request the regional authorities to order the registration of all unused Jewish properties, forcing Jewish families to move in together. The proposal was rejected, but re-emerged later in a more sinister form. On one decree after another the appearance of Josef's and Sophie's signatures showed that they had duly reported, complied, and handed in the items they were no longer allowed to possess.

No amount of staring at their names on these lists could tell me how they must have felt, forced to sign away their past in small segments, compelled to cooperate in writing off their future.

The summer of 1939 found Ernst in London, Alfred, Ella and Wally in Jerusalem and Sophie and Regina under German occupation in Czechoslovakia. It was Trude who proved to be in the worst of all possible places. For no one else in the family did the situation change so swiftly, so radically or in a manner that so utterly excluded any opportunity to escape.

Trude and her husband, Dr Alex Peiser.

Poznań had still been the German city of Posen when the Freimann family moved there in 1914 after Rabbi Jacob received the call to serve as its rabbi. The town was blessed with a thriving and prestigious community, a beautiful synagogue and a full and rich

Jewish life. Its prominence as a rabbinical seat contributed to Rabbi Freimann's growing reputation as one of the leading authorities on Jewish law throughout Europe. Trude was in her teens when the family made the move and life in Posen would have been pleasant. My mother's mother also grew up there; she was just a few years older than Trude and spoke often and with affection of her school days, which were followed on summer afternoons by a swim in the river. The daughter of the head of the Jewish Hospital, the popular Dr Caro, she was a beloved and indulged only child. Since she valued helping at the hospital, especially during the war years when many injured soldiers were brought to the town for care and rehabilitation, and was keen to become a doctor herself, she might well have encountered Trude's future husband, Alexander Peiser, a young colleague of her father.

It may have been because of his professional commitments that Alex chose not to move west when, after its defeat in the First World War, Germany was forced to cede the region to an expanded Poland under the conditions of the Treaty of Versailles. Most of the Jewish community, who spoke German and identified deeply with German culture, and who had every reason to fear the overt anti-Semitism of the National Party with its support from significant parts of the Catholic Church, opted to leave for Germany. By 1921 there were scarcely two thousand Jews left in Poznań. Among them, however, remained Rabbi Jacob and Regina Freimann. It was probably in those post-war years that Trude and Alex met. He was a doctor and a senior mason. They were married in 1921 and their only son Arnold was born in the late 1920s. The house on the Aleje Marcinkowskiego in which they had an apartment served as the masonic lodge.

Alex had a private practice and probably also worked in the

Jewish hospital. It was built from monies left in a bequest by Salomon Benjamin Latz, who, following the great fire which swept through the city in 1803, entrusted the outstanding scholar, the *Gaon* (genius) of Posen, Rabbi Akiva Eger, with the establishment of a new house of study and a Jewish hospital, to be run under his personal guidance. The building was constructed on the Teichgasse in 1829. Illustrations show a large edifice with a formal façade; it was destroyed in 1945.

Pictures from the interwar years suggest that the Peisers were a happy family. A framed circular photograph from the Sztuka studio in Poznań shows a still-girlish Trude holding baby Arnold with his head against her cheek and smiling gently. A later photo taken when the boy was six or seven has him wearing a sailor suit and sitting on his mother's lap. Trude has a round, soft face and a gentle smile.

Trude, with her son Arnold at the age of six or seven.

In the summer of 1938 Trude celebrated her fortieth birthday; she was determined to make an occasion of it. After chiding her family for their lateness in sending their congratulations, she offered them a full account of the celebrations:

Poznań

12 June 1938

My dear ones!

This time I waited before writing, as Wednesday was my birthday and I didn't want to write until after it was all over. Incidentally, I hadn't received any greetings from any of you, and only yesterday did letters arrive from Ella, Wally and Ernst, and a card from the dear Redlichs and also your dear letter. As I'd been invited out a great many times during the year I took my revenge and invited everybody to the garden of the lodge for coffee and cake on 9 June. For dessert I held out the prospect of the gardens, with maybe a few insect bites thrown in. The veranda was laid for thirty-eight people. Frau Lindner decorated it all with yellow pansies and Martha baked very fine cakes. There were two *Nusstorten*, one *Sandtorte*, one *Blechkuchen*, one *Königskuchen,* vanilla crescents, *Bisquiteroullade, Mürbekuchchen,* and Frau Chone lashed out on half a pound of very fine coffee beans and five bowls of whipped cream and gave me too a most beautiful embroidered silk blouse and stockings. I also got the following presents: Frau Wollheim and Frau Korytowski each gave me a bottle of orangeade and raspberry juice; from Frau Moses I received a brown skirt; from Aunt Freimann a silk nightdress; from Frau Lipschütz a pair of silk slippers; the Peiser family clubbed together and gave me a linoleum runner for the corridor and bathroom, a gift to which Martchen also contributed; from dear Alex I got a silk blouse in black with white [illegible] and a pair of

```
Ella u.Walli,Ernst von denl.Redlichs eine Karte und auch Euer l.Br
im Laufe des Jahres sehr vieleingeladen war habe ich mich revanchi
zum 9.Juni in den Logengarten zu Kaffe und Kuchen eingeladen.Als N
ich den Garten u.ev.einige Mückenstiche in Aussicht gestellt. In d
war für 38 Personen gedeckt.Frau Lindner hat alles mit gelben Stie
schmückt und Marta hat sehr gute Kuchen gebacken,Es gab 2 Nusstort
1 Blechkuchen,1Königskuchen,Vanillekipfeln,Biquitroullade,Mürbeku
halbes Pfund sehr guten Bohnenkaffee und 5 Schüsseln Schlagsahne s
Frau Chone,die ausserdem noch eine sehr schöne seid.Garnitur-Hemd
Sonst bekam ich geschenkt: Von Frau Wollheim und Korytowski je 1 P
u.Himbeersaft,von Frau Moses 1 braunen Rock,von Tante Freimann 1 s
Frau Lipschütz 1.P.seid.Schlüpfer, von der ganzen Familie Peiser f
und Badezimmer einen Linoleumleufer-an dem Geschenk hat sich auch
```

An extract from Trude's letter describing her fortieth birthday celebrations.

silk stockings; the same too from Frau Cohn and Frau Baum, a black silk slip from Springers, soap, eau de Cologne and cream from Lehrs, a fruit plate, writing paper, serviettes, handkerchiefs, five boxes of confectionery, waffles, chocolate, lots of flowers and pot plants from other acquaintances, I can't even count it all. At any event, everyone was happy and I can't tell you how long they stayed because at eight o'clock we went back to the flat. I wouldn't have done it upstairs as I couldn't have coped with so many people and all the chatter, but downstairs it was all nicely spread out and everyone could talk to their hearts' content and as I told you it was a beautiful day full of sunshine which was just the right weather for being in the garden.

The party, which was something of a feast, sounded as if it had also been rather an ordeal for Trude and her husband, who couldn't refrain from admitting how glad they had both been that it could be held in the garden, where the noise of so many simultaneous conversations was happily dispersed in the open air and how relieved they were to retreat after a respectable period to the calm and quiet of their apartment, leaving those guests who refused to take the hint to continue the festivities among themselves.

The letter exuded a sense of plenty: Trude clearly relished describing all the different kinds of cake, and there were more presents than she could count. I abandoned the attempt to translate the menu: even if some of the pastries did have corresponding English names this wasn't their milieu; they belonged to the unique environment of the cultured European café or teatime coterie. However, I had grown up in a little refugee enclave of German manners, albeit tucked away in North West London, so I put aside the dictionary and resorted to memory. Weren't *Mürbekuchchen* what my mother's mother who, after all, came from Posen, used simply to call *Posner Kuchchen,* those soft biscuits made of buttery, shortbread-like dough, only yellower because they were rich in egg yolk? My grandfather had loved them so much that I once saw him, when my grandmother offered him a plate with all kinds of luxury biscuits from the shops but just one such home-baked *Kuchchen,* reach over without even looking and select it from among all the other options in their shining wrappers. Wasn't *Blechkuchen* that moist base beneath the layer of dark-red plums in those delicious cakes we were sometimes offered as children, but always in the homes of other German-Jewish refugees? I wasn't sure about *Königskuchen,* but *Nusstorte* was something I'd always avoided as a child, with a sense of disappointment that just because others regarded it as a delicacy it had been allowed to supplant a treat like chocolate cake. Here was an entire culture on tea plates.

But what was Trude trying to tell her mother? This question had troubled me ever since I first set eyes on the letter. It was, after all, the summer of 1938 and she couldn't have been ignorant of what was happening in Germany. Or was it impossible without the daily experience of living within its immediate compass to comprehend the all-pervasive threat which penetrated ever more terrifyingly into the hearts of Germany's and Austria's Jews? Perhaps the letter was an attempt at reassurance: amid all her other concerns Mama had no need to worry about Trude; life in Poznań was proceeding as usual and everyone was fine. Or maybe the letter was the expression of an ongoing effort to keep not her mother but herself as calm as possible: everything was still as normal; one still made the best cakes according to the best recipes, drank coffee with cream and received the finest presents for one's birthday? Given the situation at the time, what other options could there be?

Yet there is a certain cruelty to hindsight with its often unwarranted assumptions about what must have been known at the time and its implied judgements about how people should or could or might have acted otherwise than they did. Perhaps Trude was simply telling her mother how she had celebrated her birthday, nothing more or less. After all, it wasn't just any birthday; it was her fortieth. Perhaps, too, she sensed that this would be one of the last opportunities for a celebration, before the uncertain times to come.

In fact, a more careful reading of the second half of the letter showed that things were not as calm as they might initially have appeared. Alex added a short note explaining that Arnold was busy with preparations for his Bar Mitzvah. Then a different concern emerged:

Otherwise things are very difficult here economically and one has to think about how one's going to manage. We've had good news from Palestine . . . That's it for today, with warmest greetings, Your Alex.

seine Sache hoffentlich gut machen. Es ist jetzt nur noch knapp 3 Wochen,die
Zeit vergeht schnell.Am 21. hat er schon Ferien die wohl bis zum 3.September
dauern werden.Wie schön wäre es wenn Ihr herkommen könntet.Es ist leider alles
anders gekommen als wir es uns gedacht hatten. Dir 1.Annchen danke ich für Dei
Anschrift.Bei Springers werden schon Vorbereitungen für Hochzeit,die Anfang
Juli stattfinden sol.,getroffen,d.h.wenn die Papiere in Ordnung sind.Die Trauu
wird im Waisenhaustempel stattfinden,im allerengsten Kreise. Habt Ihrmal Ceci
Sp. gesprochen,ich glaube,dass sie mit ihrer Tätigkeit nicht zufrieden ist,sie
hat das Gefühl,dass man sie als Spion ansieht,und nun hat sie noch eine wenig
sympathische Zimmergenossin bekommen. Habt Ihr eigentlich Telefon und welche
Nummer,vielleicht kann man sich mal wenigstens telefonisch sprechen,wenn es so
nicht anders geht. Von allen Bekannten soll ich Dir,1.Mama herzliche Grüsse se
und Dir 1.Annchen besonders von Springers. Bleibt gesund und schreibt bald wie
Eurer Euch herzlich grüssenden *Trude.*

Herzliche Grüsse sendet *Arnold.*

Liebe Regina!
Hoffentlich bist Du gesund. Empfange die besten Grüsse von Deiner

The second half of Trude's letter, with additions from Arnold and Alex.

The good news from Palestine was presumably an encouraging letter from Alfred or possibly from my grandmother or Wally; they were beginning to settle down in their new lives. Were they also telling their sister to hurry up and leave Poland, and to bring her family to join them before it became too late?

There were nuances of tone in Trude's part of the letter too: 'How lovely it would be if you could come here. Sadly everything has happened differently from how we imagined,' she wrote to her mother, though she may simply have been referring to their recent family tragedy. Yet she could not but have been acutely aware of surrounding events. She was one of the leaders of the Poznań Association for the Support of Jewish Women and it would be hard to imagine that people affected by what was happening just across the border, or who had crossed it in flight, had not been turning to the organisation for help. It had been founded in 1933, partly, presumably, to support those former Jewish residents of Poznań who had left when it became part of Poland after the First World War because they had felt themselves to be German at heart, and who were now being forced by the very country with which they had imagined themselves to have possessed so deep an affinity to flee back to the mercies of their former homeland. The Nazis had by now been expelling Jews with Polish nationality for years. Later that autumn they would simply dump several thousand on the border at Zbastyn; they refused to allow them back into Germany, the Polish authorities refused to admit them, and the hapless victims were left in no-man's-land to starve.

There were no more letters from Trude until the following summer, when she and Alex sent a brief card to Ernst and Eva in London, informing them of the forthcoming arrival there of a mutual friend. The postmark was smudged but it was just possible to decipher the date, 23 June 1939. Alex wrote first:

My dears!

Let me take this opportunity to send you best wishes for your birthday, from me, my mother and my sisters. Otherwise we're all in good health. One has to wait and see what's coming. My very best greetings, your Alex . . .

Trude continued:

Meanwhile you'll have received our letter and we hope to hear from you again soon. I wanted to tell you that Hilde has left to join her brother in London, bringing you greetings. Maybe one of you can go there; the address is Heinz Fink, London SW3, 36 Oakley Street. She'll tell you all about us. Our young man sends us happy letters from his summer holidays; he's already sent us several nice photos. I'm sending you my birthday congratulations in advance, dear Eva. But I'll be sure to be writing to you soon again. May everything go well for you, in so far as that's possible these days. Affectionate greetings, your Trude.

It was the last carefree summer holiday young Arnold was to enjoy; he, at least, was apparently able to feel happy and relaxed. Neither of his parents chose to hide any longer their apprehension about the future. Alex's brother Poldi would later find refuge in Shanghai, where he would live out the war. One of his sisters, Charlotte, had married a certain Felix Tuch and the couple were living in Berlin. His other sister, Susie, also lived in the capital but had come on an ill-timed visit to their mother who had stayed, like Alex himself, in their home town of Poznań. They, with Trude and Arnold, would encounter their fate together.

'One has to wait and see what's coming,' Alex had written. It wasn't long before matters became all too clear. On 1 September the Germans invaded Poland. To the many who had experienced the mud-bound deadlock of the First World War, the speed of the advance must have seemed unthinkable, although not to those Poles who remembered the German occupation in the First World War. Only one week after her brother in London listened, no doubt with deep foreboding, to Neville Chamberlain's declaration of war, Trude found herself under Nazi occupation. The Germans took Poznań on 10 September. Six days later they shut down the Jewish schools and four days after that they closed the Jewish shops. From 29 November Jews were required to wear the yellow star, a decree which came into force considerably later elsewhere. On 1 December round-ups began; ten days later the Jews of Poznań were deported east. No surviving letters, supposing Trude had been in a state of mind to write them and any kind of civilian postal service had been operating in those weeks of military rule, indicated how she, her husband and their son experienced those devastating weeks.

Hitler had announced his plans for the region even before the commencement of hostilities. An anonymous secret note recorded the gist of his briefing to the High Command of the *Wehrmacht* on 22 August: 'Destruction of Poland in the foreground. The aim is elimination of living forces . . . Have no

pity. Brutal attitude'.[1] Within a month of conquering the territory, Hitler annexed it, declaring it part of Germany proper. In
an address to the central leadership of the Nazi Party in mid-October he spoke of a 'struggle' that would not allow of normal
legal or moral restraints. This was a clear reference to the ethnic
cleansing required to ensure the racial purity of the region and,
on a more practical level, to free up sufficient housing and
farmland for the resettlement of hundreds of thousands of ethnic
Germans. In January 1940 the area was named the Warthegau;
unlike much of the rest of occupied Poland it was considered
part of the Reich proper. Other regions annnexed included East
Upper Siberia, where the small town of Oświęcim would become
notorious as the location of Auschwitz. The justification was
that the Warthegau had belonged to Germany in the past and
that its restoration to the Aryan state was just one more instance
of the righting of the wrongs of the Treaty of Versailles. However,
the Nazis drew the border 150, and in some places as much as
200, kilometres further east than the pre-First World War
boundary, thus annexing a significant further slice of land. The
rest of Poland they had meanwhile signed away, in equally bad
faith, to the Soviets.

Poznań was situated in the western part of the Warthegau, near
to the Altreich; this proved a critical factor in determining its
destiny. Here indeed was *Lebensraum* ('living space'), a fertile
domain into which those ethnic Germans scattered throughout
Eastern Europe and the Baltic States, and to whom Hitler had
promised a triumphant return to the *Heimat*, could be brought
'home' and provided with model villages, farms and houses. Here
they could create the ideal of the pure and well-ordered German

life as envisaged by Himmler, who, in addition to his existing powers as head of the SS, had that October been placed by Hitler in charge of the newly established Reich Commissariat for the Strengthening of Germandom in the country's recently conquered domains.

It had not been the German Army alone which invaded Poland on 1 September. In its wake followed a series of *Einsatzgruppen* ('task forces') – that is, murder squads – of the SS; their brief was to arrest and kill. Notorious for the mass executions of hundreds of thousands of Jews, Soviet prisoners of war and civilians following Operation Barbarossa against the Soviet Union in June 1941, their activities in fact began far earlier, in Poland in the very first days of the war. Their relationship with the *Wehrmacht* had been under negotiation since the early summer of 1939. Concerned if anything with the risk of damage to its reputation, rather than with basic moral issues, the High Command of the army failed to object in principle to the aims and actions of the *Einsatzgruppen*, but instead communicated the need to co-operate to the troops. When some officers did protest against the brutality they were witnessing, they sometimes did so under the mistaken assumption that it represented 'local excesses'; they did not appreciate that such conduct was part of a comprehensive policy in which, by virtue of their lack of consistent opposition, they would henceforth be implicated. On 18 September a meeting took place between Heydrich, subordinate in the SS only to Himmler, and von Brauchitsch, Chief-of-Staff of the *Wehrmacht*, together with Quartermaster General Wagner, who was responsible for relations between the army and the *Einsatzgruppen*. When the generals were informed that there was to be a thorough clean-out of Jews, intelligentsia, clergy and nobility, their essential demand was that this should not take place until the army had been replaced by a civilian administration.[2]

On 21 September Heydrich instructed the heads of all *Einsatzgruppen*, who by then had already been responsible for the rounding up and shooting of large numbers of Jews and Poles, that the Jews were to be concentrated in larger towns as a preparatory measure for a subsequent 'final goal' which was to be kept 'strictly secret'.[3] The explanation to be given to anyone who dared to ask questions, and to the victims themselves, was that this constituted a reprisal for the 'decisive part' purportedly taken by Jews in sniper attacks and looting. The very absurdity of the excuse was itself an indication of the extent to which Jews were demonised. The locations chosen for the concentration of Jews were all on major railway lines, to facilitate further deportations in the future.

On 21 October Arthur Greiser was appointed head of the Warthegau region. 'The German is master in these territories, the Pole is a slave,' was one of his favourite slogans; Jews were evidently not even credited with the status of the latter. Five days afterwards he was made *Reichsstatthalter* (Reich Governor). A cold, cruel and arguably insecure man who sought to consolidate his position among other initially better-connected Nazi leaders, he cultivated his relationship with Himmler with whom he came to form a strong connection, and co-operated closely with the SS. During the war years he made a series of public statements which reflected Himmler's, and his own, ideology. In July 1941, bolstered by the *Wehrmacht*'s early successes against the Red Army which pushed the borders of German-occupied lands swiftly eastwards, he encapsulated in simple terms the core aims of Nazi policy in the Wartheland:

We are in a position here to create a genuine National Socialist domain. We have before us 'virgin territory' in which the National Socialist vision must be realised. What happens here is a groundbreaking exercise for the Reich and a visiting card for the German East.

The region, with its key city of Posen, was destined to become 'the parade ground of practical National Socialism', where hundreds of thousands of ethnic Germans would be resettled within the expanded borders of their ancient homeland.[4]

A year later Greiser wrote again:

For the settlers, next to God in heaven comes Adolf Hitler and nothing more. The Führer is to them the very content of their lives, because it is impossible to them to imagine that there could exist a man with the power to bring tens of thousands home from foreign lands and to provide them with farms to which they are driven by car, where horses, cows and pigs are standing in their stalls, where the farmer's wife finds the pot ready on the stove and the children the dolls in the toy crib.[5]

Convicted of genocide by the highest court in Poland, Greiser was hanged on 21 July 1946.

But how were these supposedly ready-made idyllic havens to be provided? In order to make room for the influx of ethnic Germans, the Warthegau had first to be cleared of a significant proportion of its local population. The final demarcation lines between the Nazi- and Soviet-occupied parts of Poland were established by the end of September. Returning from a visit to the central regions of the country, Seyss-Inquart, later to be appointed *Reichskommissar* in the Netherlands, observed that the marshy area around Lublin would constitute a suitable 'Jewish reservation' which 'could induce a severe decimation of the Jews'.[6] As Himmler put it in May 1940, the area would serve well as a 'catchment basin of Germany's racially unfit'.[7]

Meanwhile, on 25 November the *Rassenpolitisches Amt der NSDAP* (the Nazi Ministry for Racial Politics) submitted a report by Dr E. Wetzel, head of its advisory service, and Dr G. Hecht, its leading scientific officer. (Many of the senior Nazi officials held doctorates, not only the theorists but also the practitioners, including fifteen of the twenty-five top officers of the *Einsatzgruppen*.) Entitled 'The question of the treatment of the populations of the former Polish territories from the racial-political perspective', it analysed the numbers of Poles, Jews and other groups currently living in different parts of Poland, their racial composition, the dangers they posed to German aspirations and the options available for dealing with them. Poles, the report explained, were by no means to be regarded as all the same; everything depended on their racial background and their degree of political engagement. The number of Jews in Poland was estimated at over three million, with a further one to one-and-a-half million Polish-Jewish *Mischlinge*: 'The political-racial and cultural significance of this high degree of pollution of the Polish people through the input of Jewish blood must in no way be underestimated,' the report noted.[8]

A measure of discrimination was to be employed in distinguishing those Poles who might be assimilated to the Aryan race from those whose blood was truly alien, and between those who were politically active and those who could safely be retained for slave labour in the Reich. Particular attention was to be given to the intelligentsia; all political, intellectual, cultural and even sports associations were to be shut down. All groups suspected of espousing national aspirations were to be suppressed, especially clergy and teachers. The latter, particularly the women, the report noted, were brilliant exponents of 'Polish chauvinism'; they were to be prohibited from practising their profession immediately and without exception.

There was to be no such differentiation among Jews; they were all 'without regard and as speedily as possible . . . to be deported to the rest of Poland'. Surprisingly, the report suggested that Jews might in some respects be treated with greater leniency than Poles because they wielded no political power. Cultural organisations were to be tolerated. The 'Jewish language', that is, Yiddish, was to be permitted, but not the dissemination of printed materials in Hebrew. Jews and Poles were to be played off against each other. Because an increase in the numbers of either race was undesirable, abortion was not to be punished and contraceptives were to be made available. 'The health situation of the Jews is a matter of indifference to us,' the authors observed.

Whether the document had any direct impact on Nazi policy in Posen is a matter of doubt, since by the time it was submitted the major decisions had already been taken and the orders issued.

On 17 October Hitler had spoken to a core group of Nazi leaders about 'a hard racial struggle' through which the new territories of the Reich would have to be purged 'of Jews, Polacks and rabble' who would be dumped in the rump of Poland and left there to rot.[9] On 30 October Himmler ordered the Warthegau to be cleared of all Jews by the following February. On 12 November Wilhelm Koppe, SS and police chief for the region, charged by Himmler with responsibility for the deportations, issued detailed instructions for the removal of Jews and Poles. All Jews were to be included, as well as 'those Poles who either belong to the intelligentsia or who, through their national-political views, pose a danger to the process of Germanisation'.[10] In spite of the fact that Hitler himself had recommended that, with regard to the Jews, care was to be taken not to harm the economic interests of the Reich, there is no evidence that they were ever treated in the more relaxed manner suggested by the report of the *Rassenpolitische Amt*. Deportees were allowed to take only what food they needed for the duration of their stay in transit camps and the train journey, a single suitcase containing essential clothing and equipment, and up to 200 zloty per head, in Polish currency only. They were forbidden to take securities, foreign currency, precious stones, jewellery and objects of art. Jews were permitted to take only 50 zlotys per person.

Five days later, on 17 November, Koppe issued a secret instruction to the heads of all local councils concerning Poles and Jews who had reported for voluntary departure to the General Government; he alleged that they had only done so to save more of their money. Their names were to be added to the lists of those due for deportation first. In a further secret order the next day he gave instructions that the people on the lists were to be 'removed from their homes by the local police and taken to holding camps. Those involved are to be informed of their evacuation only when it actually takes place. But they should be allowed time to find and pack those items they are permitted to take with them.'[11] Two days after this he imposed the death penalty on anyone caught stealing from empty properties: by order of Hitler, the money and possessions of deported Poles and Jews were now officially the property of the German Reich. Nowhere did such threats prove sufficient to preclude local 'initiatives'.

In the meantime a number of key measures had already been put in place. Following Heydrich's instructions at the end of September, *Judenräte*, Jewish Councils, were established. As everywhere else, they were intended as tools in the hands of the Nazis, a pernicious way of making its own leadership an instrument of torment to the Jewish communities over which it was forcibly appointed. Economic measures followed swiftly: boycotts, fines, the requirement to register possessions, the confiscation of businesses and wares. Jews were prevented from withdrawing more than 100 zloty per week from banks; shares and other accounts were frozen and access to safe-boxes denied. The whole process of dispossession and exclusion, which was to unfold slowly over the following three years around Sophie and Josef in Czechoslovakia, overtook Trude and her family in less than three months.

Deportations began on 1 December 1939. People were taken from their homes without warning, during the night or at dawn, to prevent any chance of escape and to deny them the opportunity to conceal their valuables. They were given between twenty minutes and an hour to prepare for leaving.

On 11 December the Jews of Posen were taken to the transit camp at Glowna where their luggage was confiscated; two days later they were deported to the General Government, the central area of Poland under the leadership of Hans Frank. The names of Alex, Gertrude and Arnold Peiser appeared on a list of those travelling in 'Wagon One'; the document was not dated. Nothing in their previous lives could have prepared them for such a journey; for most of the deportees it entailed enduring two, three or more days locked into unheated cattle wagons without food or water and with outside temperatures down to −30°C. Even the local officials who had to deal with the victims along the route complained to the Nazi leadership; not, however, out of compassion, but because they could not cope with the consequences:

The deportees had been locked in cattle cars for as many as eight days, without even the opportunity to remove their human waste. Owing to the extreme cold, one train arrived with over 100 cases of frostbite. Other reports complained that the deportees had arrived without receiving food or drinking water for the entire trip, and had been robbed of even the most basic necessities.[12]

Approximately one thousand of Poznań's Jews, Trude and her family among them, were sent to Ostrów Lubelski, near Lublin in the east of Poland. Small and remote, the town was many miles distant from the nearest railway station. There wasn't even a proper road; access was by means of horse and cart, or on foot.

The town had formerly enjoyed a rich and varied Jewish life, but this was destroyed in the opening weeks of the war. As one survivor, who fled but later returned, recalled:

The town looked very different from that which I had left. It was desolate – the shops were empty, broken doors and windows, and pieces of glass were strewn about the streets. Two days before my arrival home, the local Poles, armed with pitchforks and axes, had attacked the Jewish shops, destroying them and looting whatever they could.[13]

Mischa Eckhaus, who grew up in the town, vividly remembered the arrival of the deportees:

One Saturday morning, early, the Germans brought a carload of Jews from Poznań to Ostrów Lubelski. They broke our hearts with the stories of their sufferings on the journey. As the trains did not reach our town, these Jews had been made to walk the remaining 10 kilometres on foot. The road was very rough and all those men, women and children who for some reason couldn't walk were shot by the Germans. Those who had the privilege of reaching our town were worn-out from the beatings, hardly caring what happened to them. When the Gestapo arrived, a few Poles pointed out the wealthier Jews and helped to 'organise' a contribution of money, jewellery and other valuables.[14]

Mischa's wife Bronia was likewise unable to forget the horror of what she had witnessed:

Thousands of tortured, exhausted victims were brought to the already overcrowded ghetto in Ostrów Lubelski, where they were cramped together, condemned to hunger, cold and disease. Death in all its shocking forms was their fate. There are no words to describe their sufferings, to tell about the anguish of those people.

While all of Poznań's Jews and its Polish intelligentsia were being deported east, another group of people was also being 'removed' from the region. From October 1939 onwards patients were secretly taken from institutions for people with mental illnesses. Many were simply shot in the surrounding forests; others were brought to Fort VII, part of the nineteenth-century fortifications of the city and a convenient location in that it possessed extensive barracks and was well hidden from public view. The systematic murder of these victims, deemed in the Nazi phrase *lebensunwertes Leben* ('lives undeserving of life'), lasted into the following year; among those killed were probably a number of Alex Peiser's former patients. It was not the first such 'action' carried out by the Nazis. The policy of exterminating such racially undesirables had been established on Hitler's direct orders not later than the previous summer. A special unit had been formed under the directorship of his personal physician, Dr Karl Brandt; it was referred to cryptically as T4, an allusion to its address on the capital's prestigious Tiergartenstrasse. Though at this point the personnel responsible for the killings on the outskirts of Poznań functioned independently, key members of the T4 staff would subsequently be moved to both Poznań and Lublin. As the scholar Michael Alberti noted, 'Nowhere was the link between the so-called "euthanasia" programme and the beginning of the genocide of European

Jewry so clear as in the Warthegau.'[15] The killings at Fort VII were carried out by means of poison gas; carbon monoxide remained the preferred medium, but experiments may also have taken place with Zyklon-B.

Meanwhile the *Treuhand-Stelle Posen* had been created for the orderly appropriation of the money and possessions of deportees. On 15 April 1940 the last Star of David was ceremonially removed from the town's synagogue, where my mother's mother, by her own confession, used to ask challenging questions about God and religion of the patient rabbi. The beautiful building, too majestic even in Nazi eyes simply to destroy, was turned into a public swimming pool, which it remains to this day. Photographs of a concert of Jewish music recently held on the premises as a memorial tribute showed the audience seated around the pool, at the far end of which stood a Menorah in surreal testament to a past which the building's new function was unable entirely to conceal.

The city as my great-grandparents had known it so well, where they and their children had lived and practised as Jews for a quarter of a century, had ceased to exist.

No letters from Trude survived from September 1939 until December 1940, when she was finally able to send a detailed report about her changed circumstances to New York. Even then, there must have been a great deal which it was simply not possible for her to describe: the sudden impact of the arrival of the Germans; how Alex was dismissed from his post; how they were driven from their home; whether their possessions were stolen before, during, or after their enforced departure; what they packed; the nights in the transit camp; the journey to Ostrów Lubelski. Except for that single list, which numbered them among those allocated to Wagon

One, I was unable to discover any documentation whatsoever relating to their fate, or to that of their home and possessions in Poznań. The house itself was not destroyed; a picture from Google Earth shows it still today as a beautiful and imposing building.

The fortunes of the city's Polish intelligentsia offer some indication of what became of the homes of the town's Jews after they had been deported. Jan Karski was sent to Poznań on behalf of the Polish Underground at the close of 1939. Later in the war he was taken in secret into the Warsaw Ghetto and to a concentration camp, before being smuggled out of occupied Europe and brought to London and Washington to testify to the free world about what he had witnessed with his own eyes. His contact in Poznań explained to him that the entire intelligentsia and every Pole who owned property had been expelled from the city. Members of the middle class who did not register as *Reichs-* or *Volksdeutsche* were imprisoned without warning: 'Peasants, workers, and artisans receive a sudden notice to be ready to evacuate their homes within two hours. They are permitted to take 10 pounds of food and linen. Their homes must be cleaned and put in good order for their German successors and all their possessions must be abandoned to the new tenants. Police have often ordered children of peasants to make bouquets of flowers and place them on tables and thresholds.'[16] Nothing was to be lacking when the ethnic Germans arrived at their perfect Aryan abodes. There could be little reason to suppose that the house which had belonged to the Peisers would have been treated any differently; some ethnic German family would have been cordially invited to occupy it as their own. What they would have made of the Hebrew books, ritual objects and scrolls on the doorposts enjoining them to 'love the Lord your God with all your heart' who could know? Or perhaps these objects, in contrast to innocuous children's toys, would have been disposed of before their arrival.

Trude, Alex and Arnold must have been terrified and bewildered by the fate which engulfed them. The sheer speed with which the Nazi conquest overtook them and shattered their lives must have made what befell them all the more frightening and confusing. Yet when she did eventually write, Trude presented a picture of remarkable composure. The family had managed to regroup and settle down to a very different and far more basic, but for the time being seemingly stable, existence. Somehow, they were coping. As Regina wrote in her first letter of 1941, relaying the information to Ernst in New York, 'Thank God we're getting good reports from the dear Peisers.' Remarkably, they had found the resources to re-establish themselves and keep going. They appeared to have food, fuel, acquaintances, even books to read and, most significantly, the hope that matters might yet improve. As Trude would write to her brother towards the close of 1940, 'One just has to take care to keep oneself healthy.'

Alex had even been able to resume his work as a doctor. I ordered a copy of the *Yizkorbuch*, the memorial volume published in Israel by survivors from the town, hoping that there would be some reference to a doctor who had arrived with the refugees from Poznań at the close of 1939 and begun to serve the local population. Sadly, there was no mention of him whatsoever. The only evidence of how the family managed to survive lay in references in the letters of Regina and Sophie and the two reports Trude herself managed to send to Ernst in New York.

Had the family not been deported to eastern Poland but

remained in the Warthegau, they might have fared even worse. The Nazi policy of mass deportations was soon to prove a failure; it simply wasn't possible to transport a sufficient number of people fast or far enough to make space for the new Germany envisaged by Hitler and Himmler. The recently appointed Governor-General of the General Government, Hans Frank, didn't want any more Jews in his territories either. In a discussion with regional Nazi leaders in November 1939 he declared that it was 'a pleasure finally to be able to lay hands on the Jewish race. The more that die, the better.'[17] He eventually even managed to prevail upon Himmler to stop sending any additional Jews into the lands under his control. Meanwhile he would have to be patient; although there had been massacres, the systematic killing by the thousand lay in the future.

From the Nazi point of view, the considerable numbers of people deported still did not suffice to free up enough accommodation to enable the ethnic Germans headed west towards the promise of a new Germanic Eden to be resettled quickly enough. This led to the joke that the region should have been called not the Warthegau, but rather the 'Warte-gau', the land of endless waiting. Dispossessing the victims of all they owned prior to transporting them east also proved an error. The regional authorities in whose domains they were in effect dumped without any means of support did not know what to do with so many destitute people who had nowhere to live and no money to buy even the most basic provisions. In Kutno, spotted fever broke out among the 6,500 Jews confined in the buildings of a former sugar factory; the fear among the local Nazi echelons was that it would not be possible to contain future epidemics among the Jews, who therefore constituted a health risk to the entire population. That

October, Goebbels visited the ghetto in Lodz, the largest city in the Warthegau with over a hundred and sixty thousand Jews, and noted in his diary that:

These are no longer people. They're animals. That's why it's not a humanitarian but a surgical issue. We have to make incisions here and radical ones at that.[18]

Clearly, a different solution had to be found to the Jewish problem. It would prove to be an enterprise which would once again bring together the talents of Himmler, Heydrich, Greiser and Koppe, and what was tested out in the Poznań region would impact sharply on the course of Nazi policy throughout occupied Europe until the end of the Thousand Year Reich.

Ernst and Eva had been in London for just eight months when Britain declared war on Germany. For them, as for tens of thousands of Jewish refugees from Germany who had found shelter across the Channel, the news must have evoked complex and contradictory feelings. Appeasement was finally at an end; Britain and France had summoned the will to counter Nazism in the only manner Hitler understood, by force of arms. The vast majority of Jewish refugees of military age longed to join up and fight in the Allied cause, a fact that it took many among their hosts a considerable period of time to appreciate. On the other hand, what would now become of their relatives trapped in Nazi-occupied Europe? Many exiles had arrived in England with one thought foremost in their minds: they may have been penniless, they may scarcely have spoken the language, but they were determined to do everything possible to enable their parents, their spouses, the rest of their beloved family, to follow them to safety. What now? What escape routes, if any, remained?

It must have been strange, too, for those refugees above a certain age to contemplate how in August 1914 they had thronged to embrace the German cause and had regarded England as the great and bitter foe. Many had served with distinction against the very country which had now, albeit partly reluctantly, become their new home.

Such feelings were also accompanied by a great fear. Was Britain really prepared for this war? What if the Nazis were to catch up with them here? Had they fled the Gestapo this far only to be overtaken by them now?

From the very day of their arrival in London, Ernst and Eva lost no time in trying to secure the papers for their passage onward to America. This, the wellbeing of their children and the safety of the rest of the family were their central concerns. Ernst referred to them all when he wrote to his mother just ten days after his arrival in Britain; the letter must have reached her as she was on the very point of leaving Berlin:

7 February 1939

My dears,

We plan to write to you too once a week. There's not much new. We're still waiting for a decision from the consulate. Hopefully you've already received yours. We had a detailed letter from dear Alfred in which he describes all the efforts he has made for you and for us . . . We've had good news from the children. They're studying well over there. I'm making slow progress with my English. We're taking lessons at Woburn House, but it's not enough. Sending you my heartfelt greetings, your faithful Ernst.

Eva added:

You can't imagine how much we wait for your affairs to be completed. Especially when one sees how slowly everything moves here. For the moment we're enjoying all the lovely things there are here. It's all really interesting. Hopefully we'll be able to do something for your nephew. It looks more or less like it. We're waiting urgently for news from Josef. Send us good news soon. One doesn't just bump into people in the street over here. Greetings and best wishes, your Eva.

Aside from obtaining the necessary papers to travel onwards, the top priority for Ernst was to learn English: 'More lessons were given in the Woburn House, a charitative institution located in Central London,' he recalled in the memoirs he wrote many years later for his grandchildren. Evidently his English never did become perfect. Woburn House was home to the offices of the German Jewish Aid Committee, which supported refugees arriving from Europe.

Ernst had his eye on the American medical exams: 'I got a book with which I could prepare for the New York State Licence examination,' he recalled. But he was keeping his options open: 'In the Zionist club they started to give lectures about medicine, which I attended.' As ever, he made the best use of his time, visiting the nearby British Museum and enjoying its treasures, including 'a large collection of old Hebrew manuscripts and books'.

Meanwhile the expiry date on his temporary permit for Britain was growing ever closer; Ernst pursued the issue of his visa for the States with urgency. On receipt of a prompt reply to his request that his papers be transferred from Germany to London, he wrote at once to the American consulate in Stuttgart, enclosing the requisite remittance of four shillings and four pence. Unfortunately he sent a postal order; this was returned a week later with a note stating that it was 'an international money order that should be forwarded'. Not until the London office had been sent a receipt showing that this had duly arrived would they be able to adopt his case here in Britain. By 17 February matters were properly in order and the American consulate general felt able to inform him that a communication was that very day being addressed to Stuttgart 'asking that your alleged registration be officially verified . . . and your name entered on the waiting list maintained at this office'.

Towards the end of the month Ernst wrote again asking how long, even in the worst-case scenario, he was likely to have to wait for his visa. On 31 March he was advised that 'A few months before your turn will be reached you will be given an appointment to appear here for a preliminary examination . . . The consulate general is unable to give you any indication as to how long it will be before your turn is reached . . .' Ernst is unlikely to have felt reassured.

On 1 April Dr F. S. Perles, Advocate, acting under instruction from Alfred in Palestine, wrote to the Assistant Commissioner for Migration in Jerusalem, renewing Ernst's application for immigration certificates, category A1, for Palestine. A1 was the so-called 'capitalist' category; thanks to Alfred's efforts, and perhaps those also of Eva's relatives in London, sufficient money had been placed at the family's disposal. Alfred was still expecting his brother to join him in Jerusalem at the earliest opportunity.

Nevertheless Ernst and Eva must have felt helpless before the grinding processes of a bureaucratic apparatus over which they had no influence whatsoever. 'Especially when one sees how slowly everything moves here,' Eva had written to her mother-in-law. Regina would have been well able to understand their frustration; was she not also waiting powerlessly for news of the progress of her papers? 'Could you not also write to the American consulate in Prague? Can't one do anything in London? Somewhere there must have been some mistake since you're still there,' Sophie observed in a letter of 7 June. Refugees have almost invariably been confronted by bureaucratic processes which, often without necessarily intending to do so, hindered their progress and allowed ambivalence and negativity towards them to prevail.

How long was 'a few months' supposed to be, and how many

of them did Ernst and Eva have before the British authorities insisted that they move on? The great fear was that they would be sent back to Nazi Germany. On 12 May the Home Office granted them leave to lengthen their stay in the United Kingdom for a further three months, so long as they did not 'enter any employment, either paid or unpaid, while in the United Kingdom'. In August their visas were further renewed, no doubt once again to their great relief, until 18 December. Two weeks after they obtained this welcome information, Germany invaded Poland and Britain found itself confronting other concerns regarding the foreigners in its midst.

But at least Ernst and Eva, unlike hundreds of thousands of others, were waiting outside Nazi-ruled territory. They must have listened with horror back in March to the news of the entry of German troops into Czechoslovakia; hadn't Ernst's mother travelled there only weeks before to flee the dangers of Berlin? Why hadn't her papers come more quickly? If only they would finally arrive now!

Meanwhile they received alarming news from their children in Switzerland. Things were far from easy for the girls, as Jenny well remembered: 'All the men were out of work. There was one relative who did have a job; he used to come every Friday and leave money on the table. They looked after us well; we always had enough to eat.' But it was the boys who were the immediate concern. Hans, who was just seven, was dangerously ill with diphtheria. Ernst obtained the necessary papers and travelled out at once; the local doctor was on vacation and in their anxiety the nurses had being using too low a dosage of the vital injections. He insisted they double it immediately. It was too late to save the life of another little boy, but Hans was soon out of danger, as Ernst reported to his hugely relieved wife. 'My beloved Ernst,' she wrote on 7 July:

Thank God, I read your letter with relief; I hope everything is OK and that I got myself so worked up without cause. I'm really happy if little Hans is well enough that you can have a couple of nice days. All in all it's been a hard year and one has to take what comes. I presume you'll write to me in detail about everything the children have been saying.

Four days later she wrote again:

Hans is quite right if he feels his mother should have come too . . . A letter arrived from the American consulate inviting you to a preliminary interview on 26 July at 2.45 p.m. I'm enclosing a copy of everything they've asked for. I don't know if you've got everything and what you think about it. Since you'll be back here by the 20th at the latest, there'll be a few days' time. But there won't be a lot. Hopefully the letter will also have an effect on the Certificate, since they usually both come at the same time . . . A long letter came from Mama. Things are still not entirely clear there and one just has to wait. I think you ought to write to Holleschau. You don't have to tell them everything. I've written that you're away. Write to Jerusalem and New York too. I've got lots to do. We made strawberry jam yesterday.

That interview at the American consulate was precisely what the family had been waiting for. But what did Eva mean by advising her husband to write to Holleschau yet not 'tell them everything'? She is unlikely to have thought that his mother and sister would have been hurt if they'd known Ernst had been on the Continent but hadn't visited them. They would have understood only too well why that would have been impossible, and were surely happy that he and his family were safe. Perhaps she simply didn't want to worry them with a report about Hans' illness. Yet Sophie and

Regina must have felt deeply alone, however little they acknowledged it in their letters.

Eva had been making strawberry jam, an excellent recipe for calming the nerves. Was Sophie able to make hers that year, I wondered, as she had done from the abundant crops the previous season? Was the fruit in Holleschau equally good that summer too? Was she even allowed to keep it?

Back in London, Ernst received a heart-rending request from a former acquaintance from Frankfurt, Julius Simon. The opening words of his letter said it all: 'We are still here . . .':

I have learnt that one can obtain positions for girls between 16 and 18 years old in domestic service and as tutors in England, without having to put down a financial deposit. As I have no other connections in England I am turning to you with the request that you tell me urgently whether such an opportunity might exist for our Margot. I am assuming that you already have a sizeable circle of acquaintances and that asking among them may prove to be of help. Margot is seventeen years old; she has benefited from a two-year training apprenticeship at the orphanage here in Frankfurt, as you presumably know. I would be most grateful to you if you would stand by me and help me. To this end I am enclosing a testimonial and a photograph.

The character reference was provided by the director of the Jewish Orphanage, J. Marx. He probably spent every night writing such letters, following long days devoted to caring for the desperate children in his charge:

Miss Margot Simon, born on 24 October 1922 in Bisses, was employed in our household during the period from 14 June 1937 until 31 March

1939. It gives us particular pleasure to say that we were entirely satisfied with Miss Simon's hard work and achievements. She had occasion during her time with us to study all aspects of housekeeping, an opportunity of which she made every effort to take full advantage. During her stay she was always punctual, honest, conscientious and reliable in performing the tasks allocated to her.

There were just three weeks left before war was declared; it is unlikely that Margot ever made it across the seas to Britain. She almost certainly perished.

There was no record of the outcome of Ernst's interview at the American consulate. Perhaps, with hostilities clearly imminent, it was postponed. When, on 3 September, Neville Chamberlain announced that Britain was at war, Eva and Ernst found themselves labelled as 'enemy aliens' on foreign soil. In Germany they had been outcasts because they were Jews; in Britain they were threatened with being cast out because they were Germans. There were an estimated 80,000 'enemy aliens' in Britain at the outbreak of war. The government set up special tribunals to examine and classify them in one of three possible categories: 'A' was for those deemed a high security risk, 'B' for doubtful cases and 'C' for those judged to represent no risk at all. The greatest number, over 64,000, fell into the third group. Of these, 55,000 were refugees from Nazi oppression, the vast majority Jewish.

Ernst accordingly received a request from F. Narborough, Secretary of the Aliens Tribunal No 12 in the Metropolitan Police Area, to attend the tribunal appointed 'to examine the position of all Germans and Austrians over the age of 16 in this country, and to consider which of them can properly be exempted from internment and which of those exempted from internment can be exempted also from the special restrictions which are imposed by the Aliens Order on enemy aliens . . .' The hearing was scheduled for 6 October at 10.30 a.m. at St Michael's Parish Hall in Golders Green, round the corner from where I grew up. Ernst was allowed to bring with him a British subject who was either 'his employer or who has known him well and has been resident for a long time'. To his and Eva's relief, he was duly classified as category 'C'.

C2W6

METROPOLITAN POLICE

Golders Green Station,

To Mr. Ernst FREIMANN, Finchley Road,N.W.11.

3, Sneath Avenue,

Golders Green, N.W.11.

5th October, 1939.

Tribunals have been appointed by the Secretary of State to examine the position of all Germans and Austrians over the age of 16 in this country, and to consider which of them can properly be exempted from internment and which of those exempted from internment can be exempted also from the special restrictions which are imposed by the Aliens Order on enemy aliens, *i.e.*, the restrictions on travelling without a travel permit, on change of residence without the permission of the police, and on the possession without a police permit of certain articles including motor cars, cameras, etc.

Your case will be considered by the tribunal sitting at

St. Michael's Parish Hall,

The Riding, Golders Green Road, N.W.11.

You should attend there on 6th October, 1939, at 10.30 am and you should bring with you your Police Registration Certificate., and your Passport.

Letter summoning Ernst to appear before the Aliens Tribunal.

Ernst would not have been able to take an employer with him since he was specifically forbidden to accept any form of work. However, with war ever more imminent, the Medical Department of the Central Office of Refugees in Bloomsbury House had written to him at the end of August to say that 'The Home Office Authorities have given us to understand that in the event of a national emergency the foreign doctors living in this country without right to practise may be allowed special concessions in view of their professional skill and experience.' Ernst immediately offered his services and received a reply from the Home Office confirming that his application had 'accordingly been sent to the British Medical Association'.

Meanwhile Eva had travelled to Cambridge to help relatives who had been evacuated from London with their children on the outbreak of war. They rented a large house, paid for by subletting rooms to Jewish students for whom they also provided meals. Ernst and Eva were needed to help out; they found a place nearby belonging to a professor of botany who had created a beautiful garden with many rare herbs. It became for them a peaceful haven amid their wanderings, one they would deeply miss in the hubbub of New York. Some fifty years later, when I met Ernst and we spoke about Cambridge, he wistfully recollected how 'we had a house there with a lovely garden'.

Early in 1940 Ernst and Eva were finally able to bring their children to join them in England. 'The daughter of the President of Switzerland was a nun; she travelled with us by train through France. There was bombing on the way,' Jenny recalled, although this was months before the German invasion of France. 'Mummy came to meet us off the boat, but for security reasons she wasn't allowed to approach right up to the ship. So the captain, who didn't want to be left with four small children in his charge, took me as the eldest and walked with me down the gangplank to find my mother.' Among Ernst's papers in Jenny's flat I discovered the small pink ticket issued by the Chairman of the Port Emergency Committee in Folkestone, carrying the instruction 'Permit M. Eva Freimann to proceed from Station Entrance to Vessel on one occasion.' It was dated 14 February 1940; the family were reunited on Valentine's Day.

They were not as yet to enjoy many months together. First the failure of the Norway campaign and then the beginning of the Blitzkrieg against Holland, Belgium and France brought a surge in collective anxiety accompanied by a renewed fear of foreign agents in Britain's midst. Invasion was now an immediate threat. Subject to considerable public pressure about the dangers of a fifth column, the government took the decision to intern all enemy aliens, including those in category 'C' previously considered as presenting no form of risk. 'Now we were not Jews any more, but Germans, and in May, 1940, almost all the male refugees were imprisoned,' Ernst recalled. It was only eighteen months since he had been freed from Buchenwald. But the experiences could scarcely have been more different:

We were taken to a barn-like hall in a small town near Cambridge. There a Colonel informed us that we would be served English tea; hot, wet and sweet. Most of the prisoners were professors or students. A few asked for the possibility to eat kosher. So they gave us new pots and we cooked some vegetables.

Ernst was taken via Liverpool to the camp at Ramsay Bay on the Isle of Man for which thirty or more houses along the Mooragh promenade had been requisitioned. A report in the local *Courier* described the arrival of the detainees:

The aliens were mostly youthful or middle-aged. There were practically no elderly men among them. They were a mixed lot: some well-dressed and bearing signs of affluence, others were of lowlier mien and wore canvas

shoes. One alien had his dog with him: another – somewhat optimistically
– was carrying a fishing rod. Another carried a typewriter in his hand.[1]

Ernst was promptly elected to be leader of one of the hostels, so,
as he remembered, 'I got a better room':

The weather was often nice. They let us go swimming in the bay. We
all wrote long letters describing all the personal reasons we had to be
released; all without any success.

He wrote to Eva almost every day:

My letters are a silent conversation with you and although only seldom
I find an hour to be together with you in my thought I always enjoy
this. Don't be worried about me and do your work and the education
of our children in the same way as before in calmness as if I were with
you. Whatever happens to us we will not be separated also if much land
and sea is between us. This rabbinic style is only the effect of often
exciting days when many of my people seek my advice. I think I had
never so many good friends around myself as now and try to help as
much as possible . . . In love, yours, Ernst . . .

But separation had become a distinct possibility. The turn of the
holder of position 61 on the Czech quota had finally arrived. Yet
Ernst was stuck on the Isle of Man; what were he and the family to
do? Eva sought advice from the Jewish Refugees Committee; the reply
offered a painful choice: 'We hope that internees will soon be sent
from the camp where they are stationed now to a camp near London
from where they will be escorted to the American consulate . . . You

will have to make up your mind whether you want to sail with your children without waiting for your husband or whether you prefer to remain in this country until he has received his visa.' Amid reports that the internees were going to be sent to Canada, they wrote to Eva again on the following day, advising her against assuming that they should wait to be reunited there: 'Actually we are convinced he will eventually be able to come to London to attend his interview at the American consulate. We also think you might have a last try and apply to the War Office for the release of your husband, on the grounds that it is too difficult for you to travel alone with four little children.' The committee were no doubt acutely aware of the terrible experiences of many of the refugees who had already been sent to the Dominions. The *Arandora Star*, which sailed for Canada on 1 July, was torpedoed and sunk with the loss of many hundreds of lives. Passengers on the overcrowded *Dunera*, which embarked a week later for Australia, were treated so badly by some of the crew and subjected to such appalling conditions that there was an outcry in Parliament and a number of British soldiers were court-martialled.

As if unaware of the dilemma facing his family, Ernst wrote again on 26 July:

I am very pleased with all the things in the suitcase. Old cakes are always better. I don't think that you are right that you will see me soon. Therefore it would be best to move as quickly as possible. It is a pity that you cannot see the view of the hills and the sea out of my window. I still have plenty of work and sometimes good medical lectures but not so much opportunity to speak English.

The carefully copied text of an undated telegram read:

Photographs at Consulate wire date appointment my coming
doubtful therefore sending papers for your proceeding

Whatever might happen to him, the family were to proceed to
the safety of the New World. Ernst's response was prudent: who
could know what the fate of the South East of England might
be should Hitler decide to invade? In the summer of 1940,
following the defeat of France on 22 June and with the battle for
Britain obviously looming, anything might happen.

In the event, the Refugee Committee was proved right; Ernst was
moved to Lingfield near London and was able to attend his interview
at the American consulate, near to which he also secretly met with
Eva and the children. On 27 August the committee sent them tickets
for their passage on the *Cameronia* from Glasgow to New York, with
advice to Eva on how much money she would need per person for
food and essentials during the voyage. The boat was scheduled to
depart on a Saturday. Jenny remembered how her mother hired a
boy who pushed their luggage to the quayside in a wheelbarrow with
her little sister Ruthie perched on top, since it is forbidden to Jews
to carry outside a limited predesignated area on the Sabbath. Safely
bestowed on board, they looked down from the railings and saw
their father being marched under escort to the gangway together
with a group of other detainees. The family was reunited on board
ship. On the top deck, Jenny explained, it was all well-to-do children
with their nannies: 'we were down below in third class'. The *Cameronia*
made eleven round trips to New York during 1940. Later she would
be the largest troopship involved in Operation Overlord in June 1944.
The voyage to New York took ten days; the ship in front of them
was torpedoed with the loss of all on board.

Throughout the summer and autumn of 1939 Sophie seemed determined to make light of her situation. In June she wrote to London in what sounded like a mood of cheerful resignation. After noting that it was pleasantly cool for the season, she continued:

Here everything is fine. On Sunday we were at the wedding of our Faniuka who was in domestic service with us for seven years. Now we have to manage with someone who comes every morning from six till ten and every afternoon from one till three. Once a week she stays till the evening and it's working out fine. One slowly has to get used to managing without help. For the moment we're waiting to see what's going to happen with Mama's certificate. Hopefully, this time it'll work out, since both the Agency and the British consulate are in touch from time to time. We answer everything immediately by telegram, so that there are no delays.

Aside from concerns about her mother, she made it seem as if life was continuing very much as normal. A mere few hours of domestic help each day hardly sounded like a major sacrifice. Nothing suggested any intimation of the privations which were to lie ahead, though the Nazis had now been in Holešov for three months and their calculated determination to suppress and control the population must long have made itself apparent. Evidently it was still possible for Jews and non-Jews to mix socially, or perhaps it was a mark of special affection, as well as courage, that Frantiska invited her former mistress to her wedding and that she in turn attended. It was to prove a deeply important relationship.

Frantiska and her husband on their wedding day.

That autumn Sophie wrote to Alfred, chiding him affectionately for his failings as a correspondent; the English language lacks an adequate equivalent for the German *schreibfaul* (lazy at writing). But she must have known that he had plenty on his mind. How the letters reached him in Jerusalem was not clear, since Palestine was now enemy-controlled territory. Possibly at that stage it was still possible to write via a neutral country, or maybe she had some channel through which she managed to send the letters indirectly:

We've heard nothing from you for a long time, neither through Walter, nor via Ernst's children. You are lazy writers! So far all goes reasonably well with us. Josef fell ill at the end of August; from the beginning of September he was in hospital in Zlin for three weeks and had an operation. He's been back home for two weeks; he's supposed to be looking after himself, but he won't rest and goes in to the office. We're well prepared for winter, heating materials, potatoes, etcetera, so we're not worried on that score. We're not faring badly; only we could do with peace, and letters from all of you, especially from Trude. We have lots of visitors, so the time passes quickly. Our dear Mama is always busy. Heartfelt greetings, your Sophie.

Their concern for Trude must have been acute, though it is unlikely that they would have had any clear idea of what lay in store for her, or of the increasingly sinister direction along which the Nazis' policies would lead them. But life was not entirely simple in Holešov either. In September a curfew was imposed on the town's Jews. They were also obliged to hand in their radios, isolating them from news of the rest of the world. Earlier, in July, Jews had been ordered to list all valuables including gold, silver, platinum and jewellery; the following March they would be required to place all such items in deposit boxes to which they were only granted access by special authorisation. In November all rentals owed to Jews were diverted into frozen accounts. This must have had a major impact on the Redlich income since one of the two town houses they owned was subdivided into eleven flats and let out to tenants. They may not have been aware of it at the time, but in September the Reichsprotektor, Konstantin von Neurath, in honour of whom the name of their road had been changed from Mazaryk Street, after the hero of Czech democracy, to Neurathstrasse, had submitted proposals for the complete elimination of Jews from the country's economy. Neurath himself would soon be replaced as Reichsprotektor of Bohemia and Moravia by Reinhard Heydrich, an altogether more brutal man, whom Hitler would entrust with his ultimate plans for the Jewish population. Meanwhile, step by step, regulations and procedures were put in place which gradually but remorselessly forced the Jews out of every arena of local and national civic and economic life.

In November Regina and Sophie wrote again: 1 December would be Alfred's fortieth birthday:

My dear children!

Today I want to begin my letter with hearty congratulations to you, my dear Alfred. Just because my good wishes may not reach you in time, they are no less sincerely meant. How very different it was when our dear Papa, may the memory of his righteousness be for a blessing, used to start a letter to you every Monday and we would take it to the post in the evening so that it would go off that very night. How everything has changed, and not even the one pleasure has been left to me of hearing regularly from all my dear children. The thought that you are all together is a comfort to me nevertheless. Soon there will come round for the second time the *Yahrzeit* of our dear good Papa, may he be an intercessor for all his loved ones. We now hear regularly from Trude and family. They're trying to think of how to facilitate their emigration, but they lack all means to do so. To each and every one of you, my dear children, heartfelt greetings and blessings, from your faithful mother.

Sophie added:

On Friday Bertl Blum came to take his leave; he's moving to where you are. Dear Mama could have had a cheerful travelling companion. Hopefully Walter will soon receive the certificate for Mama's immigration so that he can get the visa in Trieste. Hearty congratulations on your birthday, best wishes from Sophie. [Walter, Josef's nephew, had managed to find refuge in Italy. The rest of the family were hoping that he might now be in a position to help them.]

They were evidently unable to send the letter as planned, because Regina continued:

My dear children!

We've been a long time now without news from you. We're with you in our thoughts today, dear Alfred, celebrating your birthday and our wish for you once again is that you should be able to celebrate it in good health and contentment together with your loved ones, until you reach the fabled age of 120. I haven't heard anything from Ernst and Eva for a long time either. Frau Meisel told me that her nephew, the doctor who visited you, has already got a position with the government. Some people have all the luck. Herr W. K. is taking an interest in my affairs; it would be very nice if you could be helpful to him when he arrives. My dear children and grandchildren, receive my heartfelt greetings and blessings, from your faithful Mama.

It must have been an immense relief to receive news from Trude and to know that she had survived the terrible onslaught of the German invasion.

Regina's letter of November 1939, with additions from Sophie.

A short note to Ernst completed the correspondence for 1939:

We were very happy to receive your dear letter. Warmest greetings to you, Eva, and to the other children. Josef had an operation; he's back at work. He was well looked after in the hospital in Zlin and at home he's recovered fully. It's very cold here and we're heating steadily. We've got all we need for the winter. We're fine; it's nice and warm and we're busy and can still be of help to others.

Zlin was a rapidly expanding nearby town. The Nazis, however, chose the older and more beautiful Kroměříž with its fine castle as their local headquarters. That may have been a further reason, besides its fine hospital, why Josef was sent to Zlin.

As much as any in the years to come, those letters from the first months of the war offered an insight into Regina's spirit. She was of course concerned for her own future and anxious to reach Palestine. But even then she was less motivated by worry for her own safety than by the desire to be close to her beloved children. They, the grandchildren and the family, comprised everything which mattered to her now, together with the memory of her husband, next to whose name she had added the Hebrew acronym *zatsal* ('may the memory of his righteousness be for a blessing'), reserved for the dead whose lives had been marked by special uprightness and learning. How different it had all once been, she recalled, not just because she was fearful about the future, but in acknowledgment of the blessings which had marked the past. Sophie's last line to her brother Ernst could have served as their motto: 'We're busy and can still be of help to others.' Those affectionate concerns served to create an alternative emotional world, painful in the light of times past, yet something of a refuge nonetheless from the immediate cruelties of the present.

From the entire year of 1940 not a single communication from Regina and Sophie survived. For a long time I puzzled over this strange fact: how could there be so many letters from 1939 and even more from 1941, when Nazi power appeared invincible across Europe, yet not even one short note from 1940? Was there perhaps a further bag of correspondence left unopened after Alfred's death? His daughter Ruthie allowed me to examine every single bundle of her father's papers preserved in the high cupboard in their flat in Tel Aviv where they stored their old suitcases, but there was nothing from 1940 to be found. Maybe, then, there was a pile of envelopes in an unsorted box somewhere in Jenny's flat? On each of my visits to New York she had set out on the table a carefully prepared selection of well-ordered documents from various carefully organised files. But it had become too painful to her and her sister Ruth to continue to sort all the papers; there remained a number of files or boxes which they had not been able to bring themselves to open. I was keen to see them, though not at the price of causing them any further sorrow. Eventually, on my fourth or fifth visit, Jenny placed before me a thicker file, the still-folded letters unarranged, the papers running into and across each other, exactly as they had been left for decades. Guided by a contradictory mixture of compulsive curiosity and reticence engendered by a kind of awe, I picked them up, gently straightened them out and read them one by one. Ernst, it became clear, had written to his wife from the Isle of Man virtually every day. My grandmother had sent long letters to America throughout the war. I copied them carefully; maybe here was something important about my father's life I had not known? There was the tiny pink ticket from Folkestone Quay. But from Sophie and Regina in 1940 there was absolutely nothing.

Yet it was hardly likely that no letters at all were written, and why should it have been harder to post them in Czechoslovakia in 1940 than it would become a year later when the Nazis were burning the steppes and racing towards Moscow? Until Pearl Harbour, America was officially neutral and, albeit via the hands of the military censors, post passed relatively freely. Perhaps Ernst was simply unable to save the letters during 1940? After all, he spent part of the year in internment, part in transit to America across an Atlantic Ocean treacherous with German U-boats, and the remainder trying to create the beginnings of a new life in the United States. But, given his and Eva's careful preservation of so much of their other correspondence, this solution seemed unlikely; had there been any post, he would have found a way to keep it.

On reflection, however, the answer appeared simpler; until virtually the end of 1940 Sophie and Regina simply didn't know where to send the letters. Britain and Palestine were both enemy territory; except via the Red Cross, no post could pass. Though Ernst reached the States in the autumn of that year, some weeks must have gone by before he was able to establish and communicate an address to which his mother and sisters could write.

How the long months of 1940 passed for the family in Holešov can therefore only be surmised by considering the impact of the Nazis' decrees, copies of which were preserved in the local archives in Kroměříž. In document after document there appeared the names of the three members of the Redlich household, Sophie,

Josef and Regina, as lists were compiled, property registered, possessions requisitioned and the free movement of Jews ever more tightly circumscribed.

From 1 March 1940 the letter 'J' had to be entered in the passports of all Jews in the Protectorate. On 17 August, all Jewish shops in Holešov were required to display a special sign. Jews were permitted to make purchases in Aryan-owned shops during specific hours only, from 10.30 a.m. until midday, and between 3.00 and 5.00 p.m. They were only allowed to withdraw small sums from their savings each week unless they obtained special permission. From 8 February 1941 Jews were permitted to shop solely during the afternoon. With supplies limited because of the war, they were not given access to the better commodities until all other customers had taken their pick and most decent lines were sold out. Obtaining basic foodstuffs became increasingly difficult. Throughout 1941 the Protectorate Department of Agriculture issued a series of proclamations precluding Jews from receiving ration cards for an ever-growing list of products: apples, sugar, vegetables, tobacco, preserves, and later, in the autumn, fish, wine, liquor, onions and garlic. It was presumably easier for Jews to find alternative ways of obtaining at least some of these items in the countryside than it would have been in Prague. So long as they were not denied access to their land Sophie and Josef would have grown fruit and vegetables of their own. But the net was being drawn tighter all the time. From the end of October the Jews of Holešov were forbidden to enter cafes, bars, swimming pools and other public places.

The measures which must have had the deepest impact on the household, at least in the initial years of the German occupation, concerned Josef's business. The firm of Adolf Redlich was founded in 1866 and produced liquors and spirits. In 1939 it had four employees. As part of the Aryanisation of Jewish enterprises in Czechoslovakia, the Economics Ministry of the Reich had decreed as early as the spring of 1939 that all Jewish companies not due for closure were to be placed under German management. A local report dated 20 January 1940 advised that, since 'Adolf Redlich's Son', as it was called after the death of Josef's father, was the only business of its kind in the region and supplied the entire locality with alcohol, it should be allowed to remain open. Henceforth, however, it was to be placed under the directorship of a certain Dr Kurt Uher, whose brief was no doubt to turn its profits over to the Nazi state (in the event that they weren't embezzled before reaching Berlin). The company letterhead now contained an extra line, explaining that the firm was '*unter treuhänderische Leitung*'. The first time I saw the notepaper I mistakenly assumed this to mean that the enterprise was sufficiently successful to require the employment of a manager. Only later did I realise that what the added phrase actually indicated was that the business had been taken over by a Nazi appointee. The note was dated 28 September 1942, by which time the manager was a certain Hans Hutler, resident at the Hotel Viktoria in Zlin. It was a handwritten instruction to the Jewish community of Holešov, requiring them to address all future correspondence concerning the business to him and him alone.

The previous year there had been some confusion about the calculation of the taxes owed by Josef. The Jewish community of the nearby town of Prosnitz wrote to him on 9 February 1941 questioning his tax return. In its view, the estimated valuation of 184,000 kroner for the business was much too low; other important figures, such as the taxable value of Josef's properties, and of the family jewellery, were entirely missing. Further, whereas in 1939 the profits had been declared as 57,000 kroner, in 1940 they had apparently gone down to 30,000 kroner, a fact which in its view demanded an explanation. Josef evidently replied that his 'manager' Dr Kurt Uher was withholding all information from him. The Jewish community of Prosnitz therefore wrote again, though the surviving document did not indicate to whom, repeating its complaint that the figures provided were too low and that the true value of Josef's assets was not less than one million kroner. The sum of 13,120 kroner paid to the community in taxes was therefore far too small.

The leaders of the Prosnitz congregation may have been concerned because Jewish communities were funded by a percentage of the income tax of their members; it would therefore have seemed to them that they were being deliberately starved of money. But the chief fact emerging from this correspondence was that Josef was now totally excluded from the running of his own business, a situation which must have been galling in the extreme, since the enterprise had been operating successfully for over seventy years and represented the achievement of two generations of his family. Yet the letters from 1941, in none of which did so much as a single sentence in Josef's own hand appear, suggested that he was still 'very busy' and working hard. Perhaps he had won the dubious privilege of being admitted as an employee to work in the business of which he was in fact the owner.

The enactments which affected the family most intimately, and

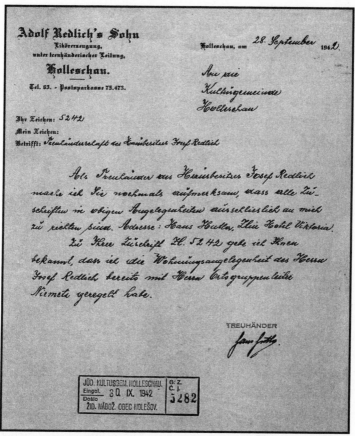

Josef's business, Adolf Redlich's Sohn, came under German management from 1940 onwards. This note, from Hans Hutler, instructed the Jewish community in Holešov that he was now the sole contact.

which would ultimately prove the most sinister, concerned the regulation of living space. On one list after another, most unfortunately undated, were recorded in great detail the properties owned or occupied by Holešov's Jews. The Redlichs possessed two houses, number 2 Freiherr von Neurathstrasse, as the street was called under Nazi occupation, which they let out to tenants; and number 3, where they actually lived. The former was subdivided into eleven flats, with thirteen rooms, nine kitchens, seven living rooms, one cellar, one garage, one stable for a horse, one utility room for doing the washing, and various shops. Part of the house served as a kind of bed and breakfast for visitors from the surrounding countryside who found themselves obliged to stay overnight in the town to complete their business at various regional offices. Like the liquor enterprise, it was decided that the guesthouse should remain open because, in the words of the German assessor, it had 'for many years been run by Aryan tenants', the current manager being a certain Maximilian Graf: 'Closing it down is not therefore recommended, and I suggest that it should be transferred to Aryan hands.' Number 3 Freiherr von Neurathstrasse, where the family resided, was also divided into two flats.

On 11 July the regional authorities in Kroměříž authorised the registration of all Jewish living space. A letter to the local Gestapo stated that the sender had duly enclosed three copies of the details of the houses inhabited by Jews in his district. It was dated 18 July 1939 and carried the stamp of the Holešov authorities. Five days later, on 23 July, the Redlich family was required by the SS to appear before them in person. Whether this was directly connected with the registration of their properties or had another equally sinister purpose was not clear. They duly reported at the required hour of 8.30 a.m. on 26 July and signed against their names in the relevant boxes. On 21 November the town council sought permission from the regional authorities to list all 'surplus' Jewish properties. The plan was initially rejected by the office in Kroměříž, but subsequently agreed in July of the following year.

Twelve days later, on 23 July 1940, the police made a register of the relevant properties. Two months afterwards, selected Jewish families were notified that they had to vacate their homes and move in with other Jews, thus establishing a network of 'Jewish houses'. A couple by the name of Fuchs and a certain Mr Steiner were resettled in the Redlich home. Thus began the process of concentrating Jews together, which would later prove of such assistance to the authorities in facilitating their deportation from the town. It also meant that all such 'surplus' accommodation could be made over to Aryans.

By the close of 1940 it must have been clear to the family in Holešov that at least on the physical plane their lives were no longer their own. Their inner world, formed of deep bonds of faith and love, must have been all the more important to them. Sadly, none of the letters, in which such feelings were no doubt expressed, modestly but strongly, remain.

More correspondence from Sophie and her mother survived for the year of 1941 than from any other branch of the family at any other period of the war. Though posted to Ernst in New York, the letters were intended for all their relatives in the free world. Direct communication with Palestine was limited to Red Cross postcards, with their maximum content of twenty-five words. Because Sophie and Regina were able to maintain regular communication with Trude, since they were all living in territories occupied by the Germans, and because it was almost certainly easier for them to send letters to America than it was for her, they made a point of including the news from Ostrów Lubelski. The correspondence thus reflected the concerns, hopes and anxieties of virtually every branch of the family during those months.

The year 1941 was the most disastrous year of the entire war for the Allies. The Nazis had consolidated their rule over mainland Europe and left Britain isolated. The Battle of the North Atlantic, which Winston Churchill described as the only theatre in the entire war which had made him truly afraid, was at its height, with U-boats causing huge losses to the Royal and Merchant Navies. Operation Barbarossa against Soviet Russia had begun well for Germany and, at least in the early weeks, it looked as if Moscow would fall and the Red Army suffer defeat before winter. Yet the tone of the letters from Holešov suggested that those branches of the Freimann family left stranded in Europe had somehow managed to develop practical and emotional ways of coping and only hoped, as Sophie wrote to her brother Ernst in early March, that things would 'stay this way for the rest of the war'. They at least were still in their own home, amid familiar surroundings and among people they knew. But Trude and her family had also managed to settle down; Alex had even been able to establish a basic medical practice which was helping the family to survive. 'We're happy still to be able to help others,' Sophie characteristically noted again.

Of course, Sophie and Regina would have been mindful of the sharp eye of the authorities; several of the envelopes bore the stamp of the Germany Military Censorship. They would no doubt also have sought to reassure their relatives, and perhaps also themselves, in so far as this was possible, that they were coping well and not in immediate danger. Nevertheless, even after making such allowances, what emerges from their letters is that Sophie and Regina were able to muster a remarkable depth of spiritual resilience. Regina's words especially conveyed a certain equanimity and wisdom, in spite of her frequent mentions of how deeply she missed her husband.

Though the letters were addressed to Ernst, Eva and their children, they made reference to numerous other relatives. These included Regina's siblings in 'B', no doubt Berlin. Greetings were frequently passed to Aron Freimann, Regina's brother, the outstanding bibliographer who devoted over three decades of his life to the curatorship of the Judaica collection in Frankfurt's municipal library, earning universal respect and a congratulatory telegram from the city's mayor on his sixtieth birthday. Yet when the Nazis came to power he was promptly 'retired' and obliged to hand over the keys to the office in which he had worked for half a lifetime. He eventually managed to find refuge in America together with his wife Therese, their only child Helene (Leni) and her husband Menny Rapp. They were extremely close to Ernst and his family, a source of great solace to Regina. On Josef's side was his nephew Walter, who sought assistance from his prosperous uncle, though the family in Holešov had hoped that from his somewhat safer location in Italy it would be he who could help them. More distantly related but closer in affection was Recha. She had been married to Therese's brother Felix, who died from diabetes at the age of 28, in the very year when the properties of insulin were first understood. She remarried in 1939, only to be widowed for a second time.

Sophie and Regina wrote to Ernst in New York three times during January.

8 January 1941

My dear ones!

There's been a long gap since we last had news of you. We hope you're well and getting on with your work in peace. I'm in the habit of answering every letter immediately, because I know that they take such a long time. Your dear children will have settled down well at school and they won't be wanting for friends. Thank God we're getting good reports from the dear Peisers. They've enlarged their place with one more room and made it habitable, so now they are all together. Dear Trude wrote to me that they sent you a detailed letter a few weeks ago and wait longingly for your answer. After I've read your letters as many times as I can, I send them on to the dear children because I know you don't have much time. Recha hears from us often, which makes her happy; she writes that she's in constant contact by letter with you and the

Rapps. My dear brothers and sisters in B write regularly and provide me with the Jewish newspaper so that I'm always *au courant*. On Friday week we'll light the little lamp for our beloved Papa and, as they say where you are, wish each other long life. I must live through melancholy memories. May his noble good deeds protect you and all the children. I receive such warm letters from so many friends. One of the leaders of the congregation wrote to me that such a harmonious personality is very much missed in the community, because your Papa was a man who won the love and respect of everybody with whom he ever came into contact. You'll see from my handwriting that writing is not easy for me. I've got very bad rheumatic pain in my right arm; it's probably caused by the exceptionally cold winter we're having. But we've probably got through the worst of the cold. Next month the winds of spring will begin to blow. We hope to hear good news from you soon, also about Alfred, Ella, Wally and all our loved ones. Your faithful mother wishes you everything good with her whole heart. *Seid innig gegrüsst* (heartfelt greetings), dear children.

Sophie added:

We'd really like to hear from you every week but sadly it takes a long time now. Everything's all right with us and we're in good health. Dear Mama's pains are probably connected with the weather. But she works harder with one arm than two people with healthy arms, even though it's quite unnecessary. How's the raisin wine turned out? Rosehip wine is much better and certainly keeps well. You boil two and a half litres of water with one kilo of sugar and pour the mixture slowly over one kilo of dry hips. You then leave it in a warm place for six weeks and filter the wine into bottles.

Holleschau

17 January 1941

[five days after her birthday]

My dear ones!

We received your dear letter of 13 January, accompanied by the loveliest pictures of the dear children, and were delighted with it. The raw winter weather through which we all had to suffer is now largely over. The Peisers wrote that after the heavy snow they suffered a lot from the water. The roads are so bad that one sinks into the mud. But the wind soon dries the country out. They write that they are in good health and keeping themselves busy. I received very nice birthday letters from our dear family in New York as well as from our dear ones in B. I don't want to be reminded of such dates; they're too painful for me. I'm entirely at one with our beloved Papa, visiting him once a month, but in my thoughts I'm with him always – and the little vase with flowers always stands next to his picture on the night table. My prayer every morning and evening is that our good gentle father should protect you on all your paths and lead you to where you can live in quiet and at peace and free from worry. You write, dear Ernst, that in Cambridge you had a beautiful home with a garden; one should never hanker after what is gone. With God's help you'll be able to live a modest life in your new homeland . . . My dears, receive my heartfelt greetings with a hearty kiss to each of your dear children, from your faithful Oma.

Sophie added:

My dear ones!

We're absolutely delighted with the beautiful pictures, but we'd love to have some of you as well. Here everything is the same as ever. I'm at home a lot and, when I have the opportunity, practise what I've learnt. We often have visitors. Unfortunately I can't send you any samples of our dishes to taste, only recipes, but you, Eva, have more than enough to do. Everyone would be happy if I could travel again; sitting at home doesn't agree with me. Some of our friends are working in hospitals and sanatoria helping with the patients, prior to being allowed to sit the exams. I'll try to get hold of their addresses.

Heartfelt greetings . . .

Holleschau

26 January 1941

My dear children!

We were delighted with your dear letters of 19 November and 3 December, which arrived last week. We're content if we hear from you once each month as we know that the post is expensive. Last week we very much missed getting your news. In such sorrowful days, since we can't be together we want at least to hear something from our nearest and dearest. The Peisers write often, as do our dear brothers and sisters who were at the Heidereuter synagogue for the *Yahrzeit*. We visited the cemetery on Thursday here; we had the path to the grave shovelled clear of snow, which lay a metre deep. May your good father be a faithful intercessor for you and all the dear children. The dear Peisers are in good health, thank God; they've had their home sorted out and Alex writes that it's comfortable. They've had very cold weather and a lot of snow but by now the worst of the winter has been overcome and the spring is approaching. They still have some fuel left for heating . . . We sent congratulations to dear Aunt Therese and dear Lena on their birthdays; we always write by airmail and as our loved ones are often together you no doubt read our letters out and give our heartfelt wishes. We had a very detailed letter from Recha; we're in constant touch. Keep in good health, hearty kisses to the dear children, all the best to you and all our loved ones; your faithful mother.

Sophie added:

Your dear lines, as ever, bring us happiness. Since September my travels have completely come to an end. In November I made one trip to Gleiwitz . . . Since then I've been nowhere. There's been a lot of snow, but I'm not doing any sport as I get plenty of exercise around the house. Apart from that everything is the same as ever.

There was something about Regina's handwriting in these letters which puzzled me. As both she and Sophie acknowledged, her arthritis was getting worse, yet it was far easier to read her writing from Holleschau during 1941 than it was to decipher what she had written during 1938 and 1939. At first I could think of no cause for this strange fact. On the contrary, why, if she was suffering more during the cold winter of 1940–41, would her handwriting not have grown considerably worse? But when I looked again at the original letters I was struck by a possible explanation: the paper she had written on in Berlin was tissue thin, whereas the writing-paper she used in Holleschau was of excellent quality. Perhaps this had made the difference. Or perhaps she simply had more time to write slowly now, in her increasingly circumscribed life bound by Nazi decrees.

Regina's letters were full of thoughts about her husband. Her feelings must have been particularly intense at this time, not only on account of the many losses which she and the family were continuing to suffer, but because this was the time of his *Yahrzeit*, the Hebrew anniversary of his death, which fell that year on 18 January. Immediately after reflecting on how deeply she missed him, she proceeded to advise her son never to hanker over what was gone. It was as if she was also talking to herself. Her abiding sense that her husband's protective presence remained close to her and the children must have provided a measure of comfort, both then and afterwards.

The synagogue on the Heidereuterstrasse to which Regina referred was Berlin's oldest Jewish place of worship, consecrated in 1714. It was here that Jacob Freimann had served as rabbi from 1928 until his death. In 1943 it became the site of a remarkable demonstration. On 27 February the Gestapo conducted one of the last major actions against the remaining Jews of the city. The round-up included Jews in *Mischehen* (mixed marriages to non-Jewish spouses), a status which had previously protected them from deportation. The prisoners were brought to the administration buildings of the Jewish community, round the corner from the synagogue, where their partners, mainly but not exclusively women, gathered to call for their release. Remarkably, the protest proved successful, probably because the by then ailing Nazi economy was desperately short of manpower. Over the following days approximately two hundred people were allowed to return to their work, mostly as slave labourers in arms factories. The building was destroyed in 1945.

The limitations imposed on Sophie's formerly highly mobile existence were evidently a cause of frustration not just to her alone; she needed more outlets for her energies. Her note about the recipe for rosehip wine showed that she had been closely involved together with Josef not only in the management but also with the practical aspects of the liquor business. Apparently it was not easy to obtain kosher wine in New York in 1941, a fact I find hard to credit. Or maybe it was simply too expensive for them to afford, so she wrote to her brother and sister-in-law explaining how to make it for themselves. The formula sounded simple enough to warrant putting to the test, not so much to produce a supply of wine as to bring back to life something of the culture of my father's family.

Two letters survived from March and one from early April.

Holleschau, 9 March 1941
My dear children!

Yesterday your dear letter arrived and that always makes it feel like a holiday. I'm about to send off what I've written to our dear children in O[strów Lubelski]; I always enclose your letters, which makes them very happy. This week brings Passover; many people in Holleschau remember how we used to celebrate it in our home. You experienced a good childhood growing up in your parents' house. In the year of '35

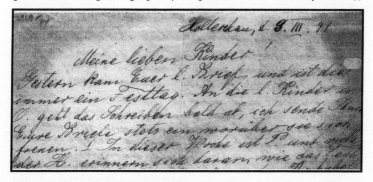

The opening of Regina's letter of 9 March 1941.

we arrived in Palestine during these very days; the joy of our dear departed Papa when he saw the land from the ship was indescribable. What has only happened since that time! You too must also be having pleasant spring weather and the darling children will be spending a lot of time in the park. The news that the dear children are thank God progressing well at school makes me especially happy. It's nice that you're often together with the dear Rapps and that your dear children are often with dear Ernst and Ruth. I can understand your feeling that you would like to have your independence, but that's how it is for most people, especially nowadays when the pressure of exams is so great. Dr Kohlhagen and Dr Herzog went a few years ago and it was easier then. My dear children, put your trust in God and everything will surely turn out to be for the best. Our dear relatives are doing everything they possibly can. The most important thing is that you're healthy and can live in peace and quiet. Letters are taking a long time to arrive in spite of going by airmail, so already today I want to send my heartfelt congratulations to darling Jenny on her birthday, with the wish that she should keep her charm and bring you, my dear children, only happiness. What you've told us about Alfred, Ella and Wally makes us happy. One's become so modest nowadays; one is content if only the family is healthy and able to keep itself going. Have healthy holy days and receive my most deeply felt greetings from your faithful Mama.

Sophie added:

Today I was in Bystritz . . . We look at the pictures of the children every day and think of you a lot. Don't give yourself any worries on our account. We're all here in our familiar surroundings, busy with our usual activities; we hope things will stay this way for the rest of the war.

We're happy still to be able to help others and to be able to send our greetings to Recha, our aunts in Berlin, Trude and my sisters-in-law, and many friends. Mama misses getting letters from Ella, Wally and Alfred terribly, and is always happy to hear your and Trude's news.

Holleschau, 24 March 1941

Today, on 23 March [the letter was presumably finished and posted the following day] your dear letter from 24 February arrived, so it took a whole month. I hope the dear little ones are well again; many people have got colds in the cold, wet weather. We often hear from Trude, Alex, and his mother and sister. According to what they wrote to us in their last letter, there's a letter to you on the way. Thank God they're all well . . . We were especially happy to receive the news from Alfred, Ella and Wally. Hopefully Robert will also be able to find something to do; I imagine he's helping in Adi's workshop. He knows a lot about precision tooling and used to make beautiful things at home . . . I'm especially grateful to the Rapps for the faithful interest they show in you, my dear children. There's nothing more noble and beautiful than family solidarity. We already sent our congratulations to your dear little Jenny in our previous letter. I'm only sorry that I'm unable to send a present. I like to remember how sweet the dear children looked in their pyjamas; the bright blue made their faces look so good with their blond hair. Keep in good health. I pray each evening and morning to our dear Papa that he should show you and all your dear children the right path and protect you. Have a healthy festival and receive my most deeply felt greetings and kisses, from your faithful mother. Heartfelt greetings to all our dear relatives.

Sophie added:

Meanwhile I expect you've received the recipe for rosehip wine, one can also use dried fruit. I imagine fruit and alcohol are cheap where you are, but Josef thinks it's better if you buy the essences ready-made; they always have the recipe on them. We're fine, thank God; we're in good health and we've kept nice and warm throughout the winter.

8 April 1941

My dear children!

There's been such a heavy snowfall today and a mighty storm; one gets such unusual shifts in the weather in April. We're delighted with your picture, dear Eva, with the dear little ones. Thank God that everything is once again in order; once again you've been through so much. I know how hard it is to make the children stay in bed and warmth is absolutely essential. There was a lot of work this week; but one really wants to help. We're getting good news, thank God, from the Peisers. They're all busy and in good health. Trude writes that she intends to answer your letter directly and then you'll be up to date. Write very soon. Your faithful mother.

Sophie added:

We've finished our preparations for Easter. The house is in order, the curtains washed; everything is gleaming. There's been enough work, because since Faniuka got married we haven't managed to get hold of any girls to help in the house. Most of our friends still have some. Dear Mama did a lot of work on the Easter gifts; we sent eight parcels, including to my sisters-in-law and Trude. Trude and her family got no foodstuffs, of that they have enough; it's only clothes and stockings and little things which one can't get there. The Peisers are gradually putting together a modest household and are grateful to be able to remain there for the moment.

A check against the calendar indicated that in 1941 Passover in fact began on the night of 11 April; the reference in the letter of 9 March was presumably a slip and Regina meant to write not Passover but Purim, the carnival festival which falls exactly a month earlier. But why in the later letter did both Regina and Sophie speak of Easter? After all, they would surely not have sent 'Easter gifts' to Trude. Was it concern for the censor? They were of course referring to Passover; why otherwise stress that the house was gleaming, if not in compliance with the strict rules concerning the removal of all leaven and the cleaning out from every nook and cranny of even the smallest crumbs? They were no doubt accustomed to receiving a lot of help with these arduous tasks from Faniuka, whose wedding they had attended in the summer before the war. Not only had they accomplished all this by themselves, they had also managed to send out parcels. In better years this would have been a large-scale operation; it was an ancient and enduring rule that no one should sit down to celebrate the festival of freedom without first ensuring that the poor too were provided with unleavened bread, wine and all the other necessaries for the observance of the holy day. But to have sent eight parcels in 1941 indicated that Sophie, Josef and Regina still had access to provisions, that they were acutely aware of the greater distress of their nearest and dearest, and that they found in these traditional tasks a sense of purpose which must have helped them cope with their own tribulations.

How much latitude did Jews still have to acquire foodstuffs, contact relatives and move unhindered within and even perhaps beyond their immediate circles? How isolated were they in fact from their non-Jewish neighbours? A list of the numerous decrees issued by the central and regional Nazi authorities would not in and of itself provide definitive information. Thus, in January 1941 residential phone-lines in Jewish homes were cut; a year later Jews were forbidden to use public telephones, and soon afterwards the phones of non-Jews sharing a household with Jews were also disconnected. But later in the year the Department of Postal Services was compelled to issue a warning which proved that some local people were helping their Jewish acquaintances to find ways to circumvent German orders:

It has been ascertained that a number of telephone-users are still permitting their phones to be used by Jews. The postal authorities wish to make it clear that such conduct is illegal and will lead to the confiscation of the telephone apparatus. All non-Jewish telephone-users are duty bound to refuse all requests by Jews to use their phones. Passing on messages by phone on behalf of Jews is also forbidden.

There were probably also other areas in which non-Jews quietly came to the aid of their former fellow citizens, such as access to foods which Jews were no longer officially permitted to purchase. Holešov lay amid fertile countryside; though to the east the ground soon climbed towards the foothills of the Carpathians, the town itself was surrounded by fields and the warm summer climate with ample rain was conducive to the growing of vegetables and fruit. Even before the war, the Redlichs had been sending poultry and other provisions to Berlin. Presumably they not only grew their own but were also able to come by different kinds of produce through long-standing contacts and connections.

The news from Trude also appeared positive; only the phrase 'grateful to remain there for the moment' sounded a warning note. Did the Peisers by now know that Ostrów Lubelski presented no more than a short respite on the downward spiral?

On 24 April Regina wrote to Ernst full of appreciation for his concern for the wider family across America. She praised him for 'giving your dear children an education so exactly in the spirit of our dear departed Papa'. Her letters reflected how deeply connected she felt to her children, imagining each of their lives from their point of view, empathising with their struggles and troubles despite her own, and saddened by the fact that she was unable to receive more regular news from them all.

A note from Sophie confirmed how important their garden was to the family:

It's always a special day for us when a letter from you arrives. I'm soon going to send you pictures of us, if we can't come in person. Everything's very behind in the garden because of the cold weather. We've got lots of violets and a few shrubs are in flower. This week we've brought some vege-tables on. I've now got a fifteen-year-old student cook; she's intelligent and hard-working. We don't have much to report from here. Life is quiet and we go to sleep in peace. We had no guests for Easter this year; people aren't travelling in these difficult times and one doesn't want to be going out in the evening. But one reads more, and there's enough work to be getting on with in the house and garden. Mrs Batscha received a ship's ticket from her daughter, for 24 May. Whether she'll be able to make use of it by that date is questionable, but we'll write to you then, when she leaves . . .

Unlike Regina, Helena Batscha did in fact succeed in reaching Palestine. After the war, Ella wrote about her and her family to Ernst.

An envelope containing a letter dated 20 May 1941 had stamped on the back: '*Geöffnet – Oberkommando der Wehrmacht*' ('Opened: Army High Command'). But the contents were innocuous enough:

My dear ones!

Your dear letter arrived yesterday – it was less than a month en route, the date you wrote was 24 April. We're glad that our letters arrive safely . . . It's a pity, Ernst, that you still haven't got the papers you need to sit your exams. Thank God you and the dear children are well, they're doing fine at school and you are happy with life as it's turning out for you. I can well imagine, dear Eva, how much you have to do; that's always been the way with us mothers who have such large families. Yesterday Boyka was ironing a large pile of laundry and she reminded me how many pairs of shoes she used to have to clean every day and how alongside the housework she had to feed the poultry and clean out the chicken run. All that was long, long ago. But how happy and contented we all were! We heard yesterday from the Peisers that they'd had news from Alfred via the Red Cross – twenty-five words – and they answered in the same manner. A while ago we heard from Annchen in the same way. Trude's letter contained sad news – her aunt Rosa in San Francisco died on 1 March. They'd placed so much hope in the good kind lady's help; hopefully she'll have remembered them in her will. Anna doesn't yet know about her sister's death. Poldi gave them the news.

. . . Although half of May has already gone by it's still very cool and all the plants in the garden are behind. I'm looking forward to being able to sit outside in the garden although the beautiful tree underneath which we always used to sit with dear Papa had to be cut down because it froze. Everywhere are memories which occupy my thoughts; my only desire is that everything should go well for you and all the dear children and that you should find happiness in how well the little, and not-so-little, ones are doing.

Sophie added:

Mama's ticket for the ship can't be renewed any longer and she's getting the cost of the fare and board back. We're leaving travelling for peacetime; then I'm going to need a whole year to visit all our loved ones . . . Today it's been raining all day; it's very good for the garden as we don't have to water. Dear Mama is in a hurry to post the letter, so Josef just sends his best wishes. He's very busy all the time and happy to be occupied as ever. My greetings to you and all our dear ones, especially the delightful children. With my love, your Sophie.

This then must have been the point where Regina finally gave up hope of being able to reach Palestine. Leaving Czechoslovakia was simply no longer possible. In fact, the Reich Security Office had been trying to place a total ban on emigration from Germany, Austria and the Protectorate since the autumn of the previous year. It might have been assumed that Sophie's reference to leaving 'travelling for peacetime' was written more in hope than in faith, but in fact she probably did believe, even at this point in the war, that through a combination of practical good sense and discretion she would be able to outlive the hostilities and survive to be reunited with the rest of the family.

A gap of two months followed. During that period the Germans launched Operation Barbarossa against the Soviet Union, attacking on 22 June with four million men, three quarters of a million horses and 600,000 armoured vehicles. It was the largest invasion ever mounted. In its wake began the systematic starvation of Soviet prisoners of war; unlike British and French POWs, they were not granted the rights due to them under the Geneva Convention and were often simply left without food and shelter to die of cold, illness and starvation. They too were *Untermenschen* (subhumans). Four separate *Einsatzgruppen*, special units with a remit to kill indiscriminately, were sent in behind the lines of the 1800-mile-long front and began the systematic murder of the Jews. The slaughter included everyone: men, women and children. Arguably the most terrible single massacre took place in the ravine of Babi Yar outside Kiev, where 33,771 Jews were murdered in the last days of September. Dr Otto Ohlendorf, commander of *Einsatzgruppe D*, testified at the Nuremberg war trials that 'the *Einsatzgruppen* had the mission to protect the rear of the troops by killing the Jews, Romani, Communist functionaries, active Communists, uncooperative Slavs, and all persons who would endanger security.'[1] A vast proportion of those murdered were Jews. In overall charge of these killing brigades, which came under the authority of the State Security Office, were Himmler and Heydrich. Hitler had asked to be kept personally informed of the so-called progress of the operation. The experiences of the *Einsatzgruppen*, together with those of the T4 unit responsible for the 'mercy killings' of thousands of people with mental illnesses and physical disabilities throughout Germany, would prove critical to the development of Nazi policy in finding the ultimate solution to their Jewish problem.

The impact of Operation Barbarossa soon made itself felt in Moravia, where units of the German SA celebrated their army's victories against the hated Bolsheviks by sacking and burning synagogues across the Protectorate. They were joined by local members of the Vlajka, or 'Flag', the Czech fascist party, who also often took the lead in initiating violence.

Nevertheless, July seemingly found Sophie in good spirits:

My dear ones!

We read your letters with great pleasure. We are doing fine; we're enjoying the weather and I sometimes make small excursions into the neighbourhood, wherever one can bathe. We've enclosed two amateur snapshots of us in the garden; unfortunately we don't look anything special in them, but the roses have come out well. We now get fish two days a week, a pleasant change. It hasn't been all that warm here yet and it rains and thunders a lot. But the fruit and vegetables are doing well all the same. We can't send you Josef's picture because he's come out double, but one will follow soon.

Regina commented appreciatively on how excellent a mother Eva obviously was, having read in the latest letters of how she had taken the children to Central Park to play in the splashing pool. She assumed a more sombre tone when she noted that, 'Today I went to the cemetery and prayed for the wellbeing of all the children and the family.' Perhaps she had particular cause to feel a sense of foreboding. The letter was dated 22 July; on the following night fascists set fire to Holešov's new synagogue, dedicated in a service conducted by her husband less than fifty years earlier. Due to the prompt and courageous action of one of the town constables and the firemen, the flames were swiftly extinguished. It was widely suspected that Vlajka supporters were responsible for the action; a number of witnesses claimed they had seen the son of the local leader, Alois

Cech Junior, in the vicinity. No one was ever apprehended and what happened after the war to Cech and his father remained unknown.

The Office of the Reichsprotektor did not support such locally inspired attacks on synagogues. This was not because it sought to preserve the buildings, but in order to ensure that whatever assets it was possible to plunder would be fed into the coffers of the Reich and not sequestered into the pockets of vigilantes and profiteers. An order had therefore been issued on 3 July, deploring the fact that:

Through misguided articles in the newspapers, certain elements are being repeatedly called upon to commit actions which, under the pretext of engagement in the struggle against the Jews, are motivated by personal and sometimes even criminal interests (such as the looting and destruction of Jewish property). However understandable the increasing rejection of everything Jewish may be as a result of events on the Eastern Front, the pursuit of a solution to the Jewish problem through more or less aggressive individual local actions must be restrained.[2]

Anger against all things Jewish was presented as even more 'understandable' than previously, because the Jews were held responsible for the evils of Bolshevism, against which Germany had just launched its valiant offensive. At any event, the instructions were ignored by local Nazis and members of the Vlajka.

The Gestapo took over the investigation into the arson attack on the Holešov synagogue from the local Czech gendarmerie; not surprisingly their efforts led to no arrests. Instead, on the night of 11–12 August, scarcely a day after the Vlajka congress in Prague where members were urged 'to finish what they had started',[3] the synagogue was set on fire again. This time it seems the Gestapo prevented the fire brigade from extinguishing the blaze and the building was destroyed. The attack came just a week after the fast of the Ninth of Av, which commemorated not only the sacking of the First and Second Temples in Jerusalem but the destruction of numerous Jewish communities across Europe during the Middle Ages. The connection would not have been lost on the town's beleaguered Jews.

Soon after the Velvet Revolution a film of the destruction of the synagogue was brought out of hiding and made public. At first it was thought that it must have been made in secret, as a testimony to the violence and destruction wrought by the Nazis. This was clearly not the case. The making of the film was entirely undisguised, indicating that it was produced at the behest of the perpetrators as propaganda footage of their successes in the battle against the evils of international Jewry. At one point it even showed another gentleman with a camera lining up his cheery subjects.

The demolition had been carefully planned; guards stood next to improvised fencing to keep the watching crowds at bay. Well-fed gendarmes clad in uniforms with shining buttons and capped in rounded helmets shared jovial conversations. A group of soldiers marched by, no doubt to join the forces tasked with breaking up the damaged but still standing structure of the house of God. Periodically, further pieces of the edifice collapsed, raising clouds of dust. A trio of Germans pointed laughingly at where additional attention was needed; individual soldiers as well as large groups of men armed with axes, picks and lengths of timber employed as substitute sledge-hammers hacked and smashed at the brick-work. A row of youths slunk by with the air of a gang anticipating the enjoyment of violence. Senior Nazi officers watched with smiling approval. It was impossible to judge the mood of the observers looking on in the distance. It seemed as if the operation continued for a long time; the synagogue showed considerable resilience, obliging the Germans to work hard at its obliteration.[4]

Two days after the assault, the town council of Holešov ordered the Jewish community to board up the ruins of the synagogue at its own expense and hand over any valuable metals left amid the debris. The damage was estimated at 900,000 kroner. A protracted row followed between the various Nazi offices concerning the disposal of the remains of the gutted building and the sale of such materials as could be salvaged from the ruins as well as the land on which the synagogue had stood. The question of who should pocket the profits from this miserable debacle dragged on into the following year.

A still from the footage showing German soldiers engaged in the destruction of the synagogue in Holešov. (Yad Vashem Photo Archive)

On the morning after the synagogue was destroyed, Regina wrote two letters. The first was to Ernst and full of family news; the second was to her brother Aron, congratulating him on his special birthday:

12 July 1941

Today on your special day, my dear brother, I'm with you in my thoughts. With the commencement of one's seventieth year of life one becomes young once again; one starts to count and after thirteen years one reaches the year of one's Bar Mitzvah. And so I wish that, by the side of your beloved Therese and united with your dear children and your children's children, you may be granted to count the years in untroubled health and happiness, free from all worries. Your dear children and grandchildren, as well as your many friends, are with you to celebrate today, but those who are far away also feel at one with you in your beautiful celebrations. I'm most grateful to your dear children for preparing such lovely days of recuperation for my grandchildren when they visited them in the holidays. My dear, righteous and good husband often used to say to me that your sweet children have a very special feeling for family and this shows itself in all life's circumstances. Keep in good health and receive, together with your dear loved ones, my most heartfelt greetings, your faithful Regina.

After adding her own good wishes, Sophie noted that:

We've experienced little heat this summer; there's been a lot of rain. Maybe there'll be a long and beautiful autumn. About us I can report that everything's fine; we're all engaged in the usual occupations and are always happy when letters come bringing good news of our loved ones from all over the world. Heartfelt greetings from your Sophie and Josef.

It must have required exceptional self-discipline to write in such a generous and warm-hearted manner on the very morning after the place which had been the focal point of their lives for decades had been burnt down. Or maybe it offered some degree of comfort to endeavour, at least during those hours they spent composing their letters, to live an alternative existence with a geography bounded not by immediate physical constraints but by the broad, embracing circle of family affections.

At the end of the month Sophie and Regina wrote again, noting how happy they were to receive an account of how the birthday celebrations had gone. One short sentence stood out amid the family news which filled the rest of their letters:

Sadly, we can no longer go into the house which dear Papa dedicated 48 years ago.

Paradoxically it was not the rapid progress of the *Wehrmacht* but the lack of sufficient momentum in its advance against the Red Army which was to prove the immediate catalyst of catastrophe for Czechoslovakia's Jews. On 18 August 1941 the Propaganda Minister Joseph Goebbels went to see Hitler to ask him to agree to the demand to remove all Jews from Germany; it suited Nazi interests to see in them a dangerous fifth column. As a first step, all Jews were to be marked out by wearing the yellow star. In response, Hitler reiterated his 'prophecy' of 31 January 1939, which he now deliberately misdated to 1 September, the day he invaded Poland, that if the

Jews were once again to provoke a world war it was they themselves who would be annihilated. It seems Hitler had been awaiting the defeat of Soviet Russia to make available some vast and desolate expanse beyond the Urals as his ultimate dumping ground for racially undesirables, where they could be left to rot and die of their own accord. But by late summer it was clear that there would be no swift victory in the steppes. Nevertheless, he made the decision to deport all the Jews of Germany, Austria and Czechoslovakia to the east. The logistical impossibilities which ensued from this impracticable policy would soon lead to even more brutal solutions, for which the moral environment had long been prepared by Hitler's repeated promise to 'remove' the Jews. Typically, he left it to others to determine the specific actions which would bring about this desired end. There were plenty of senior figures eager, in the accustomed Nazi phrase, 'to work towards the Führer'.

Thus, by order of Reinhard Heydrich, now officially appointed Deputy Reichsprotektor in addition to his position in the SS, from 1 September all Jews in the Protectorate above the age of five were required to wear the yellow star on the left side of their chest. They were also forbidden to leave their place of residence without special permission. On 11 September Josef had to sign a declaration concerning the newly forbidden objects, in which he confirmed that 'I was today made aware of the requirement to report the possession of all typewriters and bicycles. I acknowledge that, with immediate effect, it is not permitted to determine what to do with typewriters and bicycles in Jewish possession.' At first sight the two classes of object seemed to have little in common. Yet both offered access to wider horizons; a bike provided a measure of physical mobility while a typewriter facilitated the transmission of words and thoughts. The loss of both signified the further retraction of opportunities, another move in the closing of the trap.

Regina sent an uncharacteristically brief note during the week between the New Year and the Day of Atonement:

Holleschau

29 September 1941

My dear children! Tomorrow we will be preparing ourselves for the great day which I shall spend together in thought with all our dear children. Hopefully you'll have an easy fast. Do you have a long walk to the synagogue and who will be looking after the dear children? The solemn spirit of the [New Year] service in the 800-year-old synagogue was especially dignified and in accord with our mood.

Regina was no doubt referring to the old synagogue on Příční Street, known after its most famous rabbi as the Shach Shul. Built in 1560, it was destroyed in the great fire which ravaged the town, and reconstructed in the 1730s. It was extraordinarily beautiful, decorated in typical Moravian style with quotations from the prayers painted in deep colours on the walls and ceiling. The building survived the war. Neither the local Vlajka nor the Nazis considered it worthy of their attentions. Maybe it didn't contain sufficiently valuable building materials, or perhaps its unobtrusive exterior protected it from destruction. But the more obvious reason is that it had been sold off in the 1920s and the upper floor of the building had been turned into a private apartment. The main area below must have been re-opened specially for the prayers that autumn; half underground and semi-dark, its secretive atmosphere would indeed have been 'in accord with the mood' of the remnant of the community who prayed there that New Year.

Despite the generosity of spirit with which they entered into the lives of their family in the free world, Regina and her daughter must have been profoundly troubled and increasingly frightened. The simple New Year prayer, 'Remember us for life, O God of life,' must have penetrated their hearts with deep foreboding. Had they looked up to the windows of the synagogue, they would have seen written on the rounded arches the single word *Shema:* 'Hear'. Beneath it, each window frame bore a different biblical quotation: 'Hear, O God who alone dwells on high'; 'Hear, and send the redeemer of the poor.'

On 29 September, the Day of Atonement, Reinhard Heydrich demanded the closure of all synagogues and Jewish places of worship throughout the Protectorate. On 14 October, *Simchat Torah* (the day of the Rejoicing of the Law), when Jews would customarily celebrate the completion of the annual cycle of the reading of the Torah with songs, dancing, food and drink, the town council of Holešov duly carried out the order and closed the remaining synagogue down. The Nazis frequently exploited a cynically acquired knowledge of the Hebrew calendar to ensure that they inflicted not just the maximum physical pain but also the deepest spiritual suffering.

On the last day of September Sophie wrote to New York in her typically matter-of-fact manner:

My dear ones! Dear Mama always writes to you in great detail. I'm just making wine from rosehips for Easter. I'll write down the recipe for you, dear Eva. You boil up two and a half litres of water with one and a half kilos of sugar and pour the lukewarm solution over three kilos of rosehips, from which any pieces of stems or flowers have been removed. You leave the whole mixture somewhere warm for one week, then for three months somewhere cool, keeping it well covered. I always use a cucumber jar. The wine is then filtered and stored in bottles. It costs almost nothing . . . [one line in the fold of the letter is illegible]. Josef is hard-working in all matters, but I think that from November onwards his business will have come to an end. Dear Mama is busy in the household, enjoys being in the garden or going for walks, and is happy when she can give a lot away. Hopefully there's enough there. Most of all she misses getting news of the children in Israel and would love to receive new letters. On the festivals we thought warmly of all our loved ones . . .

By now Sophie had evidently mastered the art of keeping herself busy. Late September might seem a strange time to be preparing for Easter, that is to say, Passover; yet she would have had to start then if she wanted to have wine ready in good time which complied with the stringent dietary laws of that season. Or maybe it was a family tradition, a way of looking forwards by commencing the preparations for one festival the very day the previous one was over, a means of maintaining hope in the arrival of that freedom which the story of Passover faithfully promised.

There were no more letters until November. On the 12th the German authorities in Zlin dismissed the members of Holešov's town council and replaced them with Nazi officials and their collaborators. That same day they ordered them to move promptly 'to solve [the town's] Jewish problem'. This presumably meant deporting all its Jews. Almost certainly unaware of these developments, Sophie wrote to her brother in America on 25 November.

My dear ones!

Your two letters arrived at almost the same time. One of them came yesterday; the other, of 2 November, came today. Sometimes the post travels really fast. We're pleased that you, dear Ernst, have found an occupation, even though it's not at all in your line and doesn't bring in much money. But over there in your country it's the way things go; you start off shining shoes and end up a millionaire. You should have no worries or troubling thoughts about us. We're in good health and are making life as pleasant as these times of war permit. No one here has yet died of hunger. One occupies oneself with one's usual pursuits, helps where one can, and leaves it to the good God to worry. My birthday was very nice; I received many good wishes, beautiful flowers and homemade treats for the belly. In my free time I read a lot and sometimes also play bridge . . . When peace comes I'd love to come and visit you and see the city and the children. Hopefully it won't be too long; surely everyone in the whole world wants that. Warmest greetings, also from Josef, who's still very busy but will probably have more time in a fortnight, your Sophie.

Regina added to the letter the following day:

My dear children!

We are, thank God, in good health; nothing here has changed. You need have no worries on our account. Thank God, we're getting good news from Trude and her family . . . The sweet greetings of the dear children made me especially happy; so did the news that they're being strong and doing well at school. I stand by the view that, as our dear God has ordained them, so shall things turn out for good, let come whatever has been decreed for us. The day before yesterday we again received a Red Cross telegram of 25 words via Annchen from our dear children in Palestine, which I have already answered. Thank God they are all healthy and have sufficient employment, including our dear grandchildren. Keep in good health. I wish you, dear Ernst, every success. May we only have happy news to share; for that I pray and beseech God constantly . . .

Your faithful mother sends her heartfelt greetings to all our relatives.

Sophie and Regina were obviously concerned to reassure the family that they were managing at least tolerably well. Of the letters they in turn received from America not a single line survived, though I found it hard to abandon the fantasy that maybe they were still there, in some forgotten box sequestered in a dust-covered corner of the attic where Sophie hid them in case they should return, or in the event that their relatives should come to look for them after the war. Whatever knowledge of what was actually happening in Nazi-dominated Europe and whatever resultant anxieties those letters might have conveyed is hard to surmise, since Ernst and Eva would also have been wary of endangering their loved ones by attracting the attentions of the censor. But Sophie especially was at pains to be positive. Her birthday, on 11 November, may have been nothing like Trude's in the years before the war, but it still seemed to have been something of a celebration, with food and flowers, unless that was a fiction designed to set Ernst's mind at rest.

Definitely untrue was Sophie's assessment that 'everyone in the world' wanted peace. Less than two weeks later, on 7 December, the Japanese Navy attacked the American fleet in Pearl Harbour. Four days later Hitler declared war on the United States of

America. The postal connections between Axis Europe and North America were now broken. For Sophie and Regina their one relatively unimpeded avenue of communication with the family in the free world had been shut down. For all her inner faith, Regina must have been heartbroken; aside from Sophie, with whom she was living, the only one of her six children with whom she could now communicate was Trude.

On 15 December the German authorities forbade Jews access to museums, libraries and exhibitions. They were also forbidden to enter the town's main square and the Smetana gardens, or to use certain streets, including the Freiherr von Neurathstrasse where the Redlichs lived. The notice read: 'Those Jews resident in these districts may not loiter or walk about unnecessarily.' On 20 December the Nazis issued a map indicating which parts of the town were now out of bounds to Jews. Holešov was effectively divided into sections; any Jew wanting to go from one area to the other had to make a lengthy detour. Thus at the close of 1941, the elegant and energetic Sophie who had so much enjoyed travel, and her mother, who had been brought up not far away in Ostrowo but had lived in the intervening years in the beautiful and cultured cities of Posen and Berlin, found themselves virtually prisoners in their own home.

They must surely have asked themselves for how long they would be permitted to stay there. Perhaps this was implied in the seemingly calm and positive tone in which they sought to reassure their relatives:

We're all here in our familiar surroundings, busy with our usual activities; we hope things will stay this way for the rest of the war.

Meanwhile Hitler, who had now brought about the very world war which he had accused the Jews of threatening to instigate, could claim to be justified in bringing down upon their heads the threatened annihilation which he flattered himself to have prophesied. It would begin in the Warthegau and soon afterwards spread to the rest of Poland, in particular to Lublin and the towns and villages of the surrounding region, before encompassing almost the whole of occupied Europe.

The small, remote town of Ostrów Lubelski lay north east of Lublin, near the vast Pardew forest. It was here that Trude, her husband Alex and their son Arnold had been deported at the close of 1939, in the bitter cold at the turn of the year.

I visited the place with Mossy, my son, in the summer of 2015, not because I expected to find any specific records about the family or discover the place where they had lived for those two-and-a-half traumatic years, but simply to wander among the houses, breathe the air and pay homage to the members of my father's family, and the thousands of others, who had here lived out the final portion of their destiny.

Remarkably, Trude and Alex had somehow managed to establish a home of sorts. In a short, undated note, probably from mid-1940, Regina had reported to Ernst and Eva that, 'Trude and family send their greetings to you in all their letters; sadly she can't write to you from there herself.'

In December 1940 Trude finally found a way to communicate directly with her brother in New York. By then she had probably been in correspondence with her mother and sister in Holešov for several months, but from all those invaluable letters not a line remained. Who knows in what heap of rubbish they perished? Perhaps Sophie and Regina took them along when they were deported, as their final link with those they loved most, parting from the letters only when they were forced to relinquish their last, most precious belongings. Or maybe, to make room for their own meagre things, some new occupants tipped out the papers the previous people had been so messy as to leave behind and dumped their useless junk in the muddy street. Or possibly, a fantasy I have not been able to discard, the letters still lie in some dust-covered box somewhere in Holleschau.

It would have been impossible for Trude to write to Ernst any earlier. There was no postal connection with Britain, so it would not have been until she had learnt of his safe arrival in America and received an address, presumably via Sophie and Regina, that she could finally send him a proper letter. All post had to be delivered to the Jewish Council and written in Latin letters, in Polish or German, so as to be easily monitored by the German censors. No doubt the threat itself sufficed to make most correspondents cautious.

Ostrów Lubelski

8 December 1940

My dear ones,

At long last I can write to you directly. Our dear mother sent me your letter and also those of all our loved ones. We've more or less settled down here now. Alex is busy with his practice. My sister-in-law and I do all the household chores ourselves, just as you do, dear Eva – tidying up, doing the washing and the dishes and so forth. The day is filled with work and in the evening we play Skat. We've got used to the petroleum lamp, so much so that we can't imagine things being any different. In bed we always still read for a bit. Friends supply us with books, magazines and newspapers, or borrow them from us. Most of our friends are no longer here. Only Dr Cobliner has managed to emigrate from here; he's gone with his wife and daughter to San Domingo. We got the required sum of money for Shanghai from our aunt in San Francisco, Rosa Chaim, who lives at 710 Funston Ave. But here there are quite different rules about emigration than in Germany and the money for the journey to the sum of 340 dollars per person needs to be made available in a neutral country. As there are five of us, we need to wait and see if our aunt can also put this money at our disposal. Poldi, Alex's brother, has already been in Shanghai for a year and should be making efforts there towards our immigration and visas, but for the moment nothing can come of it as emigration from the General Government is not permitted. Maybe we too will come to America and maybe we'll then see each other again. Arnold is hard-working and helpful; he scrubs the floors, collects the water, chops the wood, brings peat, lights the fire every morning and cooks breakfast. There are no gas or electric cookers here. The pump is in the same street, so not very far from us. In the evening he studies. The Rothsteins have sent him various school books and he's working to a timetable. He's as tall as Alex, but very thin. I've also lost a decent amount of weight and with my winter things on weigh 102 pounds. Of our friends the Harlams and Frau Cobliner are still here. Friedl and her husband will probably soon come to you; they may already have got there by the time this letter arrives. There are of course other friends here whom you will remember, Ernst . . . Please give our dear aunt in due course, and dear Leni now, our heartfelt wishes for their birthdays. It would be lovely if we could all celebrate these dates together next year. Alex became fifty on the 25th. Sadly there was nothing for me to give him and the day passed like any other. One just has to take care to keep oneself healthy. We hope that you'll all finally be able to write to us here directly. Maybe in the meantime you'll also have news from Ella, Wally and Alfred. Meanwhile, write to them on our behalf and tell them that we're in good health and that we'd be very glad to hear from them. Greetings to everyone who still remembers us. Heartfelt wishes to you all from your Alex, Arnold and Trude.

Our address is Dr Alex Peiser, Ostrów Lubelski, Deutsche Post Osten.

Alex added just one line: 'My dear ones, to all our warmest greetings.'

The terrible experiences of their deportation had apparently receded and Trude and Alex had managed to establish a new life. Their situation even sounded more or less bearable, though utterly different from the lifestyle to which they had been accustomed in Poznań, and full of sudden terrors. Yet it was considerably better than the appalling situation which awaited the deportees in the vastly overcrowded ghettoes of Warsaw and Lodz, where for the great majority there was neither work nor sufficient food to prevent starvation, and the streets were full of the dying and the dead. Trude and Alex were not in a ghetto; they were able to make contact with non-Jewish neighbours and in this manner earn a meagre income, procure some food and gain at least some limited access to general news. The small town itself, while poor, was not utterly desolate, and the land around it, surrounded by forests, had once been fertile, with small market gardens. With Alex able to practise as a much-needed doctor whose services were greatly in demand, the family had enough to eat to stave off severe hunger, at least some fuel for heating and lighting, and even, apparently, access to books and newspapers.

My son and I, accompanied by my friend David, went to the

local municipal office just in case there was anyone there who could help us find traces of the former Jewish community whose homes had once filled the central streets around the square. A lady explained to us in flowing Polish, of which we understood not a word except the gesture showing that it existed no more, where on the map the synagogue had formerly stood, and pointed out the location of the old Jewish cemetery. We walked through the streets, expecting no obvious clues, constantly wondering if this or that small house built of thick timber beams slatted together at the corners had been Trude's home in those harsh years. I found what I thought might have been a pump; the thick metal screws protruding from the base could easily have held the heavy super-structure and the lever. I sought marks on doorposts at shoulder or head height which might reveal the fact that the small oblong box which held the mezuzah scroll had long ago been attached there. I was constantly aware that at any moment I might be passing the place which had become their makeshift refuge, where Alex had returned after his rounds and Trude brought her meagre shopping, and from which she had written with such carefully restrained longing and frustration to her brother and besought him to remind their mutual friends that in the deep forsaken east of Nazi-occupied Poland they were still alive, still hoping for those tickets and visas which might, miraculously, save their lives.

It was impossible to know what Trude had chosen to conceal from the family or considered prudent not to share with the censor. Perhaps her most poignant sentence was the brief 'Most of our friends are no longer here'; if so few people had been able to emigrate, there remained only one interpretation for their absence. The few survivors from Ostrów Lubelski testified after the war to the misery and disease which killed so many of those who had struggled, exhausted and starving, on foot and harassed by the brutality of their guards, to reach the isolated settlement. The Nazis also appeared regularly, conducting random murders and shootings and burying their victims in pits on the outskirts of the town.

Alex's mother and sister had been deported with them; somehow they'd managed to keep close to each other. Forming a family team must have given them all increased economic as well as spiritual strength. As Regina reported to Ernst in January 1941, 'They've enlarged their place with one more room and made it habitable so now they are all together. Dear Trude wrote to me that they sent you a detailed letter a few weeks ago and wait longingly for your answer.' The reference was no doubt to that letter of 8 December which Ernst had so carefully preserved.

Arnold's life had changed sharply; he was unlikely to have been used to scrubbing floors and collecting water from the river or a well. Yet there were small compensations. The following summer Regina informed Ernst that they'd heard from Trude that all was well and that 'Arnold wrote in the last letter that he's been playing so much football that he can hardly feel his legs.' But it was neither all work nor all play; a disciplined plan of studies was developed, the necessary books procured and a tutor found so that he could continue with his lessons. This was no small achievement amid conditions intended to strip the victims of every facet of their humanity.

Most important of all, the Peisers still had plans for leaving. Alex's brother Poldi had succeeded in reaching Shanghai in the early months of the war. Jews began arriving in the Chinese city in 1933 and continued to flee there until 1941. In 1939 and 1940 a shipping service was operated by the Lloyd Triestino company between Italy and Shanghai, bringing thousands of refugees each month; it was probably by this route that Alex's brother had succeeded in escaping Europe. Life for the impoverished arrivals was by no means easy, especially as the region had been occupied by the Imperial Japanese Army since 1937. Jews were subsequently restricted to a ghetto, but they were not deported or murdered. Might Poldi therefore be able to obtain the necessary papers and open the path to freedom for the rest of his family?

Or might their aunt in America be able to help? The Lublin *Judenrat*, the German-appointed Jewish Council, had announced in June that since the American Embassy in Germany was still issuing papers to those with close family in the United States, anyone with such connections should register with its Emigration Department. Yet, as Trude clearly suspected, nothing ever came of it. She was correct in stating that emigration from the General Government was not permitted. Any dreams the family might still have harboured were soon dashed when the aunt in San Francisco on whom they had pinned their hopes of providing the necessary money for the tickets died that March. As Regina noted sadly, 'They'd placed so much hope in the good, kind lady's help, hopefully she'll have remembered them in her will.' But money was not in itself sufficient without the requisite papers.

Key to the family's survival was Alex's ability to continue working. The *Yizkorbuch*, the Memorial Book of Jewish life in the town, contained a touching tribute to the local physician, the much-loved Dr Last, 'a generous-hearted man who lived the life of the Jews of the town and was no stranger to their difficulties.

He knew from whom he could ask for payment for his visit and for whom he had to hide a coin beneath the pillow with which to buy the medicine he had prescribed. The smile was never wiped off his lips; he had a comforting and calming word for everyone.' No doubt he and Alex soon formed a collegial friendship.

Alex's life as a country doctor must have been dramatically different from what he had been used to in Poznań. The winter of 1940–41 had been exceptionally cold and the subsequent thaw had turned the ground into a bog. On 24 March Regina wrote to New York that:

Alex has a lot of work; he often has to do his rounds by cart. Sometimes the wagon gets stuck and the ground is so muddy that it's almost impossible to get through. The cart also sometimes overturns; thank God nothing's happened to Alex but some of his glass instruments have been broken. The horses are used to the boggy ground, only the journeys take for ever.

In July Regina reported that 'we regularly receive good news from dear Trude and her family. Alex is able to make good use of the instruments; he's very busy.' It would appear that either Ernst or another family member had found a way of sending his brother-in-law badly needed medical equipment and that, remarkably, it had somehow reached him safely.

Yet these details no doubt concealed much of the truth. Trude referred to her weight as just 102 pounds, even in her winter coat. Photographs from before the war showed her as an attractive, but not especially slim, lady. That she had 'lost weight' was more than an understatement; she must have been extremely thin. 'I see before my eyes the victims,' remembered Bronia Waserman-Eckhaus who survived the massacre of the town's Jews,

Thousands of tortured, exhausted victims were brought to the already overcrowded ghetto . . . where they were cramped together, condemned to hunger, cold and disease. Death in all its shocking forms was their fate. There are no words to describe their sufferings, to tell about the anguish of their fate.[1]

She added, in tribute to the community of local and foreign Jews now thrown together in misfortune:

We learn about noble persons whose names will never be known . . . who to the very last moment strove to help the others, the more vulnerable – the old people, the sick, the weak, the homeless, the children, to provide them with a piece of bread, a bowl of soup, a piece of soap, medicine.

In such a context, it seemed of little importance that Trude was not able to arrange anything special to celebrate Alex's fiftieth birthday and that 'the day passed like any other'. Yet her own birthday party must have been vivid in her memory and the inability to do likewise for her husband must have affected her deeply. On the face of it, this was just a minor deprivation amid incomparably greater sufferings. Yet precisely for that reason it was a painful marker of the loss of those modest joys and freedoms which make life truly human.

Amid all the many papers in Jenny's flat in New York I found just one more letter from Trude, posted the following autumn. Between the dates of the only two letters she managed to send her brother there unfolded a sequence of decisive developments in Nazi planning which largely determined her fate, that of all the Jews of the town, and indeed of Poland and most of Europe.

Virtually since its inception, the policy of mass deportations had failed to serve the Nazis' objectives. As far back as February 1940 Reichsmarschal Hermann Göring had opposed Himmler's demand for the further speedy deportation of Jews out of the Warthegau on the grounds that the war effort required all available manpower and means of transportation. That April, Arthur Greiser, Gauleiter of the Warthe region, had also asked for the continued removal of racially undesirables; his request was deferred until August. Eventually, in November 1940, Hans Frank, head of the General Government into which the superfluous Jews of the Warthegau were due to be resettled, informed him by telegram that any further deportations would be impossible before the end of the war. No one wanted to provide the breeding grounds for disease which the dumping of so many destitute creatures would entail, or commit themselves to supplying even the most meagre and inadequate provisions.

Conditions that winter must have been appalling, since the memory was lodged even in the minds of the most senior Nazis. Thinking back to them the following July, Rolf-Heinz Höppner, head of the *Sicherheitsdienst* in Posen, wrote to Adolf Eichmann at the Reich Security Head Office in Berlin. It is hard to imagine that he was the only one to come up with the idea:

There is a danger that the Jews will not all be able to be fed. It needs to be seriously considered whether the most humane solution would not be, in so far as they are not capable of work, to finish the Jews off by means of some swiftly operating substance. At any event this would be more pleasant than letting them starve to death.

These matters, Höppner concluded, might sound part fantastical, but they would in his view be 'quite capable of implementation'.[2]

He was indeed not alone in thinking along such lines. The T4 team had by now acquired substantial experience in the liquidation of tens of thousands of mentally and physically disabled people. But public pressure had forced Hitler to abandon his so-called euthanasia programme in Germany. Both the personnel involved and their skills could therefore be deployed elsewhere, and on a far wider scale.

Operation Barbarossa provided another source of manpower for mass killings, in the form of the teams from the *Einsatzgruppen*. Operating in four separate units, they had covered the entire breadth of the front in the wake of the *Wehrmacht*'s advance across the USSR through the summer and autumn of that year. In Lithuania, Latvia, the Ukraine and Russia they had massacred hundreds of thousands of Jews. Most were driven out of their home towns into the forest and made to dig their own funeral pits before being shot in the back of the head and left to fall into mass graves already full of the dead and half-dead and flowing with their blood. But those killings, it emerged, had their price for the SS too. Shooting Jews was inefficient; it took too long, and burn-out among the perpetrators, who often found it necessary to maintain a state of constant drunkenness, was high. Himmler himself, who visited Minsk in the late summer, could barely stand the experience. As one of his companions observed to him after witnessing the killings in Minsk: 'Look at the eyes of the men in this commando, how deeply shaken they are. These men are finished for the rest of their lives.' For him it was the poor killers who emerged as the real victims of their necessary and glorious, but challenging task.[3] When progress against the Red Army stalled in the autumn, the dream of infinite expanses for German resettlement to the east had to be deferred indefinitely. So too had the concurrent notion that there would be space out of sight and out of mind beyond the Urals for the dumping of unwanted populations. Another, more radical, solution to the problem of the Jews had to be found, together with a more impersonal and effective method of killing than that practised by the *Einsatzgruppen*.

The issue was urgent; this was the very moment when the pressure on the ghettos and Jewish quarters of the cities and towns of Poland became even greater because of the policy, agreed by Hitler that September, to deport all of Germany's and Austria's Jews to the East. How, if no one wanted them, were they to be disposed of? What were the authorities in the Warthegau to do when faced with the imminent arrival in the starving, destitute and overcrowded Lodz ghetto, and elsewhere, of further tens of thousands of German Jews?

Viktor Brack had been the inspiration behind the Nazi euthanasia programme. In 1936 he had been appointed chief of Office Two in Hitler's Chancellery, which handled matters concerning the Reich ministries, the armed forces and the Nazi Party. It was he who had delegated to August Becker in December 1939 the task of arranging the killing by means of poison gas of mentally ill and physically disabled people whose genes the Nazis deemed unworthy of perpetuation. In October 1941 he proffered advice on the gassing methods employed by his personnel. It was no accident that his team was dispatched to Lublin that very month. Soon afterwards the SS began the construction of a new, even more sinister kind of camp.

By the time Trude wrote to her brother again, in what was almost certainly the last letter from her ever to reach him, the words 'final solution' had begun to acquire their ultimate meaning.

Ostrów, 31 October 1941
Herrn Dr Ernest Freeman, New York.

My dear ones! I haven't written to you for a long time, but dear Mama always encloses your letters. Hopefully by the time this letter arrives, dear Ernst, you'll already be busy with a small practice; only work can help one cope with everything. I can't tell you how much I regret that Mama and the Redlichs are not yet together with you; it's simply incomprehensible that they've waited so long. They may now have to travel and it's not so easy in this weather. I hear from acquaintances that many people are moving to Weissensee; it's more convenient for them. Hopefully all your family are healthy and already settled in their new flat. The death of Uncle Leon is most regrettable; I hope other relatives can offer you help through these early days until you are no longer in need of it. Have you, dear Ernst, had any news in the meantime from San Francisco? Maybe you can write to them again and remind them that we still exist. I'd also like to ask you to write to friends of mine in Lima in Peru; they should write to me here. The address is: J. Korngold, Calla Huarez, 428 Lima, Peru. Tell them about us. Alex has been very ill and is still not quite back to normal even today. It was a combination of a bad flu and total exhaustion; he's grown thinner but he's being taken good care of so that he gets his strength back. Hopefully he'll soon be able to practise again. Many people are waiting for him. Furthermore it's an urgent issue of survival for us because I've already bartered away our old stuff; one doesn't have much anyway and life goes on and after all we are five people. Arnold helps at home and in the practice, wherever it's needed. He helps with the washing too. I wash alone and as the river is near we go together as long as it remains warm enough. Rinsing, starching and hanging out are Susie's job; she's also the cleaner while I do the cooking and shopping. In his free time Arnold studies; he has lessons with Magister Polakowski so that he doesn't forget everything he learnt in the gymnasium. The Rothsteins have been providing us with text books as well as reading material and newspapers so that we once again possess a small library. It's my best time of day when I go to bed (that is, on the sofa) at eight, or at the latest nine, and read. Sadly the light doesn't always work all that well; we only have electricity in two rooms and as the current is provided by a mill there isn't always light, and when there is, it flickers a lot. We also have two petroleum lamps but we don't use them very often as petrol has become very expensive. We're often together with Friedl's mother; she's happy when she gets news from her children. Otherwise everyone struggles on as best they can. Most people live off the sale of old stuff that gets sent to them. Did you actually receive our photograph? Write to us here directly. Please send our greetings to all our relatives and tell them about us. *Alles Gute weiter. Seid alle herzlich gegrüsst* (every good wish and heartfelt greetings) from your Trude.

It was after Jenny and her sister Ruth found this letter while sorting through their father's papers that they decided they had had enough: 'We couldn't take any more,' Jenny told me. They had known Trude and her family well and could hear their voices in every word; they could recall the faces and features of all their dear ones who had written these final letters. I and those like me belonging to the second and third generations were free to follow our inner compulsion to know what had happened without experiencing a similar impact of immediate personal pain.

The recipients of Trude's letter would not have missed the implications of the reference to Weissensee, the vast Jewish cemetery in Berlin, to which so many acquaintances had 'moved'; to be dead must frequently have seemed easier to those struggling through each hour of every day than the remorseless, frightening and haphazard fight for survival. The passing comment about 'bartering away all our old stuff' also struck a disturbing note. When approving the expulsion of the Jews, Arthur Greiser had declared that they would remain in ghettoes 'until the possessions cobbled together by them were given back in exchange for food,' that is, until destitution had stripped them of everything they had.[4] After that, what was there for the Nazis to lose if hunger and disease destroyed them? With no money left to be sucked out of them, the time had come for them to die.

Trude still imagined that Regina and Sophie would be able to leave Czechoslovakia; she seemed to believe that they had the necessary papers but were for some inexplicable reason unable to bring themselves to depart. Her hopeful attitude regarding her own situation that late in 1941 suggested that what subsequently came to pass happened with a speed and ferocity of which she had little intimation even then. Yet there was a despairing tone to the request that Ernst should remind their relatives in San Francisco that 'they still exist'. In fact, it was already too late. Just two weeks earlier, on 18 October, Himmler had determined that there was to be no further emigration of Jews from anywhere in the Reich. The previous day Hitler had told the guests at his headquarters that they were going to get rid of the 'destructive Jews entirely' adding that he experienced no scruples and felt himself 'to be only the executor of a will of history'. This self-justification was a strange and revealing backward glance at what he despised as a weak and outdated conventional morality with its ancient injunction against murder, henceforth overridden by the superiority of the National Socialist ideal, and which anyway did not apply to those such as Jews, Slavs or Roma, who belonged to a less-than-human race.[5]

Alex's illness had clearly been serious. In November Regina reported to Ernst that:

Alex was very ill; he lay in bed for several weeks and couldn't practise. But things are all right again now; patients come to the house, and so long as he can earn, everything is fine. We can help them with everything from here except money.

The following day she added:

Thank God we are now getting good news from Trude and her family. Alex has fully recovered from his serious illness and has returned, thank God, to his practice. He's been outside too when the weather's been good; but now it's raw and wet there. Sun and warmth would obviously be better for him. A number of good friends died of the illness, the young Hirschlich, whose father has also travelled the 'way without end' and the youngest of the Neumark brothers. Trude writes that with the death of these people a piece of home has been lost.

As a doctor Alex would have been exposed to all the diseases that were rife in the ghetto. Perhaps he had caught typhoid? In any event, he had been lucky to survive. Without the income derived from his work the family would not have been able to cope.

My son and I found the small Tyśmienica river, where Trude had gone to do the family washing. Passing under a bridge close to the entrance to the town, it flowed through steep banks of grass down which stepping-stones led into the shallow water. It was not difficult to imagine groups of women doing their washing in the stream. We also found the remains of the Jewish cemetery. We ascertained where the synagogue had probably once stood, the site still bare but the building long ago destroyed or decayed into non-existence.

No correspondence existed from 1942. After the entry of America into the war Trude could no longer write directly to Ernst. Unlike her older sister in her home town of Holleschau, here in Ostrów Lubelski she was not among life-long non-Jewish friends and neighbours who might have smuggled out a letter on her behalf.

During that fateful year matters in the small over-crowded town only became worse, as Tovah Elkon recalled:

The Germans would appear twice each week in the town for what they called a 'Jew day' . . . Once they made a fire in front of the town hall and ordered the Jews to bring and burn all books written in Hebrew characters, while they drank themselves drunk and joked. They added to these their Thursdays, the market days, when they would enlist the 'Volksdeutsche' to attack Jews and destroy their possessions.[6]

As new groups of Jews were brought in, disease became ever more prevalent and hunger even more pervasive.

Meanwhile Nazi experiments in mass killing were quickly developing into a comprehensive plan for systematic murder. In the words of the historian Ian Kershaw, 'Warthegau anti-Jewish policy had run ever further into a cul-de-sac. Killing offered a way out.'[7] It will probably never be possible to reconstruct the precise sequence of suggestions, recommendations and commands as a result of which the Final Solution was implemented, but the order for the mass gassing of Jews from the Warthegau could not have bypassed Gauleiter Arthur Greiser or the SS and Police Chief of the region, Wilhelm Koppe. Their plans were almost certainly sent first to Adolf Eichmann, Reinhard Heydrich and Heinrich Himmler of the SS for approval before receiving ultimate authorisation from the Führer himself, who had repeatedly affirmed the ideological legitimacy of the mass murder of non-Aryan undesirables.

During the autumn of 1941 Herbert Lange, whose T4 team had been based in Posen since 1939, had his chauffeur drive him round the Warthegau in search of a suitable site for mass extermination. The choice fell upon Chełmno on the River Ner; it was accessible to transports of Jews yet sufficiently remote not to attract unwelcome public attention. New vans had recently been built in which the occupants were asphyxiated by diverting the carbon-monoxide exhaust gases back into the sealed saloon. These automobiles, which looked like ambulances or refrigerated trucks, were brought to Chełmno, where the killing of Jews began that December. The victims were forced into the backs of the vans, which were then locked shut. Pipes concealed beneath the wooden floor led to the driver's cabin, from where the release of the lethal gas was controlled by means of a pedal. Afterwards, fellow Jews were forced to pull the bodies out of the wagons under the blows of the SS. The dead were thrown into pits and piled 'in layers, faces down in the way that one person's legs met another person's head. If there was any tiny space left, it was filled with a child's body.'[8]

When on 16 December Hans Frank addressed the Nazi leadership of the General Government on the need to 'exterminate the Jews wherever we find them', he would have been well aware that the facilities for carrying out his instructions were already under development.[9] Although the vans employed carbon monoxide as the killing agent, the first trials in the use of Zyklon B as a quicker and more efficient method of asphyxiation had already been conducted on Soviet prisoners of war in a converted barracks next to the railway junction of Oświęcim. Rudolf Höss, the commandant of Auschwitz, testified to having observed these experiments:

A short, almost smothered cry, and it was over . . . I must admit that this gassing set my mind at rest, for the mass extermination of the Jews was to start soon, and at that time neither Eichmann nor I was certain how these mass killings were to be carried out.[10]

Höss's observation that the end came swiftly with 'a short, almost smothered cry' was a lie. As the very few survivors who had stood outside the gas chambers and heard the screams later testified, the agony of the victims was not speedily over. Their final minutes are best left to the words of the scholar Nikolaus Wachsmann: 'What happened next . . . cannot be described'.[11]

The killing of the excess Jews of the overcrowded Lodz Ghetto commenced at Chełmno in the late autumn or early winter of 1941–42. The Wannsee Conference, convened and chaired by Reinhard Heydrich in a large villa in an elegant Berlin suburb just a short time later, on 20 January 1942, was clearly not the gathering at which the Final Solution was conceived. Rather, it was here that the SS stamped its authority on the ultimate resolution of the Jewish question. The administrative responsibilities necessary to its efficient functioning were allocated and the associated organisational challenges addressed. The business plan of the Final Solution, now intended to include all of Europe's Jews, was given its essential outlines.

The task of preparing for the extermination of the Jews in the General Government had already been entrusted by Himmler to Odilo Globocnik. His ideas now took further practical shape. During the early months of 1942 three additional facilities were built; following the assassination of Reinhard Heydrich by British-trained Czech agents on 27 May 1942 they became known as 'the Reinhard camps'. On 1 November 1941 construction began near the village of Bełżec on the main Lublin–Lvov railway line. Work also commenced at Sobibór, a small settlement concealed in wooded landscape on the Chełm–Włodawa line. By the time that, in April or May, an SS team arrived to conduct initial surveys at Treblinka, a tiny station off the Warsaw–Białystok line, Bełżec and Sobibór were already operational.

The essential structure of each of these death camps was similar. Erich Fuchs, an officer in the SS who had worked in the euthanasia programme at Bernburg and was subsequently transferred to Lublin and involved in the development of Bełżec, explained that 'barracks were built as gas chambers. I installed the shower heads . . . the nozzles were not connected to any water pipes; they would serve as camouflage for the gas chamber. For the Jews who were gassed it would seem as though they were being taken to baths for disinfection.'[12] From their arrival to their annihilation, the killing process for the victims was also the same: they were deceived, shocked, bullied, beaten, robbed, kicked and harried to their deaths before most of them could fully absorb what was happening to them, let alone resist.

It seems most likely that these developments caught up with Trude, Alex and Arnold in the autumn of 1942. Deportations from Ostrów Lubelski to Bełżec had already taken place earlier, during the spring. As Mischa Eckhaus recorded:

Around three-thousand-and-sixty-two Jews had been deported from Ostrów Lubelski, leaving behind only those that were strong and able to work. Ostrów Lubelski, my former home, had the shameful fate of becoming the final station for Jews who had been deported from Poznań, Slovakia, Lubartów and Lublin.

That autumn the entire remaining Jewish population was taken to the local town of Lubartów, which lay on a railway line. From there they were transported in mid-October to the nearby death camps. An unnamed eye-witness described what happened:

The people were placed in columns of four on Lubelska Street and were led to the train. This procession of Jews, arranged as if in an army, extended from the market square to the railway station. People were thrown into cattle cars, on the floor of which lime had been scattered so that they suffocated. When the cattle cars were so overcrowded that no space remained, the Germans shot the victims on the steps of the train and on the platform. Only a few people were hidden or managed to escape during the march to the railway station.[13]

The closest camp to Lubartów was Sobibór. Yitzhak Arad recorded that 3,000 Jews were taken there from Lubartów on 11 October and murdered. However, in an official response to an enquiry from Ernst after the war, he was informed that Trude and her family had probably perished 'together with the rest of the Jews' in Treblinka. Although it was slightly further away, that seems to have been where the Nazis sent at least some of their victims that day; it lay two hours north east by train, in the middle of nowhere, surrounded by forests intended to swallow up in a thousand years of silence the murders perpetrated among its trees. Chil Raichman, who worked at Treblinka in the *Sonderkommando*, units of Jews forced under threat of death to assist the Nazis in 'processing' their fellow victims and later in disposing of the corpses, and who subsequently survived the revolt on 2 August 1943, recorded how he, too, was put on the train at Lubartów:

We travel from Lubartów station, some 20 kilometres from Lublin. I travel with my pretty young sister Rivka, nineteen years old, and a good friend of mine, Wolf Ber Rojzman, and his wife and two children. Almost all of those in the closed car are my close acquaintances, from the same small town, Ostrów Lubelski. There are about 140 of us in the car. It is extraordinarily tight, with dense, stale air, all of us pressed against one another.[14]

None of them knew for certain where the route led or where the journey would end. Among those crushed together in that wagon might have been Trude, Alex and Arnold.

Approximately 800,000 Jews and many Poles and Roma were murdered at Treblinka before it was determined that the crematoria had fulfilled their function. To hide the evidence of genocide from the advancing Red Army, the mass graves were opened and the bodies incinerated, a process taking many months. The camp was then dismantled and a farmhouse built on the site.

Perhaps it made little difference at which of the death camps Trude had died. She, Arnold, Alex and his mother and sister all perished without trace. Not a spoon, a prayer book or a final note remained. No one would even know for certain the proper date on which to commemorate their deaths. If they had managed to survive the train journey, the hunger, thirst and lack of air, worse humiliations awaited them on arrival. Parted from each other, stripped of their hair and clothes, lied to until their very last moments, they would finally have confronted the bare concrete walls of the gas chambers, heard the metal doors shut and involuntarily begun to inhale the carbon monoxide which the Nazis still used as the instrument of murder at Treblinka. Who knows on what their final thoughts came to rest, as they passed forever out of consciousness.

Five months after the end of the war Alfred wrote from Jerusalem to his brother in New York, 'About Posen there is absolutely nothing to be gleaned.'

There was little more to be discovered in Ostrów Lubelski either. We found the old Jewish cemetery; white metal markers along the periphery informed the passer-by that this was once the Cmentarz Żydowskiego. Across the bare site tall grass, weeds and wild flowers flourished. The space was simply empty wasteland. There wasn't even a memorial to remind anyone that here there had once been something to remember. Visible solely to the intrepid or heartless visitor daring or insensitive enough to walk across the unmarked ground beneath which lay the now nameless dead, and noticeable even then only from a few yards distant, lay a small pile of broken gravestones propped against each other as if in hapless solidarity. They had possibly been brought back in semi-secretive respect by men and women uncomfortable to discover, during the course of repairs to their property decades afterwards, the provenance of the materials plundered in the years of poverty after the war to pave an alley or fill a breech in a wall. The few broken stones now lay together in a haphazard pile, half a tribute on one, a Hebrew name on another. Who knows if underneath were not buried the victims of some of the Nazi round-ups, men and women seized, shot and thrown into pits around the town? A more desolate testament could scarcely be imagined to the capacity to destroy thousands of people without memory or trace.

Gravestones in Ostrów Lubelski. (Courtesy of Wioletta Wejman)

Ernst, Eva and their four children arrived at the quayside in New York in the early autumn of 1940. They were met there by their cousin Leni, the daughter of Regina's brother Aron, and her husband Menny, a fellow physician. With further help from their uncle Leon in Chicago, without whose sponsorship they would have been unable to obtain immigration papers to the United States, they found rooms in an Irish part of the city. 'The neighbours were nice to us,' Jenny recalled. 'They'd rarely experienced a really good doctor before.'

But to gain formal authority to practise professionally, Ernst had to pass a challenging series of examinations which were set independently by each state. He turned once again to his uncle Leon for guidance. In early February he received an emphatic response from Chicago. 'Don't be so impatient,' Uncle Leon cautioned him:

Don't expect to accomplish somethings [sic] in days here what would require months in other countries, after all you are here six months and if it takes a little longer don't worry you will get there in due time, be happy that you and Eva and the children are in good health.

As to Ernst's suggestion that he sit the exams in Massachusetts, that, his uncle advised him, would not be sensible since there was no guarantee that passing them there would gain him access to a paying clientele. In New York he had friends; in contrast 'the New Englanders are not that kind that will welcome you with open arms, as they don't care very much for foreigners and the Jewish are not much better than the Gentiles'. So stay in New York, he counselled, before concluding:

Enclosed find your monthly checks, as usual hope you will have good news the kind you would be pleased to write to me and if you don't happen to have that good news, write what you have, will be just as pleased with what you have . . . As ever, Uncle Leon.

His mother gave him similar advice about patience:

I can understand your feeling that you would like to have your independence, but that's how it is for most people, especially nowadays when the pressure of exams is so great. Dr Kohlhagen and Dr Herzog went a few years ago and it was easier then. My dear children, put your trust in God and everything will surely turn out to be for the best. Our dear relatives are doing everything they possibly can. The most important thing is that you're healthy and can live in peace and quiet.

I asked Jenny if she remembered whether her parents had adapted easily to life in the New World. She replied:

My parents adjusted to the US very well. They never ever mentioned all the things they used to have as did the parents of my friends. They both felt very blessed that we were all together as a family and alive when every day there was news of all the terrible things happening to people they knew. My father made a point of not speaking German and kept that to the day he died. My mother was a master at making do with what little we had at the beginning. She had come from a very wealthy home and had never cooked, washed laundry or cleaned the house before. She managed to learn how to do all these things without ever complaining. Not only that, there were always people invited to Shabbat or Festival meals who were alone. All my brothers and sisters went to Jewish school but there was none in existence for me. [Jenny was the eldest]. These schools were all built by us refugees.

Uncle Leon was by now well established in America and a man of some means; with no children of his own to support, he was able to provide the family with the financial assistance they needed until Ernst could earn a regular income. In fact, a whole year passed before Ernst was able to obtain his doctor's licence and begin to work in his new homeland. He joined the practice of a certain Dr Aaron Kaplun on West 96th Street in Manhattan. The two men became fast friends and when he died childless Dr Kaplun bequeathed his office to Ernst. By that time, however, he was no longer Ernst Freimann, the refugee from Germany, but Dr Ernest Freeman, as his naturalisation certificate indicated, 'In testimony whereof the seal of the court is hereunto affixed this 10th day of December in the year of our Lord nineteen hundred and 45, and of our Independence the one hundred and 70th.' His papers were duly signed by William V. Connell, Clerk of the U. S. District Court.

The most important event in the life of the American branch of the family was the birth of a baby daughter, Rachel, on

19 September 1943. As Jenny, the happy older sister, recalled, 'We were utterly delighted having a little baby and spoiled her terribly.' The good news reached Palestine a month later where the uncles and aunts of the new arrival were thrilled to learn about 'our first American niece' as Alfred promptly described her. Her arrival marked a turning point, a first expression of faith in the future:

Ernst's naturalisation certificate, in which he is named as Ernest Freeman.

You have my heartfelt congratulations. May you be granted to bring the child and her brothers and sisters up to be happy and contented people of whom you can be proud. Everyone tells us, dear Eva, how hard-working you are and how well you've provided for the household, up to the very last day. We hope to hear the good news directly from you soon. You're the only ones in the family who're providing for the wider long-term rebuilding; therefore, with God's help, you'll merit a happy old age in the circle of your children and grandchildren. As soon as we hear about the name, I'll write it on the family tree.

The letter was dated 1 November 1942, when the battle of El Alamein was raging and profound anxiety must have been felt across the entire Middle East, but no mention of this was made by Alfred. At 1.05 a.m. the very next morning Montgomery launched Operation Supercharge, which led, amid fierce fighting, to the defeat of the Axis armies under Field Marshall Rommel and their almost complete destruction in North Africa.

Life in Palestine, as my father recalled, actually improved during the war. The poverty which had marked the late 1930s was replaced by a local boom: 'The country was soon transformed into a huge supply depot for the British Army; the economy took off and dozens of new factories were built. Palestine supplied the British with ammunition and mines, gasoline, tyres, and spare parts. It dressed and shod the soldiers and fed, lodged and entertained them when they passed through on leave. Palestine flourished in the war; tens of thousands of people owed their livelihood to it . . .'[1] Among those who fed and lodged the British soldiers and their allies was my grandmother Ella. This she managed by renting out two or three rooms in their first floor flat on Ramban Street, the main artery through Rechavia, a district in the new part of Jerusalem settled primarily by refugees from Germany and more like a small colony than a suburb. The rooms came with board; this was no doubt part of the reason why many of the lodgers stayed for so long, since Ella was an excellent cook.

The first language in the family home remained German, as

did many of the habits, including eating a hot meal with meat at lunchtime even in the burning days of July, something I could never understand when I stayed there many years later. In the summer of 1943, Ella reported to her brother in New York that:

my day is entirely taken up with running the household. I've been letting one room to two Czechs for almost two years. I've never spoken so much Czech in my whole life as here in Palestine. Neither of them, one officer and an official from the Czech Consulate, know any German and have only poor English, so we speak to each other in Czech.

She also let rooms to British officers. They were polite and friendly, my father remembered, but also occasionally critical. 'The peas were hard today, they took many hours to go down,' was a comment which still stuck in his memory decades later. The income from the rent saw the family through the war years. 'I'm busy with the same things as before,' Ella wrote again in April 1945:

I've rented out three rooms to officers; they are very pleasant and nice tenants, considerate and grateful for every little thing. The Czech officer has been here for three years and will soon be going home. The English officers change, but one recommends another and they write me long thank-you letters about how good they felt and how hard it's now going to be for them to live somewhere else. Whenever any of them are on leave here they visit me.

My grandfather Robert, who had owned a wood mill in Germany, found it difficult to settle into the more primitive and impoverished conditions of life in Jerusalem. His skills and experience were not readily transferrable and he must have missed desperately the family business and the role it gave him. He would never return to Rawitsch, near Breslau, and see again the premises of the Wittenberg timber yard.

'Robert is still not earning anything, so he helps in the household by washing the dishes and laying the table,' Ella wrote in the summer of 1943. That cannot have been comfortable for him; as I was to learn two generations later, this was not a household where men were made to feel welcome in the kitchen. 'Robert had a job as watchman in a car park for six months. For the last two weeks he's been working as a warden in the Bezalel Museum. But the position is very badly paid,' Ella wrote again in April 1945. When Alfred informed Ernst that through such employment 'Robert is also bringing in some money at the moment, for the first time in years,' he added an exclamation mark and in another letter asked his brother what he 'thought of that' as an occupation. In a family full of rabbis, doctors and professors my grandfather was made to feel out of place. He died young, in 1954, just a month before my brother, his first grandchild, was born. 'He was so much looking forwards to the arrival of the baby,' my mother remembered. He didn't live to see the day.

My father, by contrast, was referred to in letter after letter as *fleissig* (diligent and hard-working). 'Adi is very hard-working and earns well. He's able to support himself as well as helping Eva and Steffi,' my grandmother reported to Ernst. Later in the war he was able to return to his studies, assiduously following an English curriculum by correspondence course. 'Adi is working very hard,' she wrote in early 1945. 'He's still with the same firm (freezers and cooling plants) and studies hard every night to sit

My father, Adi Wittenberg, as a young man.

his engineering exams. He receives assignments from the British Institute and sends them in. There are 45 units and he's on the 26th, so it's going to take quite a while. He's been studying for almost six months.' Refrigeration was to be his livelihood; during the siege of Jerusalem in 1948 he was responsible as a member of the *Haganah* underground army for keeping cool the emergency supplies of blood in the city's hospitals. But it wasn't until a decade later, in Glasgow, that my father was eventually able to catch up on the education the Nazis had denied him. Studying for seven years at night school, often returning home after the last train had left so that he had to walk three miles through the snow to the rooms in Kirkentilloch where my mother was looking after my toddler elder brother, he finally obtained his degree in mechanical engineering, an achievement which reflected immense tenacity and determination. 'Lore has taken the children out,' my father wrote more than once in letters to Jerusalem from Glasgow in the late 50s; 'it gives me some quiet to work for my exams.' No doubt my arrival on the scene in 1957 did not make his revision any easier.

At some point my father must have joined the British Army because he used to tell me that he had helped repair tanks behind the lines at El Alamein. He was a non-commissioned officer and once showed me a document indicating that his commission might be on the way. Sadly I was never able to trace it. By the end of the war some 30,000 Jews in Palestine had enlisted in the British Army, following David Ben-Gurion's famous declaration in 1939 on behalf of the Jewish Agency: 'We shall fight with Great Britain in this war as if there were no White Paper, and we shall fight the White Paper as if there were no war.'[2]

Among those who enlisted was my father's sister Hella, who was later posted to Italy where she apparently had the time of her life, eventually meeting her husband in the army. She also met both the pope and Field Marshall Alexander, encounters which became part of family legend: 'She spent her last leave in Rome,' her mother wrote. 'Of course, she visited the Vatican and they were all – I assume it was an organised group – received by the pope. Hella writes that the pope asked her where she came from. When she answered, 'From Palestine,' he spoke with her in Hebrew and said that he'd also been there.' The story was no doubt further embellished with each retelling. The encounter with the top military brass went less according to plan: 'Field Marshall Alexander visited the hospital and asked her whether she was "in active service". She replied that she'd only been on a motorbike, at which he broke up in laughter.'

My father's oldest sister Eva found work as a nanny: 'It's not too strenuous for her,' my grandmother noted, in a remark which sounded ominous in hindsight. Steffi, the youngest of the four siblings, was studying in a children's home, preparing to become a nurse.

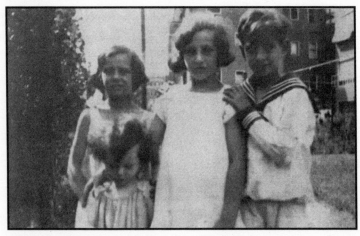

My father with his sisters, Eva, Hella and Steffi.

None of the letters from Palestine betrayed any anxiety that the Nazis might catch up with them there. More immediate preoccupations probably overshadowed such wider worries, but the family no doubt also had to comply with the rules of wartime censorship. By the mid-summer of 1942 the Afrika Korps, under the outstanding command of Erwin Rommel, had advanced threateningly near to Cairo. Hitler and Mussolini believed that the Axis strategy of a pincer movement via Egypt from below, and down through the Caucasus and Persia from above, would shortly succeed in destroying the British Empire. The population of Palestine, with its tens of thousands of Jewish refugees from Europe, would then be trapped in the middle. Ironically, the Nazi officer entrusted with liaison between Berlin and Egypt was the same Konstantin von Neurath who had initially presided over the Nazification of Czechoslovakia and after whom Holešov's Mazaryk Street, on which Sophie and Josef had lived, had been renamed. Anticipating a swift victory in Alexandria, he wrote to the Arab leadership expressing great sympathy for their cause against both the British and the Jews and promising to remove the Jewish teachers, businessmen, artists, doctors and lawyers who were devouring their nation like maggots in healthy flesh. Not an echo of those threats appeared in the family letters.

Besides the daily business of survival, the family remained profoundly worried about their relatives trapped in Europe. 'Sadly there is no news whatsoever from Europe,' noted Alfred in the same letter of November 1943 in which he congratulated his brother and sister-in-law on the birth of their daughter. But a telegram from Eva's relatives in London indicated a final period of renewed activity and desperate last hope. On 20 June 1944, just a fortnight after D-Day, Alex Heckscher wrote:

I am in receipt of your cable reading: 'MOTHER BORN JANUARY 12 1869 SOPHIE NOVEMBER 9 1891 JOSEF REDLICH JULY 15 1883 CONTACT ALFRED FOR CERTIFICATE NUMBER FROM HERE SLOW REGARDS', and have in the meantime received a cable from your brother Alfred reading: 'IMMIGRATION CERTIFICATE REGINA FREIMANN NUMBER M/4115/39'.

Whether all these efforts will have any success we of course do not know but this should not deter us from doing whatever we can. We can only pray and hope that the Almighty will soon send deliverance to all the subjugated peoples . . .

By this time neither Ernst nor Alfred would have heard directly from Europe for more than eighteen months, except possibly via the twenty-five words it was permitted to write on a Red Cross postcard. They could not have known for fact nor fully imagined the true nature of what was happening to their mother and sisters. It would have been against their inclination and contrary to the spirit of their Judaism to allow their hopes to die. Thus the following month Alfred wrote back to Ernst in New York:

It's not possible to obtain a new certificate for Theresienstadt at the present time. But we're on the list for the next one available. Annchen's mother came here this week and told us that – as long as she was still in Hamburg – that is until January of this year, she still heard from Mama. From her we learnt too that the Redlichs were also in Theresienstadt with Mama, but that they were sent away from there. The only thing one can do is to keep getting parcels sent, even if one receives no confirmation. One or another of them might get through.

The news was accurate, but by this point many months out of date. Yet how had they known that their mother had been in Theresienstadt? Probably they had received the information via other refugees, who had likewise heard about the fate of their own families through a long chain of messages, connections and chance encounters. Alfred was also correct about the parcels; some did indeed reach their addressees, where their contents were often carefully measured out among those in the same bunk or barracks, providing desperately needed calories and life-saving vitamins.

In August Alfred wrote again to his brother; he was determined to leave no possibility untried.

Jerusalem

14 August 1944

My dears!

Following our last letter we were informed by the authorities on 31 July that the Passport Control Officer in Istanbul has been advised that he may issue Mama with an immigration visa for Palestine. We telegraphed the Red Cross in Geneva so that Mama should be informed. We're now waiting for a telegram back from Geneva. In addition, I contacted the representative of the Jewish Agency in Istanbul with the request that he should do what he can to help. Meanwhile, Turkey broke off diplomatic relations, but we're hoping that there'll be the opportunity for an American or some other transport, or that at the very least her deportation will be prevented. Today we met for the first time with Annchen's mother. One would rather hear nothing at all, because what the refugees relate seems as if calculated to destroy one's final remnant of hope. The reports in the newspapers are bad enough.

The offices in Istanbul to which he referred were a collaborative effort between the American Joint Distribution Committee (a charity offering aid to imperilled Jewish communities abroad), the Jewish Agency, the United States War Refugee Board and The International Red Cross. They were together engaged in trying to locate and rescue Jews and other endangered people who might still be in a position to escape Nazi Europe. They were also responsible for organising and sending thousands of food parcels to Theresienstadt, Bergen-Belsen and elsewhere. Alfred's reference to the breaking off of diplomatic relations was in regard to Turkey's decision on 2 August to sever its official links with the Third Reich, which it had been supplying with chromite, since it was clear that the Allies were going to win the war and the Red Army was anyway on the point of cutting off its land routes to Germany.

As if unable to bear the implications of what he was writing, Alfred swiftly changed the subject: 'How have you spent the summer with the baby?'

On 20 March 1945, he wrote once again:

My dears!

We just received a letter from Aba Heckscher in which he informs us sadly that, according to what Recha reports, since January 1944 Mama is no longer in Theresienstadt. Once again this time the certificate arrived too late, a fact that we with our human limitations were unable to prevent and cannot fathom. About the Redlichs Recha appears to know nothing. Nothing is to be gleaned from the Red Cross in Geneva.

Recha herself had been deported to Theresienstadt with her second husband, whose slow death she had to witness there, a trauma which haunted her after the war. She worked in the ghetto as a nurse and became a close companion of Regina. In an exchange of prisoners financed by the Jewish community in America she was eventually brought to safety in Switzerland, from where she made contact with the family and sent the news which stripped away all but the last vestiges of hope.

Meanwhile, during the final year of the war the family in Jerusalem had been experiencing a tragedy of its own. It had fallen to Alfred to inform the relatives in New York:

July 1944
We've been living through difficult days with the Wittenbergs. As you well know, Eva has suffered from heart problems for many years. After being bed-bound for much of the last year and spending many months in hospital, last Thursday, 13 July, she succumbed to her illness. For the child it was a release, but the sorrow is nevertheless great.

It was nine months before my grandmother could face writing about her loss:

I've finally got myself together to write you a proper letter. You'll know from Alfred how stressful the time was when Eva lay ill at home and then in the Hadassah. Fortunately, she didn't realise quite how things were for her and still had big plans to sit her school leaving exams and study. It'll soon be a year now and the time has gone very fast.

As if to escape the painful subject of her eldest daughter's death, she turned to the future: 'The war will soon be over and then we'll have news of what's happened to all our loved ones.' Alfred had expressed similar hopes when wishing his brother a Happy New Year the previous Rosh Hashanah:

May peace come soon so that we can know that all our loved ones are safe from danger and we can see each other again.

He must have known that such knowledge would almost certainly not be forthcoming.

Once America entered the war Sophie and Regina were cut off from the only branch of their family in the free world with whom they had regularly been able to communicate. It must have been an immense blow to their morale, Regina's especially; nothing mattered to her so much as to be able to keep in touch with her beloved children. It was not only Ernst and his family with whom she could no longer correspond. This was also the channel through which she learnt about what was happening to everyone in Palestine; from now on she would have no news, however indirect, from Alfred, Ella or Wally either. From the autumn of 1942 she would also have ceased to receive any response to her letters to Trude. The loss of these channels of communication would have been as much or more of a torment to her than virtually all the other privations which she had been forced to undergo. With regard to Trude, one can imagine Sophie and Regina trying to configure the meaning of the silence: 'She's been forced to move somewhere else'; 'I hope they've been able to stay together.' What they actually knew, or what in their private imaginations they feared, it is impossible to assess.

Since they were no longer able to write to America, the fortunes of the family in Holešov during 1942 can only be gleaned from the general restrictions to which all the Jews in Moravia were subject. On 7 January a decree was promulgated requiring Jews to hand in their warm clothing, including furs, muffs, woollens, warm socks and ski wear. Decent winter clothes were in short supply and desperately needed both by the German Army on the Russian front, where they were laying siege to Leningrad in the north and Stalingrad in the south, and by the civilian population at home in the Reich, which was now facing increasingly well-planned and effective attacks by RAF Bomber Command. The Jews of Holešov had four days in which to comply with the order. A list of articles submitted shows that Josef was the twenty-eighth person to come forward; he handed over one fur jacket, one sports fur, one travel fur, four pullovers and waistcoats, one pair of gloves, four pairs of socks, one pair of trousers and two base layers.

In March all Jewish organisations were dissolved and their assets transferred to the *Auswanderungsfonds*. First established in Vienna by Adolf Eichmann, such funds were purportedly intended to support the emigration of Jews too poor to pay their own way out of the country (in the event that it would have been possible for them to leave in the first place). In actuality, they were one more channel through which the Nazis contrived to steal the assets of Czechoslovakia's Jews. A document stamped with the seal of the Jewish community of Holleschau on 12 January 1942 certified that shares belonging to Sophie Redlich had been transferred to the *Auswanderungsfonds* at the end of the previous September. Further money was moved across later. After the war, Ernst was informed that:

your mother, Mrs Regina Freimann, had a sum to the value of 92,608.50 kroner in account no. 658 at the savings bank in Holleschau which was transferred on 27 July 1943 into the emigration fund for Bohemia and Moravia. I have [illegible] fund in the name of the Jewish community of Holleschau.

The money was simply removed from her account and banked together with other stolen capital in what was effectively a Nazi war chest.

An order of 22 March warned local police that the failure to punish Jews found in places forbidden to them would be penalised with a fine. Such locations included public spaces as well as the more gracious streets of the small town, among them the road where Sophie lived. That such a reminder should have proved necessary more than three months after the original decree had been issued was a further indication that the Czech population was divided; just as there were those who joined the fascists, there were others who quietly helped their former Jewish neighbours, even at risk to themselves.

In the same month, whatever walls and plinths of the new synagogue had been left standing after the attacks of the previous August were dynamited by the German army. Nothing was to be left as a reminder that a Jewish house of worship had once existed there. The rabbi's house, however, remained untouched, probably because it looked just like any other building in the street.

On 27 May Czech agents trained by the British Special Operations Executive and supported by the Czechoslovak government-in-exile carried out an attack against Reinhard Heydrich, Acting Reichsprotektor and leader of the SS. He was not killed outright, but died a week later on 4 June from injuries to his lungs, into which asbestos from his motorcar seat had penetrated. The backlash against both the Czech and Jewish populations was ferocious. Following alleged intelligence connections with the assassination, the villages of Lidice and Ležáky were selected as the main target of the Nazis' revenge. All the men and women in Ležáky were

murdered; all the men over sixteen in Lidice were killed and virtually all the women deported to Ravensbrück. The villages were then
burnt to the ground. On the night of 10 June a thousand Jews were
seized in their homes in Prague; except for 120 men selected as fit
for work when the train carrying them passed through Lublin, all
were murdered at Sobibór. Holešov did not escape vengeance either;
on 15 and 16 June a number of Jews were taken to the Kaunitz
College in Brno, where four of them were shot. Sophie, Josef and
Regina would have known them and their families for years. Death
was drawing palpably closer. A local policeman who pointed the
Jews out to the Nazis was killed in a reprisal action after the war.

From July onwards it was forbidden to teach Jewish children,
even for free. From August it was no longer permitted to sell, or
even give, Jews all kinds of foods, including fruit, nuts, juices and
syrups, alcohol, jam, marmalade, cheese, fish, poultry and sweets.
It was also forbidden to provide them with games.

It was probably the cumulative effect of all these measures
which eventually undermined Sophie's sense that they might
manage to see out the war in their home town and come through
more or less intact. At some point during those summer months
of 1942 she turned for help to the non-Jewish friends and neighbours among whom she had spent virtually all her life. No doubt
she had assisted many of them when they in turn had been in
difficulties. Among them was a certain Helene Vodičkowa; it was
to her that Sophie came unannounced one day in 1942. As the
town notary, Dr Mojmir Bernatik, recorded after the war:

Helene Vodičkowa claims that sometime in the year 1942, without
previous arrangement or prior request, Sophie Redlich brought [her]

various items of family jewellery and silver tableware. She explained to Helene Vodičkowa that she was afraid that the Germans might confiscate these objects because of an order issued during the occupation that Jews had to hand them over to the authorities. She begged Helene Vodičkowa to look after them.

Sophie might no longer have felt confident that she and her family would be able to survive the war in Holešov, but she had not lost her down-to-earth practical sense of what needed to be done. However, nothing in any of her letters indicated that Sophie was pursuing plans of her own to get out of Europe. There were many references to Regina's frustrated hopes, but regarding any attempt to gain papers of her own there was not a word.

What would have happened to Sophie's belongings had she not given them to non-Jewish friends for safekeeping? A report, unnamed and undated but written by a senior German official some time after February 1943, since that date was referred to in the document, described in detail what the Nazis did with the possessions of Prague's deported Jews.[1] A cadre of skilled assessors was kept back in the capital from among the Jews due for transportation and formed into small, specialised teams. Those forced to leave were obliged to hand over the keys to their homes. These were held in a central location and signed out on a daily basis to one of the teams, who went into the now empty property, graded it as superior, average or inferior and listed everything in it, from expensive objects of art down to half-eaten jars of jam. Food was, after all, precious in wartime. Everything was duly classified and sent to a range of warehouses across the capital where it was further categorised and either used, that is to say stolen there and then, or placed in storage. The report noted with pride that the packaging and transportation of goods had become so efficient that breakages in transit had been reduced to the same low levels as those of the pre-war postal service. On the subject of the shattered lives of those who had once lived in those homes and painstakingly acquired their contents over a lifetime of hard work, not a single word in the entire report, which ran to over thirty pages, was wasted. There was only a brief reference to the fact that work often proceeded slowly because the task-force was weak with hunger. This was noted not with pity but solely to explain the inadequacy of the manpower available in relation to the scale of the task with which the Nazi administration was confronted. There is no reason to suppose that homes vacated in the provinces would have been subject to significantly different treatment. It was presumably because he had heard about this process that my father was convinced that Sophie's Shabbat candlesticks and other Judaica were lying somewhere in the vaults of the Jewish Museum in Prague, where certain objects stolen by the Nazis eventually came to be stored.

It is impossible to know how Sophie, Josef and Regina experienced the remainder of 1942. Perhaps news of the British victory at El Alamein and the successes of the Red Army in raising the siege of Stalingrad and encircling von Paulus' Sixth Army somehow reached them and lifted their spirits with the knowledge that the fortunes of war had finally turned and that liberation, however long it might take in coming, was now definitely on the way.

But they were not to witness it in Holešov. On 14 January 1943 Sophie wrote what she knew would be her last letter from her home town. She chose to send it to Alfred; maybe she thought it would be more likely to reach Palestine than America. How she was able to post it, and by what route it eventually reached its destination, remained a mystery.

Dear Alfred,

We're leaving here on 18 January. We're travelling to Ungarisch Brod; there we're being gathered in a school and after three days sent to Theresienstadt. Whether we'll stay there or be sent on further to Poland remains very uncertain. All Jews have to go; only thirteen people in mixed marriages are staying. The Jews of Zlin, Napagedl and Gaya are travelling with us. It's not clear if Josef is going to remain with us. Hopefully dear Mama will be able to go to an old age home in Theresienstadt in Bohemia and meet up with our dear aunts from Berlin.

In this manner we want to say farewell to you all and tell you, my dear ones, where you may be able to look for us after the war.

We're leaving behind two houses, no. 2 and no. 3 in the Zöpergasse, free of mortgage, with fields (as can be seen in the land register). Approximately 8 kg of silver (cutlery etc.) and jewellery (including things belonging to Mama, Annchen and Ernst) are with Frau Helene Vodičkowa. Glass and china and one carpet are with the vet, Dr Ludwig Volak. About clothing and linens, including Mama's fur coat, as well as about many other things, Bozka, who's now called Buchta and lives in Holleschau, can give you more accurate information.

Mama's savings from her pension are in the bank in Holleschau and amount to some 92,000 kroner. Our money is in the same bank; there are about 150,000 kroner. That can be confirmed in the books.

We pray to God that he will allow us to overcome successfully this trial which has been placed upon us and that we will see each other again in peace. We send you all our most heartfelt greetings. Your Sophie and Josef.

The letter concluded with a short postscript from Regina:

My dear children,

Today I took my farewell from your beloved and good father; may his spirit hover over us in these difficult times. *Seid innig gegrüsst von Eurer Mutter* (heartfelt greetings from your mother).

On 17 January lorries took the luggage of Holešov's Jews to the transit camp at Uherský-Brod, the central town in the district and the assembling place for all transports of Jews from the region. The following day, the Jews of Holešov were forced to board a train to the nearby small town of Hulín. Only a few kilometres distant, it was situated on the main railway line between Vienna and Prague. From there they were taken to Uherský-Brod, and, a few days later, to the town of Terezín, better known as Theresienstadt.

With what thoughts did Sophie, Josef and Regina leave their home town? Did the happy memories of their youth and young married lives come back to fill them with longing, or had the harsh years of attrition and dispossession together with fear for the future displaced all gentler associations from their hearts? They must have realised that they would not return. How else could Sophie's words 'and tell you, my dear ones, where you may be able to look for us after the war' be understood? What other meaning could Regina's postscript bear? Or perhaps this was not the case. Maybe they truly hoped that in Theresienstadt they would meet up with 'their dear aunts from Berlin'. The Nazis had, after all, spent a great deal of effort on deception. Calling the place 'Theresienbad', they obliged many elderly Jews to sign a home purchase contract, charging a high rate in advance for supposed board and lodging and luring many people into making over their life's savings.[2] Even if they were, as Sophie partly feared, 'sent on further to Poland', it is impossible to ascertain whether they had any accurate knowledge regarding the fate which awaited them there.

Theresienstadt was not a death camp. Although within the ultimate control of the Reich Security Office, the town was under the authority of the Zentralamt, the Central Office for the Settling of the Jewish Question in Bohemia and Moravia. It was established in the autumn of 1941, following a conference in Prague chaired by Reinhard Heydrich on 17 October of that year. A note, carefully marked *Geheime Reichssache* (state secret), recorded that the Jews of Bohemia and Moravia were to be gathered in a transit camp for evacuation. For that purpose the secluded town of Terezín was to be cleared of the units of the German army garrisoned there and the Czech inhabitants ordered to move elsewhere. It was estimated that the place would be capable of accommodating between 50,000 and 60,000 Jews. But there was never any intention that they would be allowed to remain there. In a secret minute of a report given by Heydrich in Prague in October 1941, he was noted as concluding that after the final 'evacuation [of the Jews] to Eastern territories . . . the whole area might be used for a model German settlement.'[3]

Unlike other camps, which were purpose-built or converted out of disused barracks, Theresienstadt was a carefully laid out town. It was constructed during the 1780s as a fortress forty miles north-west of Prague on the orders of the Austrian Emperor Josef II, who duly named it in honour of his mother, the Empress Maria-Theresa. Off the beaten track and self-contained, it served the Nazis' requirements perfectly. It consisted of two unequal

Sophie's last letter from Holešov on 14 January 1943, with a postscript from Regina.

parts. On the far side of the river Ohře the Small Fortress had long been in service as a prison for torturing enemies of the Reich. Now the rest of the town could be put to good use as well. The local population of 7,000 non-Jewish Czechs was relocated and the entire town turned into a ghetto. A contingent of Jews from Prague, known as the building commando and composed of 342 skilled craftsmen including engineers and physicians, arrived in the ghetto on 4 December 1941 to prepare the main fortress on the eastern bank of the river for the first of the many thousands of inmates due for internment there. The group was led by Jacob Edelstein, a man of undaunted courage and a committed Zionist; he and his fellow leaders determined to save as many Jewish lives as possible. Their aim was to create a self-sustaining and productive community which would survive the war.

The Jewish leadership was responsible for administering municipal services including housing, water, electricity, sewage and the post. As a result of the combined skills of the internees, the town had better sanitation and medical care than any other ghetto. As the community developed, an extraordinary range of cultural and artistic activities began to flourish, partly underground and partly in the open. Yet, as the number of transports increased and the population grew to almost 60,000 in 1942, it became clear that it was not the intention of the Nazis to allow Jews to survive there in even remotely tolerable conditions. They were not systematically murdered in Theresienstadt itself. But during the three and a half years of the ghetto's existence 33,000 people died as a result of malnutrition and disease. There were also many executions, and a further 88,000 Jews were sent onwards to their deaths in Auschwitz, Treblinka and elsewhere.

The ghetto was effectively sealed off. Though it was possible for inmates to receive parcels, all post was strictly controlled to conform to the aims of Nazi propaganda. A contemporary scholar of Czech Jewry, Livia Rothkirchen, noted that from the Nazi perspective the town in fact had at least three functions: to act both as a *Siedlungslager* (a place where Jews could be settled), and as a *Sammellager* (a gathering point from which to deport them further), as well, after the Wannsee Conference, 'as an alibi – to camouflage the ongoing annihilation process before the eyes of the free world.'[4]

It is therefore unlikely that Sophie would have been aware of the true nature of what awaited her and her family should they subsequently be deported further. This was known only to part of the *Judenrat,* the members of the Jewish leadership council. Since there was nothing they could do to stop the trains, most of them considered it wisest not to spread hopelessness among the population by sharing the bleak truth about the death camps. Sophie's suspicion that they would be sent onwards to Poland was probably based on reports which had made their way back to Holešov, or on speculations about the fate of Trude and her family, from whom they had, by the time of their own deportation, heard nothing for several months. It is impossible to know what they really thought was going to happen to them. Of those who were party to rumours about camps where Jews were routinely murdered by the tens of thousands, many found them too monstrous to believe.

The train which carried Sophie, Josef and Regina away from their home town probably left Holešov in the late morning. At least as far as Hulín the view must have been familiar to them down to every field, house and barn. From there onwards the main line took them to Uherský Brod. Here the full shock of their condition must have made itself felt. Sophie had referred in her letter to a school in which they were to be gathered. They would have had to sleep on the floor amid crowds of fellow deportees, without proper food, bedding or any kind of privacy. It was mid-winter and the weather would have been bitterly cold. When the train arrived to take them to Theresienstadt, it might even have come as a relief.

'Small places soaring high in the mountains. Beautiful the varied contours of the wooded heights,' wrote Philipp Manes of his journey by train to Theresienstadt, where he was deported from

Berlin in 1942. His chronicle *As If It Were Life* described the day-by-day realities of existence in the ghetto until the narrative came to an abrupt end, presumably when his own turn came to be 'sent east'. 'After a few moments,' he continued, the train reached 'a small station: Bauschowitz–Theresienstadt.' The prisoners had to walk the final two miles to the fortress. At the close of January the road must have been icy. Sophie, Josef and Regina would have had to carry or drag whatever few possessions had not yet been stolen from them. Appointed by the Nazis to the ghetto police, the Czech guards had the reputation of being Jew-haters some of whom were even more dangerous than the Germans themselves. There were apparently also others who showed a measure of compassion towards the elderly.[5] Eventually there emerged before the exhausted victims the moats and walls of Terezín:

Over a narrow passage guarded by inhabited casemates, the Bauschowitz gate. We passed through, unsuspectingly. Now, Theresienstadt – the ghetto, our new home – took us in.[6]

The first impression, according to Manes, was not too bad:

One could live here, we thought. It seemed that we had not been lied to . . . when the community officials spoke of the 'paradise of Theresienstadt' and congratulated us because we had been privileged to come here instead of being sent to Lublin.[7]

Once within the walls, new arrivals were taken to the Aussig barracks, known as the *Schleuse* or 'sluice'; it was here that they were registered. '*Schleuse*' was Theresienstadt slang; the SS imported the term in 1942 and it quickly took hold. To be 'sluiced' meant to be inducted into, or out of, the ghetto, a process which lasted anything between a few hours and a few days. Luggage was checked and any items regarded by the Nazis as 'forbidden', that is, desirable to them, were seized.

Deportation of Jews from Uhersky Brod, Czechoslovakia, to the Theresienstadt ghetto, January/February 1943. (Yad Vashem Photo Archive)

Sophie and Josef were never formally listed as inhabitants of the ghetto. Jenny told me that the family believed they were shot soon after their arrival because they were rich and the Nazis wanted to be rid of them so as to seize their properties. There were no gas chambers at Theresienstadt. A low building in a nearby field housed a crematorium where the bodies of those who died as a result of hunger, illness or the brutality of the guards were incinerated. This then is where the remains of Sophie and Josef would have been taken. I visited the building several years ago, shortly after the death of my father. In my memory I still see the bare field in the middle of which I recall it being situated, the semi-dark room, the blackened pipes and the ovens. A friend chanted the memorial prayer in a deep, resonant voice:

> God full of mercy who dwells on high,
> grant due rest beneath the shadow of your wings
> to the souls of those who were murdered, slaughtered,
> and burnt to death for the sanctification of your name . . .

Afterwards the ashes were dumped in the adjacent river.

In fact, Sophie and Josef were not shot in Theresienstadt nor had the Nazis any need to kill them in order to take possession of their wealth. They had already robbed them of everything they owned and could be entirely confident that the couple would vanish sooner or later in one or another of the death camps. There was no cause to single them out for special treatment. Like tens of thousands of others, Sophie and Josef were sent east to Auschwitz just days after arriving in Theresienstadt. Their transportation cards, which I first saw in the archive at Auschwitz itself, showed that they had arrived in Theresienstadt on 22 January 1943 with transport Cn 309 and left just four days later on 26 January with transport CS 469 for Auschwitz-Birkenau. Sophie's card was marked *OCC* 26/50, *Ordner Nr.* 24, *Seite:* 122. Josef, who was indicated as arriving on transport Cn 308, was listed as departing on the same train as his wife, only his card was marked *Ordner Nr.* 24; *Seite:* 125.

The journey onwards from Theresienstadt to Auschwitz must have been incomparably worse than that which had brought them to the Bohemian town a few days earlier. Whatever hope they might have managed to preserve up to this point must have been quashed by the knowledge that they were now trapped and bound for death. It was only the detail which they were unlikely to have known, the exact place and manner of their murder.

They might have succeeded in staying together in the trucks into which they were forced before the doors were locked and they were shut in together with a hundred others, hungry, thirsty and starved of air. There would have been some comfort for them if they had been allowed to remain together. They would have been parted in the violent uproar of the first moments after their arrival in Auschwitz, amid the screamed commands, the barking and growling of dogs and the random beatings by guards and SS men to which survivors consistently testified.

The planned expansion of the already vast camp of Birkenau was far from completed in January 1943. The railway track did not yet enter the camp and the new and huge crematoria with their specially designed rows of triple ovens supplied by Topf and Sons had not yet begun to function. Crematorium II was scheduled to become operational at the end of the month and Crematorium III two months later. Although all hope of a German victory in the East had vanished and plans for the building of German towns and settlements to colonise the area for the thousand year Pax Germanica envisioned by Hitler and Himmler had been abandoned in everything except Nazi rhetoric, work was nevertheless moving swiftly ahead on the killing facilities of what was to become the largest and most notorious of the camps, so that the Jewish question could be resolved once and for all time. As the historians of Auschwitz-Birkenau, Debórah Dwork and

Robert Jan van Pelt, wrote: 'Previously the "Solution" had been a means to an end [the colonisation of the east by ethnic Germans.] But now, getting rid of the Jews, cleansing Europe of them, was an end in itself.'[8] The prevailing killing facilities were simply not adequate for the attainment of the one German war aim which still seemed achievable; the annihilation of the Jews.

Sophie and Josef were delivered up to Birkenau in the midst of these developments. Rudolf Höss himself testified to what then happened to the victims:

Two farmhouses which were in a secluded part of the Birkenau area were sealed and converted into gas chambers with strong wooden doors, and the windows bricked up. The transports themselves were unloaded at a side-track in Birkenau, outside of the camp. The prisoners fit for work were selected and marched off to the camps; all the luggage was put down and later brought to the securities warehouses. The others, destined for gassing, went by foot to the facility 1 kilometre away. The ill and those who couldn't walk were transported to the farmhouses on lorries. When transports arrived at night all were transported there by lorries.

In front of the farmhouses all had to undress behind erected walls made from brushwood. On the doors 'Desinfektionsraum' ('Disinfection room') was painted. The Unterscharführers on duty had to tell the people by interpreters that they had to have a close eye on their belongings so that they can be found again after the delousing. This calmed the people, and they were fooled into thinking they really were going to be deloused. Then the naked entered the rooms, according to the size between 200–300 people. The doors were screwed shut and 1–2 cans of Zyklon B scattered in through small openings.[9]

After half an hour, the doors were opened, the corpses taken out and any gold teeth or rings removed. The bodies were then incinerated on pyres, the ashes pulverised and the residue thrown into the Vistula River.

In this manner my father's aunt Sophie, born on 11 November 1891, married in Holešov on 25 December 1912, 15 Tevet 5763 according to the Hebrew calendar, vibrant, elegant, practical and popular, was murdered in the gas chambers of Auschwitz-Birkenau. She was 51. Her husband Josef, born on 15 July 1883, a soldier of the Austro-Hungarian Empire in the First World War, a patriotic Czech, town councillor and successful liquor manufacturer, was 59 when he was killed. The couple had no children. No gravestone marked their final resting place on earth; they had none.

In late January 1943 Regina was released from the sluice into the small, hungry and over-populated town. Her profile fitted the image the Nazis wished to present of their model ghetto better than that of her daughter. Although originally conceived as a convenient location at which to gather all the Jews of Bohemia and Moravia prior to their further deportation, Theresienstadt had been designated at the Wannsee Conference in January 1942 as a centre for Jews over the age of sixty-five. The average age of the German and Austrian Jews sent there on the first transports that June was in fact still higher, at seventy-one. Many were in their eighties or even nineties and completely unable to cope with the conditions they encountered. But the bitter reality awaiting them remained unknown to the uninitiated, who were simply told that they would be taken to a home for the aged in Bohemia where they would be properly looked after. Sophie's hopes that her mother would be reunited with her relatives 'from B' were only too easy to understand.

Instead, Regina now found herself separated from the last of her children to have been able to remain with her. It is uncertain whether she did in fact find any members of her close family in the ghetto town, but it seems unlikely. She did however meet her sister-in-law Recha, and the two became close companions.

No documentation survived regarding Regina's residence in

Terezín; the SS destroyed whatever evidence of their crimes they could before the Allies were able to seize it in 1945. But Otto Zucker, who chronicled life in the ghetto, recorded how 'Most of the elderly and feeble people were not able to use the many-tiered bunks prepared for mass accommodation.' They therefore had to live in 'attics in a state of total neglect with no insulation against cold or heat, no wiring for lights, no plumbing and no lavatories . . . [M]any were unable to use the stairs in order to take refuge from the rooftop quarters during the peak of heat. More than 6,000 persons were put up under the rafters.'[1]

The sole written testament to Regina's sojourn was a postcard sent to her relative Siegfried Horovitz in Basel, in neutral Switzerland. The card was typical of the many similar missives the Nazis compelled their victims to write to reassure their relatives and deceive the world into believing that they were well cared for and in good health and spirits. The date was hard to decipher, but appeared to be 22 November 1943.

Theresienstadt, Hauptstrasse 22
My dears!

I'm often together with dear Recha; we talk a lot about you and all our dear ones. I'm most anxious about our dear children. I've been in the old age home for a while and I feel fine there. Heartfelt greetings from your faithful Regina Freimann.

The word 'dear', *lieb*, occurred four times in the forty-eight words of the message.

The front of the postcard carried the red seal of the *Oberkommando der Wehrmacht* with the Nazi eagle and swastika.

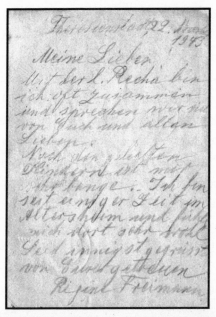

Regina's last postcard from Theresienstadt, to her relative Siegfried Horovitz in Basel.

In black over the postage stamp with Hitler's picture was the date on which the card had passed through the hands of the military censorship, 25 February 1944. Evidently it had first been sent to Berlin where its contents were duly scrutinised before it was posted on to its proper addressee. The instruction, also stamped in red ink, 'Replies only on postcards and in German' was purely for show; by this time Regina was already in Auschwitz.

My father used occasionally to refer to that card: 'It was the last we ever heard of her,' he would say. It was the tangible symbol of all the family he had lost.

The sender's address, Hauptstrasse 22, was that of the Dresden barracks, a huge building with 243 rooms around an open court-yard, in which women were interned. There were prison cells in the basement for those who broke the rules of the ghetto. The barracks were often so overcrowded that newcomers were left to sleep on the floor of the attic. But space was set aside for a theatre and other cultural performances. An extraordinarily rich artistic, intellectual and spiritual life took place in the ghetto; there can have been few such concentrations ever of so much musical, literary and academic talent in any one place at any one time. Concerts and lectures would have offered Regina a few scattered hours of respite and consolation in her harsh surroundings.

Deportations from Theresienstadt began in 1942, when Jews were sent to Riga, Minsk, Warsaw, Lodz and Białystok and gener-ally murdered on arrival. It soon became more practical to put them on trains directly to the death camps of Treblinka, Majdanek and Auschwitz. Almost 90,000 people perished in this manner.

In December 1943 Regina's name appeared on list OCC 26/47 of those due for resettlement in the east, the euphemism employed by the Nazis to reassure their victims that no harm would befall them in the so-called work camps to which they were being transferred. By this time many must have understood what actually awaited them. Jenny told me that Recha offered to go in Regina's place. Regina refused to allow it, arguing that Recha was still young, whereas she had completed her tasks in this world. Separated from her beloved children and their families, she may have felt that there was nothing more she now wanted from life except to be reunited with her husband in that better world beyond the grave in which they both deeply believed.

Regina left Theresienstadt on Transport DR-573 which departed for Auschwitz-Birkenau on 15 December. The train reached the camp on the following day; by this time the tracks had been completed which led through the notorious gates beneath the iconic watchtower into the centre of the camp. It would have made sense to assume that the day of her arrival marked her final hours on this earth. At the age of seventy she would not have passed the notorious selections, in which only those young and strong enough for hard labour were chosen to survive for as long as their starved bodies could bear the misery, diseases and arbitrary violence to which they were ceaselessly subject. She would have joined a long queue moving helplessly and ineluctably forward towards one of the large gas chamber and crematoria complexes which had been commissioned that spring and summer.

However, in contrast to the fate of virtually every other transport to Auschwitz-Birkenau, it appears that no one was taken directly from DR-573 to be gassed. Instead, the passengers were marked with numbers and sent to the so-called Theresienstadt Family Camp, section BIIb of the vast and bewildering Birkenau universe, situated close to Crematoria III and IV. This strange camp within a camp had been established the previous September when five thousands deportees, also from Theresienstadt, had been placed in a separate area where men, women and children were allowed to stay together and were spared the painful and dehumanising process of having their heads shaved and being forced to wear prison clothing. With the exception of the position of Camp Elder, a role filled by a German criminal, the internal running of the *Familienlager* (or 'family camp' as it was euphemistically known) was, as in Theresienstadt itself, left in Jewish hands. It was here that Regina was probably brought that December, together with hundreds more deportees from the ghetto in Czechoslovakia. That such a place should have existed at all within the confines of Auschwitz-Birkenau has never received an indisputable and logically compelling explanation.

Name: F R E I M A N N, Regina S.		
geb. am: 12.1.1869 in: -	Nat: -	
Eingelief. in Gh. Theresienstadt am: 23.1.43 (310/Cn) von: Uhersky Brod überstellt am: **15.12.43** (**Dr.**) zum KL-Auschwitz	Transportlisten des Ghettos Theresienstadt OCC 26/47	
Beruf: -	Ordner Nr. **17**	Seite: 13

Deportation document for Regina's journey from Theresienstadt to Auschwitz.

The reprieve from death did not last for long. On 7 March 1944 all those who had been brought to the *Familienlager* the previous September were forced to write postcards to Theresienstadt or to family and friends elsewhere in the Reich, no doubt assuring them that they were alive and well looked after. They were then all sent to the gas, without any further selections. Their cards were postmarked 25 March, over two weeks after the senders had been murdered and their bodies burnt.

At this point it must have been clear to the remaining deportees from Theresienstadt, who were joined in May by two further transports, that their own days were numbered. They were effectively penned in and waiting for their deaths, without any chance of reprieve, without even the hope of the unlikely possibility that they might somehow prove healthy enough or possess an occupation sufficiently beneficial to their tormentors to be spared. It is impossible to imagine in what mood they passed their days, virtually adjacent to the gas chambers in which they knew they were shortly to be killed.

Events turned out only slightly differently. In fact, when in July the turn came for the remaining inhabitants of the family camp to be liquidated, selections did take place. The shortage of manpower had become so acute that those capable of hard physical labour were sent as slaves to Germany, where some managed to survive until their liberation.

Regina could not, however, have been among their number. She must have perished on that day in July 1944 when the *Familienlager* was dissolved and everyone except the fittest few were murdered. The Ninth of Av fell that year on 29 July. This was the date for which my father had instructed me to make the list of the names of all the members of the family who were martyred and to place it next to the memorial candle. It was perhaps an even more appropriate day on which to remember his grandmother than he had realised.

Otto Kulka, who was a young boy at the time, survived the family camp and subsequently became an eminent historian of the holocaust, suggested a possible explanation for its strange and anomalous existence. Letters between the International Red Cross in Geneva, the German Red Cross, and Eichmann's office in the Reich Security Department showed that it was almost certainly established, rather like Theresienstadt itself, of which it became a grotesque extension, 'to serve as allegedly living proof that reports about the annihilation of the Jews deported to the East were false'.[2] It was maintained by the SS to cover the possibility that the Red Cross might decide to make a visit to inspect Auschwitz, just as it had to Thereisenstadt on 23 June 1944. In the event, the inspection of Auschwitz-Birkenau never took place. The Nazis proved so successful at deceiving the Red Cross, or the latter so gullible or weak-willed, that they were never required to repeat the exercise. The Nazis prepared the ghetto for weeks before the visit, creating a jollified small-town scenario replete with café, band and Jews who smiled (on pain of death should they fail to do so) so successfully that the Red Cross delegation was almost entirely deceived. The team from Geneva, whose credulity seems hard to comprehend, and who must have wanted to choose the easier option of believing what they were told, published upon their return a report so positive that it even apparently included a repetition of the German assurance that Theresienstadt was 'a final camp' from which there were no further deportations east. The Red Cross therefore duly decided to drop the notion of any further visits of inspection to other Nazi camps. Hence there was no longer any cause to maintain the illusion that decent living conditions also pertained at Birkenau. Upon receipt of this welcome news the family camp was summarily dissolved, its inhabitants gassed, their bodies burnt and their ashes thrown to the wind.[3]

The difficulty with Kulka's explanation is that it too seems scarcely credible. It might have been possible to deceive the Red Cross in the carefully laid-out fortress town of Theresienstadt, but surely not at Birkenau, deep inside the perimeter of the camp, surrounded by rows of barracks filled with the sick and dying, with the whole area permeated by the smoke and smell of burning bodies and the crematoria and ovens just yards away. Perhaps the Nazis had plans to relocate the deportees from Theresienstadt, should the Red Cross determine to proceed with a visit. Or perhaps the family camp was one further mad feature of a crazy world whose very creators had ceased to be capable of realising how depraved it was.

At any event, Regina Freimann, whose life had been devoted to her husband and their six children with a love and concern which extended in time to their spouses and her grandchildren, and whose contact with them was progressively pared down first to parcels accompanied by letters, then only to letters, thence to indirect news, and finally to no news at all, took her final journey amid the smoke and smells from the chimneys of Birkenau.

I imagine she was not alone in her thoughts. She was going to join her husband, her children's beloved Papa, in a dimension of existence in which, despite everything, she firmly believed, and from which even the Nazis with all their physical powers of detention had no means of cutting her off. Her heart may have been broken, but I imagine that as she walked towards her imminent end she was slowly and lovingly entrusting each of those to whom her life had been a service of love, her husband, her children, their spouses and their children, into the unassailable and unending care of God.

I visited Holešov with my daughter Libbi in order to see the town where my great-grandfather had served as rabbi for twenty years, and which had been home to Sophie and Josef virtually all their lives. I imagined myself following my great-grandmother as we took the path past the small house and the barn with the loudly singing birds through the Jewish cemetery to the grave of Jacob Freimann. I had always heard that as a mark of honour he was buried next to the Shach, Rabbi Shabbetai Hacohen, the celebrated commentator on the great sixteenth-century code of Jewish law, the *Shulchan Aruch*. In fact, there was one intervening grave between them, that of Josef Redlich's father; the two fathers-in-law lay peacefully side by side. There in that tranquil *Bet Chaim*, the House of Life, my great-grandfather rested, undisturbed by the turmoil of the terrible years and the bitter destiny which overtook his family so soon after his death. The inscription on his gravestone read simply: 'Here lies Rabbi Jacob, son of Rabbi Avraham Chaim Freimann. He wrote several books and taught Torah in important communities.' Only a certain rough quality to the lettering could be taken to suggest that the stone had been carved and erected in more haste and by less-expert hands than those which surrounded it, during a time of trouble for the House of Israel.

The words on Josef's father's stone were more fulsome, describing him as: 'A man of noble spirit who loved righteousness; a God-fearing and kind man of learning and humility, our teacher

Abraham Redlich, son of the judge of our community Rabbi Menachem Leib. He died ripe in years, aged 89, and was buried on the eve of the Sabbath on the 7 of Av, 5687. May his soul be bound up in the bond of life.' The date corresponded to 5 August 1927, the year when Josef inherited his second house.

I passed the site where the new synagogue had once stood, of which not a stone remained. Nearby was the former rabbi's house. Cars were parked outside it now; a century ago my great-grandfather would merely have had to take a stroll past the vegetable garden to reach his place of worship. The old synagogue, on the other hand, was as beautiful as ever, the walls and ceiling decorated with paintings in typical Polish and Moravian style. Only the place conveyed a certain forlornness, a palpable sense of having been spiritually and emotionally forsaken, unvisited for decades by the melodies of prayer and the affections and foibles of community life.

I wandered through the town late that night, leaving behind the main streets where a few people still lingered over coffee or beer. Close to midnight I found myself at the small crossing where the railway tracks traversed the road. I followed them for a couple of hundred yards to the deserted station. It can never have been a particularly busy junction; nevertheless there were several platforms, some clearly unused for many years. A branch-line ran into the precincts of a nearby factory. A single track stretched in either direction past the last buildings into the darkness of the nearby fields. I stood between the rails on one of the old wooden sleepers and stared. Was it from here that Regina and Sophie were taken, or, as was so often their practice in order to conceal their cruelties, did the Nazis herd them behind the gates of the factory with their bundles of baggage and make them wait out of sight of their former neighbours for hours or days without food or water before forcing them onto the train? Did they leave their home town in proper passenger cars, or were they removed like animals or packages, in dirty windowless trucks?

'We pray to God that he will allow us successfully to overcome this trial which has been placed upon us and that we will see each other again in peace,' Sophie had written in her final letter. It was not to be; they were not destined to meet again when the war was over.

But if a trial can be overcome by accepting one's fate with faith, fortitude and love, then I believe they will have succeeded in so doing in the most profound manner of which humanity is capable.

Recha Löwenthal-Horovitz

In his letter of 15 March 1945, Alfred had written to his brother that 'according to what Recha reports, since January 1944 Mama has no longer been in Theresienstadt,' adding that 'about the Redlichs Recha appears to know nothing'.

That Recha herself had managed to survive and reach a country from which she was able to write freely to the rest of the family formed in itself an unusual and unlikely story which, were it unique, would scarcely be credible amid the violence in which Europe was consumed in early 1945. She was part of a group of prisoners ransomed and transferred that February from Theresienstadt to the safety of neutral Switzerland. Before the disbelieving eyes of the prisoners counted among this fortunate number, a proper passenger train actually drew into the station at Baushowitz and carried them, weak, sick and weary, westwards across a devastated Europe, traversing a bombed-out Germany to reach the Swiss border at Constance, where they apparently received a warm welcome.

The initiative which led to this strange and remarkable act of mercy appears to have originated with a different Recha, Recha Sternbruch, a resident of Montreux. Before the war she had been imprisoned by the Swiss authorities for her efforts in helping to smuggle Jewish refugees across the borders from Germany and Austria into Switzerland. In September 1942 she and her husband

Yitzhak used the channels they had established via the Polish diplomatic pouch to pass information to the *Va'ad Hatzalah*, the Jewish Rescue Committee in New York, about the mass deportations from the Warsaw Ghetto. In 1944, with the victory of the Allies virtually assured, they persuaded the former President of the Swiss Confederation, Dr Jean-Marie Musy, who knew Himmler, to travel with his son Benoît to Germany and negotiate the release of Jews from concentration camps. Their lives were to be spared in return for money raised by the Jewish community in America which would be deposited in Swiss bank accounts. The SS personnel involved were apparently induced to participate in the project, which ran counter to the policies they had been pursuing without remorse for several years, by the promise either of complete immunity or of prosecution not before a military tribunal but in a duly constituted American court. Whatever the details of the complex negotiations which ensued, an undertaking was apparently made to deliver transports of a thousand Jews to the Swiss border every two weeks. No less a figure than Göring himself is said to have accompanied the first train as it made its way across southern Germany. The plan came to an abrupt end when news of it reached an infuriated Hitler.

Nevertheless on 7 or 8 February 1945, 1,210 former inmates of the Theresienstadt ghetto arrived safely at Constance, among them Recha Löwenthal-Horovitz. Their names were promptly published in New York in that month's edition of *Aufbau*. As soon as she was able to do so, Recha made contact with the family and her reports were immediately passed from London to Palestine and the States. Even then, as she later acknowledged, she refrained from telling them all the bitter details of what she knew, because she lacked definitive evidence and because, in her own words, she had 'neither the strength or the inclination to say anything about it'.

Her letters admit a grey half-light onto the inner landscape of those who had returned from the camps and ghettoes and now had to face a daily round in which they could not escape the pressure of images and feelings which, while still in the midst of the daily struggle to survive, they had not had the mental space or the time to allow into their consciousness. For many, liberation meant not joy but the merciless absorption of the devastating awareness that there was no one left, that they had no home, that there was no place to go and that they had no, or virtually no, companions from the past, except among the dead. As Hadassah Rosensaft was to write of her experience of freedom, 'The liberation had come too late, not only for the dead, but for us, the living, as well . . . We were alive, yes. We were liberated from death, from the fear of death, but the fear of life started.'[1] By July the war in Europe had been over for two months and Recha had managed to exchange letters with the family in New York. They had obviously been extremely close when they had all lived in Frankfurt before the war. It had been Recha who collected Eva and the children and took them to safety after Ernst's arrest following Kristallnacht.

Basel, 4 July 1945

Dear Eva, Dear Ernst,

I was so happy to receive your dear letter and I thank you from the bottom of my heart. Deepest thanks also for the little picture. You, Ernst, look just the same as ever; the children have grown so big and the little one is gorgeous. She looks just like I remember your youngest when you went away. Now he too will have grown up. I'm glad all's well with you, thank God, and I'd be so happy if I could help you. I've settled quite well into the household here. I do my work each day and in the afternoon, if all is well, I sort out my own affairs. I'm always so terribly tired; I've never known anything like it before. My head feels so numb, I feel the whole time as if I'm wearing a hat. I could sleep on my feet if I had the chance. Hopefully it'll soon pass. I much prefer my aches and pains. The one nice thing is when one can sleep, then one doesn't have to think; because one's scarcely opened one's eyes and everything begins all over again. As happy as I used to be, and as well as I succeeded in holding myself together, now I just can't do it anymore. In Theresienstadt it was as if one surrounded oneself with a wall the whole time in order to see and hear nothing so that one could get on with one's work. But now I can't manage to do that any longer. It was all too much; one can never get over it. And I've never before had so little sense of what it is that I want as I do now. I don't think that's going to change. Before then I had my home, my familiar surroundings, my parents, then only my mother, but I still had her. You were all there, my good friend was there, and my life travelled along its accustomed tracks with more or less ado. But now it's all gone, all of it; there's nothing there any more to remind one of what was once so lovely. It's gone as if it had never ever been, and there's a terrible emptiness inside. One is filled with horrors and grief. I can never forget the eyes with which dear Joe looked at me as he said, 'I'm going to manage it OK.' When one sees how the people most dear to one starve in front of one's eyes, and one stands there and can't do anything about it, one can't get over it and no kind of work can stop one from thinking about it the whole time. What I succeeded in doing in Theresienstadt, I can't manage to do here, where I'm fine . . .

A former domestic of Sophie's kept sending parcels. Do you know who the girl could have been? Maybe she might know something about what happened to Sophie; maybe they wrote something to the girl – it might be possible to find out where they went? Sophie's friends the Baers also all went on the transport; otherwise we could have sent a telegram to Holleschau. It's too terrible. May all go well, and from now on only good news! I'm looking forward so much to the picture you mentioned. Warmest greetings, your Recha.

The girl who sent the parcels must surely have been the same Faniuka whose wedding Sophie had attended several months after the German occupation. Her own letter to her mistress, tucked into an envelope together with a solicitous note from Josef, showed her to have been kind and faithful, as much a companion and friend as a housekeeper ('you left your slippers behind . . . you missed the skiing season,' she had written while Sophie was in Berlin helping her mother to pack up her affairs). No doubt it was her parcels which had enabled Regina to stay alive in Theresienstadt for almost a year, until her turn came to be taken on the fatal transports. Faniuka had probably thought that Sophie and Josef were with her in the ghetto too during all those months.

It is impossible to know if the family ever tried to get in touch with Faniuka after the war. By 2014, when I visited Holešov, it was simply too long ago to discover who she was and where she had lived, though the mayor kindly instructed his staff to look through all the relevant ledgers in spite of the fact that I didn't know her surname. 'Is it possible she could have been gypsy?' they asked me. 'Of course,' I answered. But would a gypsy have survived the Nazi tyranny untouched? I would have liked to trace

Faniuka's descendants and thank them for the help their mother, or perhaps it was by now their grandmother, had once given to my family.

Seven weeks later Recha wrote again from Switzerland:

26 August 1945
Dear Ernst and Eva,

I hope that you and your children are well and that you've had a good rest over the holidays. With me things are unchanged. One joins in with everything, but what one really wants to do is to crawl away somewhere and hide. It's impossible to put into words quite how one feels. One is so burdened by all those years, so tired, that one doesn't even know what one wants. I still don't think that working is going to make any difference, or at least not work which needs only one's hands rather than one's whole self. Now the Festivals are coming, which were anyway hard for me. Now I'm frightened of them; one isn't so strong that one can bury away inside oneself all the horrors which have happened over the years, and especially exactly a year ago. Every day something new stands before one's eyes, and one never knows anything about any of it; it drives one to despair. Write to me with Trude and Sophie's dates; maybe one can find something out through the International World Congress. They may have other avenues. One can't write to G [Geneva?] either; there are still a lot of people there, but one doesn't get to hear of anything. For me no one's going to come back, but maybe I could be of some assistance to somebody else. One has no right to be selfish. Nowadays we all need each other's help. And I know all too well just how happy one is if one still has someone with whom one can say all one needs to say, and weep. Your Recha.

What exactly it was which had happened just a year earlier in the summer of 1944 Recha did not say. The holidays were probably hard for her anyway, as they remain today for someone widowed young who has neither partner nor children with whom to share the days on which everyone else appears to be rejoicing in their perfect, happy families. On 31 January 1946 she wrote again. Her work had by now become more distracting, but this hadn't provided any serious comfort. Eva and Ernst had told her what they had gleaned about the fate of the family, but to Recha it had not come as news:

My dear ones,

Many thanks for your letter of 9 December and the lovely parcel, which arrived yesterday. I should have written to you again long ago. But sometimes I just don't know where to find the time. Work makes the day go by so quickly and in the evening I'm so tired that I sometimes just can't get my thoughts in order . . . But I'm happy to have things to do, otherwise it would be impossible to bear it all. I often find it quite exhausting, but what does that matter? What you write to me about our loved ones is sadly only all too true. I knew it already, but as I myself had no precise news I had neither the inclination nor the strength to say anything about it. Sadly, it'll be the same with the Pinchowers and Frieda Chapsky . . . I've now had news from Geneva, after I wrote about all the people I knew were missing, concerning a child who was deported with her mother from Th. I wrote to her. She's now in Prosnitz. She replied that the entire transport except for a very few went immediately upon arrival straight to the gas chambers, her mother included. The child is now eighteen; after Auschwitz she was in several camps, also in Mauthausen. She writes dreadfully badly. Now she's married a man whom she met at Mauthausen . . . Hopefully she's actually doing as well as she says. Poor child! She always wanted to study, and now all this has happened. How many more poor children are there like that? . . . How one can bear it all over time I really don't know. I would be happy if I were already with you all. Then I could properly pour out my heart . . . I'm enclosing a small picture for you so that you can see that I still look pretty good. If only it were the same inside. I hope to get another picture from you. The little one is so sweet. Oh, if only I could see you all already. Be well and keep healthy. Once again many thanks. All the best and heartfelt greetings, your Recha.

In his heart-rending study, *The Liberation of the Camps*, Dan Stone quotes a survivor of Theresienstadt who later became a rabbi:

I remember after liberation, I suffered probably more from the loneliness and the isolation, more than during the Holocaust period . . . Feeling of, yes, I'm alive, but that's it. The rest doesn't matter. No ambition. For what? For who? No initiative. If I am to stand, I'm standing. So I am standing. If you tell me to sit down, I'll sit down. That was for a long time.[2]

In 1948 Recha was finally able to join Ernst and Eva in New York, where she became a replacement grandmother to their children. She continued her work as a nurse, helping for many years in an old age home in the Bronx. 'We loved her,' Jenny told me; 'for years she lived in our house.' She died of heart failure in 1973, in Ernst's arms. I have a photograph of her from late in her life; she looks beautiful, and wise.

In the months and years after the war Ernst and Alfred wrote to each other frequently. Only the letters from Alfred survived, safely preserved in the New York home where Ernst kept everything in careful order. The brothers sent each other detailed news and pictures of their families; they wanted the cousins to grow up as close to each other as the thousands of miles between them would allow. The children also often added a few lines. Their wives were good correspondents and many letters survived written in Nelly's clear hand and warm, down-to-earth style. Ella, and occasionally also Wally, joined in the correspondence. In this way I learnt much about my father, such as his hopes of obtaining a scholarship to study in the States after the war. I had never heard him mention any such plans; maybe the fact that they came to nothing, probably for lack of funds and because of the challenging situation in Palestine, led him to bury them together with the memory of his disappointment.

Life in Palestine was never easy and became increasingly difficult as the end of the British Mandate approached. Alfred described his work, how the family celebrated the festivals, and the progress being made toward the creation of the new state, soon to declare its independence amid the growing violence. Yet in virtually every letter, in between descriptions of day-to-day life, lay small pieces of information about Europe gleaned from friends or relatives

abroad, from visitors, or from general reports: who had returned
to where; which acquaintance had heard from a surviving relative;
speculations about what, if anything, the family ought to do.
Their questions and observations served as a kind of frame, a
series of reference points, around an unfathomable and incomprehensible void. Even if they had been aware of all the facts, it
would have been impossible for them or anyone else who had
not undergone the experience fully to grasp what had happened
to their relatives and communities. 'Nobody tried to stop the
Germans from the annihilation of European Jewry,' Ernst noted
in his memoirs. 'The extent of the persecution of the Jews by the
Nazis was not known to us. [There were] some rumours about
the way the Nazis killed many of the German, Eastern European,
and later Hungarian Jews, but what really happened and what
afterwards was called the Holocaust only slowly got to us.'

On 17 August 1945 Alfred wrote to mark the first anniversary
of Eva Wittenberg's death, adding:

From Europe there is no longer any news, although we regularly go
through the many lists. We received indirect news from Annchen's brother
Leonhard and a sister and child who were in Bergen-Belsen . . .

Such lists were the preoccupation of survivors everywhere. In
Europe they were posted in railway stations, in centres where
handfuls of returning Jews gathered in the hope of finding that
at least some other member of their family had come back to the
one obvious place of rendezvous, their former home town. They
were compiled by Jewish communities and committees and by
the Missing Persons Office of the Red Cross. They were published

in the papers and, above all, carried from mouth to mouth by other survivors and those who encountered them. On 5 October Alfred wrote again:

On Rosh Hashanah a woman from Holleschau, born Beermann, visited Ella and reported that she had heard from Ernst Michalovsky that twenty Jews had come back to Holešov. She hadn't been told their names. Ella asked a Czech tenant of hers to write to the town authorities but she hasn't yet received an answer. If the Redlichs were there we would have heard from them long ago. About Posen there is absolutely nothing to be gleaned; apparently even now there are hardly any Jews there.

A month later Ella herself wrote to New York, referring to the same report but interrupting her reflections to bring news of her children:

I hadn't given up hope, but now I don't know what there is to say. Hella's been here on leave for fourteen days . . . Adi is working, now that it's got cooler in the evenings. In the summer he was so exhausted during the day that he couldn't study in the evenings . . . One of my Czechs has already gone home, and the other will probably go back to Prague in December. Both intend to do some research on our behalf . . .

Ella never did hear from her former lodgers. A letter she subsequently sent to the address he had given her was returned 'addressee unknown'.

It wasn't until the following spring that the family learnt anything more. One March morning a letter from Czechoslovakia arrived in Alfred's post box. He must have felt a simultaneous sensation of dread and anticipation when he picked it up. What could it mean, an envelope in his sister's handwriting, after all those years? Could it be possible that she was still living after all? Wasn't one hearing all the time of people emerging as if from the dead, long after the family had abandoned all hope? As Ella had noted the previous month, 'We did write to you that Nelly found the name "Regina Freimann, Lublin" in a list of addresses. Here people often turn up whose relatives have heard nothing from them for years.'

Had any such hopes flared up in Alfred's heart, the date and opening sentence must instantly have extinguished them. The letter was from the beginning of 1943: 'We're leaving here on 18 January . . . In this manner we want to say farewell to you all and tell you, my dear ones, where you may be able to look for us after the war.' Alfred already knew that his mother and sister had been sent to Theresienstadt. But why had that letter reached him only now? How had it been transmitted? And who was the sender? He shared his puzzlement with Ernst.

27 March 1946
My dears!

In these last days we received a letter from Czechoslovakia; according to the postmark it was evidently sent from Brno on 23 February 1946, but without the name of the sender. The address is in Sophie's handwriting. A copy is enclosed. We don't know who had the letter in their keeping and why it was sent off only now. Josef didn't write anything. What Mama wrote is in her handwriting; the same with Sophie . . .

Sophie had many contacts both within and outside the Jewish community. It seems probable that she gave the letter to a trusted non-Jewish acquaintance who kept it until such time as it could be forwarded safely to its intended recipient. Brno was less than forty miles from Holešov. Postal services could not have resumed the very day the war was over. But by early 1946 the unknown individual who faithfully performed this act of kindness felt sufficiently confident to carry out what he or she may perhaps have realised was tantamount to a dying person's final wish.

By that time the family must surely have known for all but certain that they would never again hear from Sophie, Josef or Regina. The letter from beyond the grave must have moved and distressed them, but the basic reality remained as it was before: they were dead and gone.

It was at about the same time that Ernst sent an enquiry via the Polish Consulate in New York to the President of the city of Poznań. He too must have had to wait until postal services were fully operative in a Europe divided by what Churchill would shortly denounce as the Iron Curtain. The newly re-established Polish authorities must have received thousands of such requests for information. On 6 August the president of the city wrote back to the Consulate General in New York:

Ernest Freeman of 251 West 87 St. New York in his letter of 28 April 1946 requested information about his sister Gertruda [Trude], married to Dr Alex Peiser, and their son Arnold, who before the war of 1939 lived in Poznań at 27 Al. Marcinkowskiego. They were resettled by the Germans to Ostrów Lubelski.

Please inform the enquirer that the above mentioned lived in Ostrów Lubelski until 9 October 1943. On that day all Jews were forced to leave town and they went to Lubartów from where they were transported to the camp in Treblinka, where they probably perished together with the other Jews.

Please collect an administrative fee of 200 zloty for the above information to be paid to the city office with the reference X/1-4909/46.

For the City President, Department Head /-/ MA Dropinski

This reply did not reach the family until several months later. On 17 November the Central Address Locating Bureau of the Consulate General of the Republic of Poland, New York, wrote back to Ernst acknowledging receipt of his cheque for $2.20, presumably the equivalent of 200 zloty, and forwarded him the letter.

At least in Trude's case the family now had information as to her final fate. Perhaps such knowledge provided them with a small measure of comfort. Knowing where and approximately when she died would have enabled them to establish a date on which to observe the annual memorial customs of her *Yahrzeit*, the anniversary of her death.

But the information was almost certainly inaccurate. In the first instance, by the autumn of 1943 the death camp of Treblinka was no longer operational. On 2 August of that year the prisoners forced to work for the SS in the *Sonderkommando* 'processing' the trainloads of prisoners who kept arriving day and night, the barbers who shaved their hair, the dentists who had to pull the crowns off their teeth, and those made to drive their fellow Jews along what became known as 'the tube' or 'the road to heaven' which led to the gas chambers and who had to take the bodies out afterwards to be burnt, staged a revolt. News of the Red Army's victories brought them not the hope of imminent liberation but the conviction that their own time to be killed had arrived, because the Nazis would surely destroy the camp and murder everyone connected with it in order to remove all evidence of the atrocities they had committed. They had not long left in which to act.

The revolt was carefully planned. The *Sonderkommando* succeeded in forging a spare key to the storeroom where the guards kept their weapons and managed to seize guns, but were discovered before they could prepare themselves fully for their intended attack. Nevertheless, more than three hundred prisoners succeeded in escaping, though two thirds were later recaptured and killed. The Germans then made the surviving prisoners dismantle the camp. The uneven earth with its vast burial pits was sowed over with lupin seeds. When the writer and reporter Vasily Grossman arrived at Treblinka with the Red Army at the end of July 1944 the sound of the bursting pods from the ripened flowers which now filled the space behind the barbed-wire fence sounded to him:

as if a funeral knell – a barely audible, sad, broad, peaceful tolling – is being carried to us from the very depths of the earth. And, rich and swollen as if saturated with flax oil, the earth sways beneath our feet – earth of Treblinka, bottomless earth, earth as unsteady as the sea . . . The earth is casting up fragments of bone, teeth, sheets of paper, clothes, things of all kinds. The earth does not want to keep secrets . . . And over all this reigns a terrible smell of decay, a smell that neither fire, nor sun, nor rain, nor snow, nor wind have been able to overcome.[1]

Trude's remains were probably buried in that same restless earth. But she and her family had almost certainly been brought to Treblinka and killed there almost exactly a year earlier, in October

1942, when the great majority of the Jews of Ostrów Lubelski were taken to Lubartów and sent in cattle trucks to the nearby death camps.

It is hard to comprehend that for the gracious favour of receiving the information that his sister had been murdered Ernst was made to pay an administrative fee of 200 zloty.

There was one further grim letter the family was yet to receive. Ella had heard via relatives in Santiago that Alex Peiser's sister Charlotte, Trude's sister-in-law, had somehow managed to survive the war in Berlin. Sometime during the second half of 1946 she wrote to her there. By February of the following year she had all but given up hope of receiving a reply and must have assumed that her enquiry had gone astray, when a letter arrived from Berlin.

Charlotte Tuch
Berlin-Schlachtensee (1)
Ilsensteinweg 4a
10 January 1947
Dear Frau Ella,

I received your letter of 14 September at the end of November. I beg you not to be angry that I'm only answering it today. As a result of everything we've been through my husband and I have been in such a wretched state, both physically and mentally, that we are only gradually able to answer the many letters from abroad. The last letter I received from my dear mother and sister Susie, and also from Alexander, Trude and Arnold, was in August 1941, after we'd corresponded regularly and also sent parcels throughout the previous year. Your dear mother and Sophie still received a letter in October 1941; then they too heard no more. Soon afterwards we received a farewell letter from them as well, prior to their deportation to Theresienstadt. Your dear mother wrote the following words: in spite of everything my faith in God remains unshakeable. These words accompanied me through the long years of persecution and bombing, when more than once our life hung by a silken thread, and gave me the strength to bear it all and come through. We lived illegally for more than two years, that is, without reporting to the police and without ration cards and in constant fear of the Gestapo. But we retained the hope that when it was all over we would find our families. Only now, when everyone who has returned from the camps has been registered with the Jewish community in Berlin, have we finally buried our hopes, and I have to [sic], however painful it is, that my brother Poldi in Shanghai and I are the only survivors of our entire family. I doubt if it's possible ever to get over it. Your dear mother and sister were overtaken in terrible fashion by the same dreadful fate. We can only hope that all our loved ones did not have to suffer too much more. My husband, who is the representative in the Jewish community, has, as you can well imagine, done everything humanly possible to find out anything about our relatives. There is nowhere which can help you further. We had, incidentally, written over the past years to your brother Ernst in New York, but we never received a reply. It was the only address we had for any of Trude's brothers and sisters. The letter probably got lost, like so many others. I would be glad to hear from you again, and I send you greetings from my husband.

Most warmly, your Lotte Tuch.

This letter was one of the first I drew out of that linen bag in the Jerusalem flat. As a result, its words haunted me even more than any of the others, demanding that I pursue the details of the destinies of the members of my father's family until I could somehow at least partially lay them to rest amid the story of the final years of their courageous, shattered lives.

Charlotte herself left Germany with her husband a year later, sailing from Bremen on 22 September 1947 for the United States on board the *SS Marine Flasher*. But whether the terrors of Nazi Germany ever left her was a very different question.

Sophie and Josef were dead; nothing was going to bring them back. But that was no reason for her family not to lay claim to her former home as their rightful inheritance; it was all that they could now regain of the lives of their loved ones and, as her last letter indicated, it had clearly been Sophie's wish that they pursue the matter. The fact that they had been powerless to prevent the murder of their nearest and dearest was no cause to accede to the theft of their possessions. Furthermore, most of the surviving family were now struggling financially and the couple had been wealthy; money would be useful in restoring whatever they could still redeem of the opportunities stolen from them. But unless one of them could take the matter in hand by going to Holešov in person, which for the time being seemed impossible, how could they lodge a proper claim? Alfred was mistrustful of the intentions of the new Czechoslovakia and doubtful about the benefits of hiring a lawyer. 'Is there any institution in the States which with government assistance can take over such a claim?' he asked his brother:

I'm very sceptical about the outcome, because without such help the Czech authorities won't let anything leave the country, as the good neighbours who took everything into safekeeping haven't yet made themselves known and will no doubt deny everything. Nevertheless we shouldn't leave anything untried, so that at least the personal items (jewellery etc.) don't remain in the wrong hands.

Sophie's final letter had provided the family with the names and addresses of the friends to whom she and Josef had entrusted the most precious of their possessions. The family could now write directly to those individuals. In August Ernst wrote to Mrs Helene Černocky, born Vodičkowa, with whom Sophie had, according to her letter, left 'approximately 8 kilos of silver (cutlery etc.) and jewellery, including items belonging to Mama, Annchen and Ernst':

Dear Frau Černocky,

Forgive me for writing to you in German but sadly my knowledge of Czech is not sufficient to do so in that language. As my sister Frau Sophie Redlich, who sadly did not return, informed us in her final letter, she gave you a number of valuables for safekeeping prior to her deportation. Since it partly concerns jewellery belonging to my mother, my wife and a cousin of mine, I would like to ask you to hand over to the court in Holešov all objects you received from my sister, so that they can be returned as part of her legacy. In any case, I would like to thank you with all my heart for this act of friendship which you performed for my sister. Any costs which you may have incurred as a result will of course be made good. Should any aspect of this matter be unclear to you from a legal point of view, I would ask you to be in touch with our attorney, Dr Frantisek Pokorny in Holešov, who, I am sure, will be glad to provide you with any information.

Respectfully your

Dr Ernest Freeman

Helene must have replied immediately; at least with regard to her Alfred had been unduly cynical.

Prague

27 September 1946

Esteemed doctor!

In response to your letter of 8 August of this year which I received on my return from the country let me tell you the following:

Before her departure your sister gave me a number of things for safekeeping. Sadly she left me no instructions concerning whom I was to give these things to in the event that she didn't return. I was therefore waiting for the results of [illegible] when your letter arrived. The articles are here with me in Prague and I intend to give them to the relevant court in Prague and to inform your lawyers in Holleschau. In your letter you also mention making good any costs I may have incurred. Your sister was so kind to me that I was glad to perform this task of friendship for her and to look after the articles she entrusted to me. For an act of friendship like this one doesn't expect any repayment.

Early the following year Helene did exactly as she had promised, handing over the items not in Prague but in Holešov itself. The event was recorded in a statement dated 15 January 1947 and drafted by 'Doctor of Law Mojmir Bernatik, student notary in Holleschau, representing Jan Bernatik, notary in Holleschau and magistrate under the act of 26 September 1946'.

Protocol D 301/46

Drawn up concerning the legacy of Josef Redlich, producer of liquor in Holleschau, Masarykowa 652, who died on 1 February, 1943.

The proceedings took place in the flat of Helene Vodičkowa, of 631 Masaryk Street. The subject under discussion was the presentation of jewellery and valuables of the deceased, which he, through his wife Sophie Redlich, had left for safekeeping with Helene Vodičkowa. The proceedings began at 14.00 hours.

Helene Vodičkowa claims that sometime in the year 1942, without previous arrangement or prior request, Sophie Redlich brought Helene Vodičkowa various items of family jewellery and silver tableware. She explained to Helene Vodičkowa that she was afraid that the Germans might confiscate these objects because of an order issued during the occupation that Jews had to hand them over to the authorities. She begged Helene Vodičkowa to look after them. But she gave her no list and left no further instructions, especially regarding what was to be done with the items should she and her husband both die. She also did not state which objects belonged to her and which to her husband Josef Redlich.

Helene Vodičkowa then set out before the magistrate the following objects which had been given to her for safekeeping by Sophie Redlich:

A long list now followed. Personal items included: 'one silver men's snuff box; one silver ladies' snuff box engraved with the initials S.R; one small silver bowl; two golden ladies' necklaces; five golden ladies' rings, three with diamonds, one with a pearl set in black onyx, and one wedding ring; one metal bowl for ritual purposes with an inscription in Hebrew'. There were also twelve silver dessert forks, twelve small silver fish knives, and much further cutlery.

The magistrate took all the above-listed items into his safekeeping from Helene Vodičkowa in order to have them valued by the court. As confirmation of the receipt of these objects the magistrate has given Helene Vodičkowa a copy of these protocols. Helene Vodičkowa has asked for no payment for the safekeeping of these items.

These protocols were duly read and signed. The proceedings closed at 16.00 hours.

The list described the treasures accrued over the best part of a lifetime in a household of substance. Many of the items were functional, knives, forks and spoons. One or two served important religious functions, such as the silver laver for the ritual washing of hands before eating bread. Most were personal, family gifts and heirlooms, tokens of affection, presents chosen by Josef for Sophie for a special birthday or anniversary. Among them was the jewellery left in safekeeping by Eva and Annchen in what had seemed the most secure household in the family. Other items which the couple would certainly have owned were not included, such as their Sabbath candlesticks and the silver *Becher*, the goblets used for the blessings over wine at the Shabbat table. Perhaps these objects were too intimate, too resonant with memory, for Sophie, Josef and Regina to bear to be parted from them. Anyway, they still had need of them. Not to see them on the table, not to hold them in their hands each week, would have meant letting go voluntarily of an essential part of their identity before it was stolen from them. Sophie must have kept them, and whoever stripped her home of its wealth and grace after she had been deported must have taken them and either had them melted down, or put them to some functional use in which their sacred purpose would never again shine through.

Helena presumably forwarded a copy of the deposition to Ernst.

That sheet of paper was all he would ever see of his sister's possessions. Thereafter all trace of the items vanished. The following
year the Iron Curtain descended across Europe and Czechoslovakia
was sealed behind it. For decades there was nothing more the
family could do.

After the fall of communism Ernst, by then over ninety years
old, took up the matter through the services of an international
firm of lawyers, Colico a.s. They replied to his enquiry in rather
clunky English on 8 July 1993:

Dear Mr Freeman,

From the documents you have sent us and from the personal investigation relating to competent public authorities, we found that the
property you had inherited after your sister in Holešov, had been confiscated according to the Decree of President of the Republic No. 108/1945
Coll. and had been transferred to the Czechoslovak state. Czechoslovak
acts of Restitution then do not relate to this case.

Objective immovable in Holešov, those are houses no. 651 and 622
and real-estates no. 1747, 1748, 1749/1 and 1749/2 are at present in the
ownership of the town of Holešov. We attested in the town hall house
in Holešov that you had not asked in deadline provided by the Act /
till September 30, 1991 for returning these things to you; also for the
case it would have been the property to which the Act No. 87/1991 Coll.
related. With regard to real state of the matter it is not possible to claim
returning above-mentioned immovable.

As to your further demand – return / eventually financial compen-
sation / of jewels, which the friend of your sister Mrs Helene Cernocky
set by the state safe in Prague, as she mentioned in her letter from
the 27 of November 1946, we could not find out any information or

notice of these things. The letter of Mrs Cernocky is very general and indefinite and on its base only is not possible whatever to find out claim.

Not long after receiving this response, Ernst, too, went to his eternal rest.

But the question of the whereabouts of Sophie's silver and jewellery continued to trouble me. It wasn't that I desired them for their monetary value. Rather, I wanted to touch something which my father's aunt Sophie and her family had once touched, as if those knives and forks, or the silver laver, were repositories of their love and courage and would have the power, notwithstanding the passage of so many years, to communicate them to the beholder who cared about their history.

My father was convinced that Sophie's Shabbat candlesticks, together with her other Judaica, had ended up in the vaults of the Jewish Museum in Prague, where its courageous staff had managed to hide a number of the treasures stolen by the Nazis from the vacated homes of deported Jews. 'Bring back Sophie's silver Sabbath candlesticks,' he told me when I first visited the city several years before the Velvet Revolution. The matter clearly rankled, even after almost half a century. But the Prague of the early 1980s was heavily patrolled by communist soldiers and the notion of so much as knocking on the locked doors of the forbidding building which I took, perhaps in error, to house the museum seemed too bold to contemplate. I did attend all the Shabbat services at the ancient Altneu Synagogue, where a small gathering of almost exclusively elderly men, and a few women, presumably all survivors, sang the traditional melodies at the close of the sacred day with a vigour and spirit which resounded through the small room where they were congregated, before disappearing within seconds of the conclusion of the nightfall prayers into the metro stations and narrow alleyways of the haunting city. But regarding Sophie's silver, I did not even meet anyone to whom I could have posed a question.

The surviving family did their best to get on with their lives. By the end of the war Ernst, now Ernest Freeman, had settled down to his fresh routines in the United States. Of all the six siblings, he had made the most successful transition to a different life. He and his immediate family were beginning to prosper in the New World. In September 1941 he had successfully passed the State Board Examination, allowing him to be employed as a doctor. Through a fortunate recommendation he had begun to work in the practice of Dr Aron Kaplun, where he would remain until his retirement in 1982, treating patients from all over the world. He even learnt Spanish in order to be able to communicate with clients from Hispanic communities without the need of an interpreter. By 1942 he had been able to pay back the money the Jewish Women's Organisation had given his family for the rent of their first apartment in New York. By the summer of 1943 the family were able to take holidays in the Catskills. His eldest son joined the American Army, later settling in Israel and becoming a well-known and much-loved scholar and teacher in the strictly orthodox community of Bnei Brak.

With the liberation of Europe, Ernst's first thoughts were for the fate of his mother and sisters. A secondary matter was the question of the possessions he had managed to pack up and place in storage in the last frightening weeks in Frankfurt before his escape to England. He would never have got them back, I was assured by a scholar of the period. They could not possibly have survived the war; they would either have been looted or blown to pieces by the RAF. In the best case scenario they might have survived until 1941, when they would have been distributed among bombed out Aryan Germans, either the genuinely needy or those on the look-out for easy profit.

But in this regard too, Ernst was fortunate. He must have shared the news with his brother, since Alfred wrote back at the beginning of 1946, 'We're really happy that you see prospects for getting your things. At least that's something.' The return of these possessions must have symbolised the survival of at least some residue of their former lives. That summer Ernst received an invoice from the international storage and removals company T. H. Hofman. The bill itemised the cost of packaging, customs, taxes and the rental of storage space from 1 January 1939 until 31 December 1943. There were two further charges of 327 marks for the removal of the boxes from the city to Oberrosbach and their return, presumably after the war, to a depot on the Main Quay in the heart of Frankfurt. It was a strange inversion of priorities that in the middle of the war, when Jews were being transported almost daily from Germany's cities (transports of Jews from Frankfurt were still leaving in February 1945) the boxes with Ernst's possessions had been kept safe from danger. One wonders if the company knew to whom the items which they had carefully removed to a less vulnerable location actually belonged. A further invoice dated almost exactly a year later carried the additional expense of sending the boxes to America.

When they eventually arrived at his New York home it must have been with complex feelings that Ernst unpacked their familiar, half-forgotten contents. These were indeed fragments shored against the ruins, and their very power to evoke memories must itself have been tainted with the odours of fear and destruction, just as the smell of smoke never leaves an object found strangely undamaged following the ravages of a great fire.

Throughout the post-war years Ernst maintained a close correspondence with his family in Jerusalem, especially with Alfred. He and Eva regularly sent their struggling relatives gifts. 'Heartfelt thanks for your parcel which arrived safely', wrote Nelly in January 1947, just one of many such expressions of appreciation:

We were all really pleased. Alfred can really do with the shirts and the same goes for me with the stockings. I gave Wally her stockings and I'm sure she'll be writing to you herself. At the first opportunity I'm going to ask someone who's travelling in your direction to take you some money, and I'm going to ask you, dear Eva, to send me some more pairs in the same size. Here they cost more than four times as much and are hard to get hold of. Thank God, we're all in good health. The children brought home good reports. Alfred is, as ever, very busy. Apart from his teaching commitments, he gives a lot of lectures and he has no lack of other concerns and people who drive him crazy. I do as best I can to keep them away from him, but there are some very obstinate characters among them. Keep in touch.

As the country prepared for independence, Alfred was becoming an increasingly important public figure. In 1942 he had been appointed lecturer in Jewish law in the Humanities Faculty of the Hebrew University. Later he was offered the directorship of the National Library, but refused on the grounds that this would not leave him sufficient time for his studies. He was a candidate for appointment to the Supreme Court upon its planned establishment following the declaration of the state.

Alfred Freimann

He loved the country. In November 1943 he had described how, on a brief holiday by the sea at Herzeliya:

we saw another part of our beautiful countryside; the whole strip of land along the coast is like one flowering, fertile garden. If they let us work in peace and quiet, and didn't prevent immigration, we'd soon have one of the most beautiful countries in the world.

Shortly before the end of the war he had sent a further description of some of his many travels and activities:

Over the last period of time I've had to travel around the country a great deal. Right now the entire countryside is in flower. Just the day before yesterday I got back from a five-day lecture tour in the Bet Shean valley. Life in the kibbutzim is indeed hard, but the people there are happy and feel entirely taken up with the thought of building up the country. We're too spoilt and too individualistic for such a life, but for the young it's for sure the one best way . . . I've a lot to do at the university, especially because of my involvement in the Encyclopaedia of the Bible for which I'm writing the article on the development of Jewish law. You're the first and only people over there to confirm that you've received my book . . .

This must have been the volume over the preparation of which he'd been labouring during the war years, as he'd informed his brother: 'I hope to begin working in the coming days on preparing my book for publication, if the issue of obtaining paper is resolved by the publishers. It comes to more than 600 pages in manuscript, but it's going to shrink in the wash.' Almost a year later, in August 1944, he'd written: 'The publication of my book is moving forwards, even if very slowly.'

Sadly, the Allied victory in Europe did not bring peace to the Middle East. As the end of the thirty-year British Mandate neared, the question of what the future would hold for the burgeoning Jewish State became ever more acute and the intensity of the local violence grew. Both sides sought to arm themselves for a conflict which was seen as inevitable. The British were still limiting the number of Jewish refugees they allowed to enter Palestine. Survivors of the Holocaust were desperate to escape the continued anti-Semitism of Eastern Europe, where the tiny remnants of once-thriving Jewish communities who managed to return home after the ravages of Nazism were quickly given to understand that they were not welcome. In many places, Jew hatred didn't die alongside the murder of its victims. In July 1946 a pogrom took place in Kielce involving police, militias and civilian mobs, in the course of which forty-two Jewish refugees were shot, bayoneted and bludgeoned to death. Now labelled 'displaced persons', fugitives and survivors were often stuck for months or years in camps in Germany, where the majority grew increasingly more anxious and impatient to leave Europe permanently behind them. Others, intent on reaching Palestine in any manner possible, joined small groups led by members of the underground Aliyah movements. Crossing the Alps on foot, often with harrowing climbs by night, they waited in Italy for passage on board scarcely sea-worthy vessels to the shores of Palestine. Few of the boats managed to evade the British blockade; thousands of homeless and stateless Jews found themselves interned in Cyprus or in other British camps.

Meanwhile, life in the burgeoning state was far from easy. The temporary war-time boom was over and daily existence became a battle for basic essentials. My father vividly remembered the shortages of food and fuel. Even the most ordinary possessions were precious, as Alfred testified in March 1946:

The Wittenbergs had a break-in during the night last week; various clothing and coats were stolen. These days that's an irreplaceable loss.

On another occasion, a burglar jumped into their apartment via the bathroom window, but fell straight into the toilet. Like the occasion when he bought a canister of paraffin in case of emergencies, which on being opened proved to contain nothing more flammable than dirty water, my father was able to recall the incident, no doubt extremely annoying at the time, with much laughter decades afterwards.

On 29 November 1947 the United Nations voted by a two-thirds majority to end the British Mandate and partition Palestine, creating both a Jewish and an Arab state. Among the Zionist leadership the plan was immediately accepted; the towns and villages of what would soon become Israel were filled with dancing all night long. But the Arab nations refused to acknowledge the creation of a Jewish state in their midst and the outlook for the new country remained frightening and uncertain. On 23 December, exactly ten years after the death of their father in what must have seemed like a different universe, Alfred wrote again to his brother:

I'd better not write about the political situation – you can read it all in the papers. We're very confident that the current sabotaging of the UN's decision will be broken by the Yishuv's powers of resistance. Sadly this battle is going to cost many more victims, but nothing comes for free in this world.

On a happier note, the letter included a detailed account of the wedding of my father's sister Hella, the first such celebration in the family since the war.

In the meantime we celebrated Hella's wedding on 14 December. Everything was really nice and the day passed in a spirit of harmony and celebration. None of the guests from elsewhere could come, as travel here is not without its dangers. Our bride was very beautiful and happy. If the groom stays the way he's been so far, she's made a fortunate choice. Now we can turn our thoughts to Adi and Steffi.

But it wouldn't be until 1952 that my father would meet my mother at the home of mutual relatives in Jerusalem.

The months before the end of the Mandate were increasingly tense: 'Some of the British supported the Arabs, but others favoured the Jews,' my father recalled. 'They used to come round with metal detectors searching for hidden weapons. So members of the *Haganah* would tape them underneath the lids of toilet cisterns; they were made of solid iron, so the guns couldn't be discovered. The *pagazim* (shells; but my father always referred to them by the Hebrew term) made a terrible noise. Many people lost their lives.' During the siege of Jerusalem in 1948 he was responsible for the refrigeration of the blood banks kept ready for emergency transfusions. 'We were always hungry,' he recalled. He once took me to a pill box overlooking the Valley of the Cross, an area well within today's city limits. 'This is where I stood guard,' he explained. 'They fired at us from over there.'

On 19 February 1948 Alfred wrote to his brother:

You're no doubt reading about our life and the goings on here in the papers. We've become so used to the war and the siege that we're surprised when we hear no gunfire, especially at night. These horrors too will pass over us. In the meantime we're already working hard at the preparations for the Jewish State. I'm responsible for the department of religious, family and inheritance law. There are many difficult issues that could be resolved if only our rabbis were of the right calibre. University activity has been severely curtailed. In between I try to keep up some scholarly pursuits. Consideration is being given to setting up a law faculty.

A month later he wrote again:

My dear ones,

Many thanks for your dear letter. You can form no real impression on the basis of the news reports of what our life is like. In so far as possible everybody keeps to their usual work and activities, even when there's shooting in the middle of it all and bombs explode. The streets are as busy as in normal times, the buses run regularly, the shops are open; only what's for sale gets less and less, especially foodstuffs and fuel. Jerusalem is to all practical purposes already divided into a Jewish and an Arab zone. The borders are carefully guarded. The entire population is divided into its duties. The younger age ranges, from 17–35, are properly mobilised, the streets are full of our soldiers; they have handsome uniforms and are well trained. We older people too are back in service, in so far as we are still capable of it. University activity is sharply curtailed because most of the students have been called up. Sadly many students have fallen in the fighting for the surrounding kibbutzim. Our young men have no interest in the higher politics. We know that we will only be able to hold on to what we can defend and they won't be able to take that away from us either, as no one is prepared today to go to war on behalf of others. Bands of foreign robbers plunder the Palestinian Arabs and then make off when they realise that there's nothing to be stolen from the Jews. You can read about the behaviour of the English in the papers. Without the intervention of a hostile major power (England) the partition, which exists already de facto now, will remain as it is today. The nation is prepared for sacrifice and confident; everyone has to tighten his belt. But for the first time we're fighting our own war and not that of the Gentiles. Our initial legislative preparations are complete; only little of the current legislation will be changed. There's much discussion of the longer-term future, but first of all we need to establish our state and make it secure. Now I have to leave a bit of space for Nelly and Ruth.

This was the last letter Alfred ever wrote to his brother. On 13 April Alfred was among seventy-eight scholars, students, doctors and nurses travelling to the Mount Scopus site of the Hebrew University. The area had been cut off for some time from the Jewish sections of Jerusalem. Regular convoys had therefore been arranged to relieve the small presence staffing the Hadassah Hospital and the academic campus. The British military had undertaken to guarantee their safe passage.

The convoy which gathered that morning consisted of two ambulances, three buses with reinforced windows in case of snipers, a number of lorries containing supplies including medical provisions, and two small cars. A British officer posted at the entrance to the Sheikh Jarrah neighbourhood which divided East from West Jerusalem signalled that the road ahead was clear and the line of trucks and coaches began to move forward. Soon afterwards the leading vehicle went over a landmine, bringing the entire convoy to a standstill and leaving it an easy target for attacks by gunfire, handgrenades and Molotov cocktails.

The disaster unfolded within sight of the watching British Army, a fact my father could never forgive. For several hours

British soldiers at their post less than two hundred yards away apparently stood by and watched. The Supreme Commander of the British Army in Palestine drove past without stopping. When the Jewish Agency asked to be allowed to send in units of the *Haganah* to evacuate the wounded, they were prevented from intervening. The President of the Hebrew University, Professor Judah Magnes, phoned General MacMillan and asked for assistance, only to be told that the British Army was trying to reach the scene but that a battle had developed. There was in fact no fighting. Eventually the buses caught fire and almost all the passengers, most of whom were already wounded and dying, were burnt alive.[1] It was four days after Dir Yassin; this was seen by some as an act of revenge.

It fell to my grandmother Ella to inform the family in New York:

My dears,

I find it unutterably hard to tell you of the terrible disaster which has befallen us all. We still can't grasp the fact that Alfred was among the victims who lost their lives in the convoy to the university. His body hasn't yet been identified, but he's confirmed as missing and as we've heard nothing from him since 10 o'clock on the 13th, the time of the attack, and as he hasn't come back, we've given up all hope. This afternoon all the unidentifiable bodies will probably be buried and we'll sit shivah. There are no words to express the pain felt by Nelly and the children. What he meant to us all and how we all loved and treasured him I don't need to tell you. May the good God protect us all from further misfortune. With love, your Ella.

She also sent a radiogram which was delivered by messenger as soon as it reached New York:

```
Alfred fatally wounded burial took place yesterday letter
follows
```

I've held that telegram in my hand and stared at it, with its large red writing.

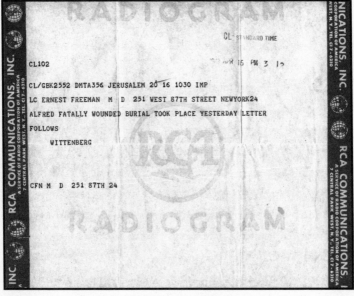

The telegram to Ernest informing him of Alfred's death.

Thus Alfred, who had employed all the energy, resources and ingenuity he could muster to try to rescue his family from Nazi Europe, and who had devoted his life to the study of Judaism and justice, perished in those very struggles to create a Jewish homeland of which he had just written that 'sadly they are going to cost many more lives'. Like his sisters and his mother he would have seen death approaching, and most likely, as with them, it would have been the fumes which killed him, before his body was burnt.

I looked in the memoir Ernst wrote for his family to see how he had reacted to the murder of his brother. I could not find one single reference to the event; it was as if Alfred had simply ceased to exist. Eventually I asked his daughter why her father had passed over this terrible tragedy without a word: 'It was just too much for him,' Jenny replied. 'Alfred's death was pointless and my father could never come to terms with it.'

My own father could not do so either. That day in Jerusalem must have been branded on his consciousness; to the end of his life he remained angry not only with those who carried out the attack but also with the British who 'stood by and did nothing'. This was despite his great love for Britain. The depth of hurt with which he referred to the event suggested that Alfred's death had come to represent to him all the murders and all the dispossession which had decimated the family's life in Europe and cut their numbers in half.

For his grandmother, for Sophie and Josef, and for Trude, Alex and Arnold, there were no funerals or rites of mourning. There were only the enquiries afterwards, the conjectures and presumptions of those who last saw them alive. Their deaths belonged to history, and to silence. But Alfred was murdered scarcely more than a mile from where he lived, and my father would have stood alongside Alfred's children Dani and Ruthie, the closest of his cousins, at the funeral and sat together with them in the silence of the house of mourning.

Memory is wilful. I don't know if it is the truth, but it seemed to me that until the last decade of his life my father did not speak all that often about his years in Israel, although he lived there from 1937 until 1955. When he did so, he became at once an eloquent raconteur. He was even more reticent about his childhood in Germany. It was as if these phases of his former existence occupied a distinct domain of his heart and mind, with its particular dramatis personae, separated from his years in Britain mainly by the urgent preoccupations of trying to create a new and better future for his family, but also by a certain inner reticence, over the causes of which I sometimes found myself puzzling: bewilderment, grief, a complexity of losses and sorrows difficult for him fully to fathom and explore, and a measure of guilt at having been carried to safety and eventual prosperity by a different destiny.

My father died in 2007. In the course of the years, as time has filtered my memories, three conversations with him have come to epitomise my understanding of who he was. They were so brief as scarcely to warrant being classified as conversations; 'exchanges' might be a better description, and the last was not even that. Once when he came to my room to say goodnight he asked me if I was doing my homework properly. I must have been sixteen at the time and was a diligent student; I could therefore reassure him with a clear conscience. 'Remember,' he said, 'everything can be taken from you except what's inside your mind.' Pondering his words, which have stayed with me ever since, I've modified his observation only slightly, to include the contents of the heart alongside those of the brain. But for him the issue was the opportunity to gain a proper education, a possibility stolen from him by the Nazis, and which he was able to regain only many years later by studying for seven years at night school.

Not long afterwards, and once again as he was wishing me goodnight, he asked me if I still said the *Shema* prayer before going to sleep. He'd taught me the words, the first in Hebrew most Jewish children ever learn, line by line when I was five, in the weeks after my mother died. I still remember how he would come upstairs to the room I shared with my brother to fulfil his promise to teach me one further phrase each evening, but only if I'd been good. As a small child I had regarded this as an exciting treat and had been an eager learner. But I was different in my teens, and hadn't yet learnt to cherish the importance of this bedtime ritual. I expect I hid the truth from my father with an uncomfortable 'yes'. But since that night I have never consciously omitted saying the words before letting myself fall asleep: 'Hear O Israel, the Lord our God, the Lord is one. And you shall love the Lord your God with all your heart, with all your soul and with all your might.'

In a lifetime of attrition these were the principles which mattered to my father most: to fill the mind with what could not be stolen from it and remain faithful to one's people and to God.

A few days before he died, as I was sitting beside his bed during that stage of decline when he was no longer sufficiently conscious to make conversation, my father struggled to raise himself off his pillows and said in Hebrew the line from the daily prayers *Umekayyem emunato lishenei afar* ('God keeps faith with those who sleep in the dust'). The words emerged from somewhere beneath the rational consciousness. This happened twice while I was with him; it was the only manner in which my father ever indicated that he might be aware of the imminence of his death. Or maybe he was thinking chiefly of his family, of all those who had perished, but were not entirely lost, because God was silently keeping eternal faith with them, and that it therefore also behoved us to keep our faith with God, in whatever meagre manner we could manage during the course of our limited years.

Then my father, who by the age of forty-one had lost two of his aunts, the uncle to whom he was closest, his grandmother, the eldest of his sisters, his father, and his first wife, went to meet his maker. I remember lying on the floor next to the bed where his body lay, listening to the birds that April dawn and feeling guilty that he could not hear them, yet knowing that this chorus of songs in his beloved garden would have brought him joy.

There was to be one more letter to add to the correspondence about the fate of Sophie. It came to my attention almost by chance, sent by an archivist at the Jewish Museum in Prague in reply to my general enquiry 'in case they had any materials bearing on the fate of my father's family'. It had been filed over a decade earlier among responses to an appeal carried by the Czech daily newspaper *Pravo* asking for information about lost neighbours. It had been posted from Bystřice pod Hostýnem, a village approximately ten kilometres east of Holešov on the first slopes of the Carpathian Mountains, a beautiful place which Sophie and Josef regularly used to visit. As it happens, I had also been there with my daughter Libbi during our visit to Holešov. We had climbed a steep woodland path high into the hills to gain wide views of the countryside below.

The letter was dated 1 January 2002.

Dear Sirs,

Having read the announcement in the newspaper *Pravo* dated 29.12.2001 'Help us to locate lost neighbours' I would like to express my memories of my mother Frantiska Sitkova (nee Bednarikova) for the period 1932–1939.

My dear mother, who is presently bed-bound due to her age, lived for seven years with the Jewish family of Mr Josef Redlich as their cook. Mr J. Redlich was the owner of a rum distillery in Holešov, in the district of Kroměříž, and with his wife Sofie Relichova [*sic*], the daughter of a rabbi from Germany, belonged to the fairly numerous Jewish congregation in this town. Judging by what was said about them, they were very decent people. They never harmed anyone and had very good relationships with those around them. The marriage was childless. They gave financial support to poor Jewish families with children. Throughout their lives they travelled (regularly) to Palestine, where they met their friends. When Hitler came to power they were warned from Germany to leave quickly. To start with, they thought about emigrating. They even had tickets to go to Palestine and all the formalities were completed. However, they never left; they were unable to leave their house, their friends and their home and in this way they sealed their own fate. My dear mother, who during the period of the war was no longer with them, heard that they were taken to a concentration camp. She made every effort to help them, at least by sending food parcels which she posted to them regularly. But she never received any news. These two good and hard-working people disappeared without a trace.

My dear mother talked about them all her life, mainly because they were very good Jews, but also about the suffering and the horrors to which they were exposed. These memories she passed on to us and she is at this moment, at the close of her life, happy that you are taking an interest in this human tragedy and that you won't allow this matter to be forgotten. It is possible that these fragments of memories are not exactly what you are trying to collect. But I considered it my moral obligation to speak of the destiny of these people from whom, together with others, the right to live was taken away. On behalf of my mother, her daughter Dana Freliskova.

So Sophie had possessed the papers which would have enabled her and Josef to escape; they had even taken care to procure them early on; so at least their former cook had believed. But she and Josef could not bring themselves to make use of them. Afterwards it was too late; it probably became too late far more quickly than either of them had anticipated. No wonder then that Sophie made no mention of her own attempts to get out of Europe when she wrote lamenting the failure of her mother's documents to arrive. 'We told Sophie not to go back to Czechoslovakia,' my father recalled, 'but she insisted. Her husband imagined they would be safe.' Here, then, was evidence to bear out his words. But can one blame people for loving their neighbours, their home and the town and countryside in which they have spent all their lives? Only those who have little respect for refugees can think that they leave their houses and homelands without good reason.

I replied to Ms Freliskova at once. I explained that I was a descendant of the Freimann family. I told her about her mother's affectionate letter to her 'mistress' in 1938 and of how my great-aunt Sophie had attended her parents' wedding in the summer of 1939. I recounted what I knew of Sophie and Josef's final fate. I copied her the sentences from Recha's letter in which, while reflecting on her tragic time in Theresienstadt, she referred to how:

a former cook of Sophie's kept sending parcels. Do you know who the girl could have been? Maybe she might know something about what happened to Sophie; maybe they wrote something to the girl – one might be able to find out where they went?

'These,' I wrote to Dana:

must be the parcels your dear mother so generously sent. They could not save poor Sophie or Josef, but they did help save Recha, and they must have made a huge difference to Regina's morale. She must have known that she and her family had not been forgotten by their friends.

From what you wrote in 2002, it seems unlikely that your dear mother is still alive. If she has gone to her eternal rest I pray that her memory is a blessing for you and all the family. I would like to thank you, in the name of my own family and my people, for what your mother did, and for what you yourself wrote about it.

For a long time I heard nothing back. I watched the post with anxious uncertainty, wondering if the address for Dana which I had taken from her letter was still current, of if, God forbid, she too might have passed out of this world. It was after all over twelve years since she had replied to the request in *Pravo*. Eventually I learnt that it was not my letter, but hers back to me, which had gone astray. She was alive and well and eager to be in touch.

I met Dana in the summer of 2015 when I travelled to Holešov with members of my community. We held services in the beautiful Shach Synagogue, filling the ancient building with the melodies of the Sabbath prayers, perhaps for the first time since 1942, and reading from the Torah the portion about the prophet Balaam who was hired by the King of Moab to curse the Children of Israel but was ultimately forced to concede that its dwellings were blessed and good.

Dana came with her daughter, son-in-law and grandchildren; they all travelled to Holešov specially for the occasion. 'I wept for two days when I received your letter,' she said, and she wept as she spoke. 'My family could not console me. I never thought history would come back to life after seventy years.'

Dana talked about her mother, a woman raised in poverty who nevertheless shared with Sophie her fondness for elegant clothes. The two women also shared a similar figure, in spite of the difference in years. 'Sophie loved to purchase the latest fashions, much to her husband's annoyance because she kept spending all his money. But she didn't like to put the garments on when they were still completely new; she had a thing about brand new clothing. So she asked my mother to wear them first, which she was glad to do, parading them in the town's most elegant streets and turning the eyes of the finest young men.' When the war came, Dana's father was taken to Germany for forced labour. 'My mother was left alone with the baby to look after and there wasn't much to eat. But she baked simple cakes with whatever ingredients she could find and sent them to the camps.'

Dana took a small box from her bag: 'This is the necklace Sophie gave to my mother on her wedding day. I'd like to give it to you.' I carefully opened the blue package she handed to me; it contained a long, fine chain of tiny seashells. All at once Ariel's song in *The Tempest* came into my mind:

> Nothing of him that doth fade,
> but doth a suffer a sea-change,
> into something rich and strange . . .

How strange and rich and gracious this encounter had proved. 'It was more than a professional relationship between the two women,' Dana concluded. 'They truly cared about each other.'

Had it not been too late, I could have told my father, who had asked me on my return from my first journey to Czechoslovakia twenty-five years earlier whether I'd succeeded in bringing home any of Sophie's valuables, that I hadn't found her silver candlesticks, but had brought back a token of her love, a love which had proved immune to the depredations of both violence and time.

'My mother's family couldn't afford to give her a good education,' Dana explained. 'She took home from the Redlich household many phrases and expressions we wouldn't otherwise have heard. There was one which my mother used to like to repeat: "Whoever helps a single person helps us all."' It was a popular version of an ancient teaching from the second-century Mishnah: 'Whoever saves a single life, saves all the world.'

Then Dana left, explaining that she was going to the cemetery 'to tell my mother everything'. I wanted to ask if I might accompany her, but a friend intervened: 'Talking to a dead parent is a private matter; I wouldn't want anyone with me when I visit my parents' graves.' It struck me then that for my part what I had to do was to go and tell Sophie. But to what burial place was I supposed to direct my steps? Several times I'd visited that vast domain of concrete posts and blackened barracks. Was that where Sophie now resided? On the last occasion, the frogs inhabiting the pond which had formed in the broken remains of the cracked and sunken gas chambers had sung so loudly that we couldn't even hear our own memorial prayers. I had left the immediate precincts of the camp and gone out into the flat lands where the ashes of the murdered had been dumped, in an attempt to listen to the voices which I believe must somehow be there even now, muffled in the silence, calling out to us still.

But that was not where I wished to look for Sophie. Instead, I set out late that night on a solitary walk, leaving Holešov behind me and turning off the road to take a footpath through the fields. It was past the middle of the month and the right-hand edge of the moon was marked with a rind of darkness like the scab of a wound. I could hear small birds rising startled as I passed and the sound of fleeing deer, but I saw nothing, only the long moon shadows which kept pursuing me. I was seeking other shades. Sophie, Josef and Regina, was there some residue of their presence here amid the landscapes of which they had been so fond that they would not willingly be parted from them, even then? Was there anywhere I might discover the vestiges of their lives?

'So that you shall know where to find us,' Sophie had written. I could look for the ghosts of my father's family in places marked by violence and hatred. Perhaps that in itself was a duty. I could, and would continue to, seek their spirit in letters, many undelivered or lost but, remarkably, not all, and decipher in the faded ink and grey-black typescript the tenacity of their faith, their courage and their unyielding love.

But from mainland Europe, they were gone.

SUGGESTED FURTHER READING

Alberti, Michael, *Die Verfolgung und Vernichtung der Juden im Reichsgau Wartheland, 1939–1945* (Wiesbaden: Harrassowitz Verlag, 2006)

Aly, Goetz, *Hitler's Beneficiaries: Plunder, Racial War, and the Nazi Welfare State* (New York: Metropolitan Books, 2006)

Arad, Yitzhak, *Belzec, Sobibor, Treblinka: The Operation Reinhard Death Camps* (Bloomington and Indianapolis: Indiana University Press, 1987)

Browning, Christopher, *The Origins of the Final Solution: The Evolution of Nazi Jewish Policy 1939–1942* (Arrow Books, 2005)

Cesarani, David: *Final Solution: The Fate of the Jews 1933–49* (London: Macmillan, 2016)

Friedlander, Saul, *The Years of Persecution: Nazi Germany and the Jews 1933–1939* (London: Phoenix, 2007)

Friedlander, Saul, *The Years of Extermination: Nazi Germany and the Jews 1939–1945* (London: Weidenfeld and Nicolson, 2007)

Gruner, Wolf, and Osterloh, Jörg (eds), *Das 'Grossdeutsche Reich' und die Juden* (Frankfurt/ New York, Campus Verlag, 2010)

Kershaw, Ian, *Hitler, the Germans and the Final Solution* (Jerusalem: Yad Vashem; New Haven/London: Yale University Press, 2008)

Rothkirchen, Livia, *The Jews of Bohemia and Moravia: Facing the Holocaust* (Jerusalem: Yad Vashem, 2005)

NOTES

CHAPTER 2: AN UNWELCOME LETTER

1 Saul Friedlander, *The Years of Persecution: Nazi Germany and the Jews 1933–1939* (London: Phoenix, 2007), p. 272.

2 Obituary of Rabbi Jacob Freimann by Martin Salomonski.

CHAPTER 3: THE ROOTS OF A RABBINICAL FAMILY

1 Jüdischen Gemeinde zu Berlin, *Festschrift zum siebzigsten Geburtstag von Jakob Freimann* (Berlin: Viktoria, 1937).

2 Rabbi Jacob Freimann, *Commentary on the Torah* (unpublished).

3 Dr Ernest Freeman, *Memoirs* (unpublished).

CHAPTER 5: STRUGGLING TO DECIDE

1 Friedlander, *The Years of Persecution*, p. 182.

2 Ibid., p. 183.

3 Francis R. Nicosia, *The Third Reich and the Palestine Question* (London: I. B. Tauris & Co Ltd), p. 160.

CHAPTER 6: INTERNED IN BUCHENWALD

1 Friedlander, *The Years of Persecution*, p. 274.

2 Harry Stein, 'Das Sonderlager im Konzentrationslager Buchenwald nach den Pogromen' in Monica Kingreen, *Nach der Kristallnacht, Jüdisches Leben und antijüdische Politik in Frankfurt am Main 1938–1945* (Frankfurt/New York: Campus Verlag, 1999), pp. 36–7.

3 Robert Smallbones, *Memoirs* (unpublished).

4 Goetz Aly, *Hitler's Beneficiaries: Plunder, Racial War and the Nazi Welfare State* (New York: Metropolitan Books, 2006), p. 48.

CHAPTER 7: AN UNDERSTANDABLE CHOICE

1 Friedlander, *The Years of Persecution*, p. 312.

2 Ibid., pp. 309–10.

3 Ibid., p. 317.

CHAPTER 8: 'GONE AS USUAL TO THE TAILOR IN OLMÜTZ'

1 Livia Rothkirchen, *The Jews of Bohemia and Moravia: Facing the Holocaust* (Jerusalem: Yad Vashem, 2005), p. 99.

2 Ibid.

3 http://www.jewishvirtuallibrary.org/jsource/History/whitepap Reaction.html

CHAPTER 9: A BIRTHDAY PARTY TO REMEMBER

1 Christopher Browning, *The Origins of the Final Solution: The Evolution of Nazi Jewish Policy 1939–1942* (London: Arrow Books, 2005), p. 15.

2 Ibid., p. 18.

3 Ian Kershaw, *Hitler, the Germans and the Final Solution* (Jerusalem: Yad Vashem; New Haven/London: Yale University Press, 2008), p. 62.

4 Michael Alberti, *Die Verfolgung und Vernichtung der Juden im Reichsgau Wartheland 1939–1945* (Wiesbaden: Harrassowitz Verlag, 2006), p. 85.

5 Ingo Loose, 'Wartheland', in Gruner, Wolf and Osterloh, Jörg (eds) *Das 'Grossdeutsche Reich' und die Juden* (Frankfurt/New York: Campus Verlag, 2010), p. 243.

6 Browning, *The Origins of the Final Solution*, p. 45.

7 Ibid., p. 69.

8 Dr E. Wetzel and Dr G. Hecht, *Die Frage der Behandlung der Bevölkerung der ehemaligen polnischen Gebiete nach rassenpolitischen Gesichtspunkten*, report issued by the Rassenpolitische Amt in Berlin, 25 November 1939.

9 Kershaw, *Hitler, the Germans and the Final Solution*, p. 62.

10 Alberti, *Die Verfolgung und Vernichtung der Juden im Reichsgau Wartheland, 1939–1945*, p. 130.

11 The details of exactly how the deportations were to be carried out and what the victims were to be allowed to take with them are taken from the orders issued by Wilhelm Koppe to the Police High Command, Posen, in a series of letters during November 1939.

12 Browning, *The Origins of the Final Solution*, pp. 55–6.

13 The accounts of life in Ostrów-Lubelski are taken from the Ostrów-Lubelski Memorial Book (New York/Amhurst: The New York Public Library: National Yiddish Book Center Yizkor book project, 2003), and from the website of the Nizkor project:

http://www.nizkor.org/hweb/places/poland/ostrow/

14 Yizkor book project, p. 391.

15 Alberti, *Die Verfolgung und Vernichtung der Juden im Reichsgau Wartheland, 1939–1945*, p. 324.

16 Jan Karski, *Story of a Secret State* (London: Penguin Classics, 2012), p. 90.

17 Alberti, *Die Verfolgung und Vernichtung der Juden im Reichsgau Wartheland, 1939–1945*, p. 132.

18 Ibid., p. 133.

CHAPTER 10: 'WE WILL NOT BE SEPARATED'

1 See http://www.airfieldinformationexchange.org/community/show-
thread.php?6891-WWII-Internment-Camps-in-the-Isle-of-Man

CHAPTER 12: 'NEVER HANKER AFTER WHAT IS GONE'

1 https://en.m.wikipeida.org/wiki/the_Holocaust_in_Ukraine

2 Ibid.; see also the testimony of Otto Ohlendorff at the Nuremberg
Trials.

3 Jan Machala, 'Unbearable Jewish Houses of Prayer: The Nazi
Destruction of Synagogues based on examples from central Moravia',
Judaica Bohemiae, Jewish Museum in Prague, Issue no. 49–1 (2014),
pp. 59–87.

4 https://www.youtube.com/watch?v=SZc4qFg2EPI

CHAPTER 13: MAKING A HOME IN OSTRÓW-LUBELSKI

1 See http://www.nizkor.org/hweb/places/poland/ostrow/

2 Kershaw, *Hitler, the Germans and the Final Solution*, p. 66.

3 Yitzhak Arad, *Belzec, Sobobor, Treblinka: The Operation Reinhard Death
Camps* (Bloomington and Indianapolis: Indiana University Press, 1987),
p. 8.

4 Alberti, *Die Verfolgung und Vernichtung der Juden im Reichsgau
Wartheland 1939–1945*, p. 110.

5 Browning, *The Origins of the Final Solution*, p. 370.

6 See http://www.nizkor.org/hweb/places/poland/ostrow/

7 Browning, *The Origins of the Final Solution*, p. 371.

8 Ruta Sakowska, *Dwa Etapy* (Wrocław: Zakład Narodowy im.
Ossolińskich, 1986), pp. 112-131.

9 Kershaw, *Hitler, the Germans and the Final Solution*, p. 69.

10 http://www.jewishvirtuallibrary.org/jsource/biography/Hoess.html

11 Nikolaus Wachsmann, *K. L.: A History of the Nazi Concentration Camps* (New York: Farrar, Straus and Giroux, 2015), p. 317.

12 Yitzhak Arad, *Belzec, Sobibor, Treblinka: The Operation Reinhard Death Camps*, p. 24.

13 http://www.holocaustresearchproject.org/ghettos/lubartow.html

14 Chil Raichman: *The Last Jew of Treblinka: A Memoir* (New York: Pegasus Books, 2010), p. 4.

CHAPTER 14: LETTERS BETWEEN JERUSALEM AND NEW YORK

1 Tom Segev: *One Palestine Complete: Jews and Arabs under the British Mandate* (London: Abacus, 2001), p. 449.

2 Tom Segev, *The Seventh Million: the Israelis and the Holocaust*, tr. Haim Watzman (New York: Henry Holt and Company, 1991), p. 83.

CHAPTER 15: FAREWELL TO HOLEŠOV

1 *Sinn und Zweck der Gründung der Treuhandstelle im Rahmen der Erfassung des jüdischen Vermögens*, (undated), obtained from the Institut für Zeitgeschichte, München-Berlin, Archiv, Fb 82.

2 Rothkirchen, *The Jews of Bohemia and Moravia*, p. 239.

3 Ibid., p. 234.

4 Ibid., p. 233.

5 Philipp Manes: *As If It Were Life*: A *WWII Diary from the Theresienstadt Ghetto*, tr. Janet Foster et al. (New York: Palgrave Macmillan, 2009), p.22.

6 Ibid., p. 23.

7 Ibid.

8 Debórah Dwork and Robert Jan van Pelt, *Auschwitz: 1270 to the Present* (New York/London: W. W. Norton & Company, 1996), p. 327.

9 www.holocaustetptfinal.com/auschwitz-birkenau.html

CHAPTER 16: EASTWARDS FROM THERESIENSTADT

1 Rothkirchen, *The Jews of Bohemia and Moravia*, p. 240.

2 Otto Kulka: *Landscapes of the Metropolis of Death: Reflections on Memory and Imagination* tr. Ralph Mandel (London: Allen Lane, 2013), Appendix: Ghetto in an Annihilation Camp.

3 Ibid.

CHAPTER 17: AN EXTRAORDINARY EXCHANGE

1 Dan Stone, *The Liberation of the Camps, the End of the Holocaust and its Aftermath* (New Haven/London: Yale University Press, 2015), p. 2.

2 Ibid., pp. 5–6.

CHAPTER 18: INFERRING FROM THE SILENCE

1 Vasily Grossman, 'The Hell of Treblinka', in *The Road* (London: Maclehose Press, 2011), pp. 176–7.

CHAPTER 20: BUILDING NEW LIVES

1 See the account of the incident by Amos Oz in his *A Tale of Love and Darkness*, tr. Nicholas de Lange (London: Chatto & Windus, 2004), pp. 354–5.